HACKING
ISIS

HACKING
ISIS

HOW TO DESTROY THE CYBER JIHAD

MALCOLM NANCE

AND

CHRIS SAMPSON

FOREWORD BY ALI H. SOUFAN

Skyhorse Publishing

Skyhorse Publishing books may be purchased in bulk at special discounts for sales promotion, corporate gifts, fund-raising, or educational purposes. Special editions can also be created to specifications. For details, contact the Special Sales Department, Skyhorse Publishing, 307 West 36th Street, 11th Floor, New York, NY 10018 or info@skyhorsepublishing.com.

Skyhorse® and Skyhorse Publishing® are registered trademarks of Skyhorse Publishing, Inc.®, a Delaware corporation.

Visit our website at www.skyhorsepublishing.com.

10 9 8 7 6 5 4 3 2 1

Library of Congress Cataloging-in-Publication Data is available on file.

Cover design by Rain Saukas
Cover photo credit iStock

Print ISBN: 978-1-5107-1892-0
Ebook ISBN: 978-1-5107-1893-7

Printed in the United States of America

Contents

Foreword

by Ali H. Soufan

Hacking ISIS is a critical book on the dynamics of the cyber caliphate for all cyber warriors. It is a timely book, as ISIS is collapsing and its physical caliphate is passing into history. The potential for a new cyber-based world, a Ghost Caliphate, will definitely allow a physically defeated force to rise from the ashes as a cyber-warfare force.

Malcolm Nance, one of the world's top terrorism intelligence professionals, and Chris Sampson, a terrorism cyber media expert who has studied ISIS and al-Qaeda for more than eleven years, have produced a brilliant resource to educate cybersecurity specialists, politicians, and the general public about the future risks of how ISIS's ideology may spread further in the cyber world. Malcolm and his team have engaged and destroyed ISIS's cyber warriors in direct and indirect cyber combat. Though the ISIS warriors are amateur and young, and generally limit their work to propagating their hateful ideology, they have the basic skills to expand from a general nuisance into a credible threat so long as we ignore their potential. As we continue to take this fight with this terrorist enemy to the electronic battlefield, this book will help our cyber warriors and decision-makers defeat them once and for all.

Chapter 1

The Keys to the Cyber Caliphate

When he woke for dawn prayers on 17 May, 2015, "Caliph" Ibrahim, a.k.a. Abu Bakr al-Baghdadi, the commander of the forces of the Islamic State of Iraq and the Levant al-Sham, a.k.a. ISIS, would be informed of a massacre that had occurred near Deir ez-Zor in eastern Syria. US Special Operations forces had completed a bold and daring direct action, penetrating directly into the heart of the territory occupied by the self-proclaimed "ISIS." The Americans had not just carried out a raid but had flown hundreds of miles behind ISIS lines to capture a man named Abu Sayyaf. When the smoke cleared, the Delta troopers had killed every terrorist present including their intended target, but the mission was still considered a resounding success. The *New York Times* and the *Wall Street Journal* reported that even though Abu Sayyaf had not been taken alive, during the sensitive site's exploitation, the intelligence team collected four to seven terabytes of computer data that gave US intelligence a treasure trove of information about the financial workings of ISIS.

There was nothing routine about the mission to seize or kill Abu Sayyaf, whose real name was Fathi ben Awn ben Jildi Murad al-Tunisi. He was a Tunisian jihadi and keeper of the keys to the

ISIS oil wealth. Abu Sayyaf worked out of the offices of the Euphrates Oil Company at al-Omar, the largest oilfield in Syria. As treasurer to ISIS, it was his job to produce, collect, and distribute hundreds of millions of dollars in profits throughout the caliphate from illicit oil, sale of antiquities and slaves, and levying taxes on Christians. He was a very high-value target, but the generals at the Pentagon would have been reluctant to risk the lives of the most elite soldiers America possessed, the National Mission Force, just to recover a pile of financial data. That could be electronically collected by NSA or purchased by gold or cash from CIA assets. No, there had to be something far more valuable and important in his possession that made the mission an imperative. Whatever it was would have to be a game changer.

The most critical indicator of the importance of the mission and its objective was the fact that the President was moved to sign the order. The intelligence community does not undertake these missions on a whim, and, even with solid intelligence, the payoff would have to exceed the risk by an order of magnitude. The amount of people, intelligence, and weapons dedicated to this type of mission is staggering.

To approve the al-Omar raid would require solid, triple-checked intelligence from multiple sources from inside ISIS itself. The sources would have to be considered extremely reliable and their information triple checked. Once confidence was high, the Director of National Intelligence, the CIA, and Pentagon would have to convince the President that the success-to-failure ratio exceeded ninety percent or more before he would sign the "Go" order to invade ISIS-controlled Syria.

Why would the notably cautious "No-Drama Obama" authorize such a momentous mission? He must have been convinced that it would result in something so damaging to ISIS that the risk would outweigh the potential for disaster. The objective could only be one thing—the intelligence 'keys to the caliphate': a softcopy database, not linked to the Internet, containing the personal data of every man, woman, child, and slave in and under the control of ISIS, as well as the communications and financial links to its affiliates worldwide.

THE INTERNAL SECURITY DATABASE

When Samir Abd Muhammad al-Khlifawi, whose nom de guerre was Haji Bakr, became the shadow commander of ISIS's military wing and its Chief of Spies, he emphasized that ISIS should gather all possible information about every person in their society in order to control behavior, blackmail the influential, or eliminate resistance. He sketched out the design for a massive paper database detailing each member's biographical, social, and psychological data.

Derived directly from his experience as a loyal spy under Saddam Hussein, he put together an organization identical to the Baathist intelligence apparatus, but one that could compile information with much more detail on the religious and family aspects of the ISIS communities. He wanted to create a hybrid al-Qaeda-Saddamist religious extremist police state impervious to foreign intelligence penetration and resistant to rebellion.

He was the right man for the job. To this end, he did a complete brain-dump of everything he had learned as a Baathist and implemented a new network for the religious terror nation. In this respect, Haji Bakr was pitch-perfect. *Der Spiegel's* discovery of his handwritten notes on how ISIS collects intelligence and databases the histories of all who fall under its control were found after he was ambushed and killed in 2014.[1] He ordered his intelligence division Emirs ("Princes") and subordinate cells to check and cross-reference information on all levels of ISIS society to ensure the trustworthiness and loyalty of its subjects.

ISIS's internal spying effort was extraordinary, eclipsing even Saddam Hussein's lust for manipulative information. It evolved into an incredibly complex operation that Haji Bakr detailed in dozens of notes. ISIS depends on slavish loyalty of all official oper-atives throughout each "Wilayat" or "State." The ISIS chain of intelligence reporting relies on sources, starting at the street level, prepared to inform on anyone in the caliphate for a reward. This information goes up from the individual jihadi to the regional Emirs, through a chain of Deputy Emirs, sub-Emirs, and their assistant subdeputies in the intelligence apparatus. Every level cross-checks the accuracy and reliability of the person below to guard against deception or penetration by enemy agents.

The entire ISIS spy chain of command is backed up by highly experienced officers who can fill the roles of those who are mar-tyred. This is a very old-school al-Qaeda system to ensure no link in the chain is lost. Add to this the ability of virtually any jihadi to spy for the apparatus and the result is a world that *Der Spiegel* cor-rectly called an "Islamic Intelligence State."

But in a financial system collecting and disbursing billions, each written dossier on a member of the internal security arm had to be placed in a modern computer database in order to ensure that people collecting and spending money were closely monitored. Each database had to be compared to the regular financial activity of ISIS's subjects for anomalies. Abu Sayyaf's remote oilfield was the perfect spot for compiling the financial and intelligence infor-mation fed into the database.

A second component of the ISIS personnel database was already well known to US intelligence since Americans had created it at a cost of billions during its occupation of Iraq. The Iraqi gov-ernment implemented computerized databasing and biometrics of all citizens in 2005. It recorded personal information including digital photos, fingerprints, and even some retina scans of anyone who registered to vote, served in government or the military, col-lected pensions, and received a passport or the new digital Iraqi national identity card. Additionally, anyone with a terrorist or criminal background or held in a detention center was entered into a national criminal database. During the battle for Mosul, ISIS had either rapidly seized or already had in their possession these databases. Additionally, the army and police biometric databases for each solider were located in three major headquarters lost to ISIS in Mosul, Tikrit, and Ramadi. To this end, Haji Bakr employed everything he had learned as a Baathist to create a new intelligence and security network for the religious terror nation.

ISIS regional databases integrated the information in the Iraqi databases found in the intelligence and security offices at Camp Kindi, headquarters of the Nineveh Operations Command and in the Iraqi 2nd Army Division and the Iraqi Security Forces Intelligence office in Mosul. A third database was located at the intelligence and admin branch headquarters of the Iraqi 12th Division at Camp Speicher near Tikrit, and the fourth was located in the ISF offices in Ramadi. All of these gave ISIS knowledge of Sunni loyalists in the government and Shia who would need to be killed. The loyalist Sunni soldiers who came over to ISIS would have their biometrics and personal data compared and kept in the ISIS database.

When Mosul was taken, ISIS members were videotaped openly checking the national identity cards of Iraqis in the city against this database held in laptops at roadblocks to determine who would live or die.

ISIS immediately tried to take precautions against the loss of Abu Sayyaf and the databases. They immediately banned Wi-Fi by all outside of approved Internet cafés in Raqqa. Most interestingly, it included the prohibition of the use of private Wi-Fi by all ISIS members and commanders. This move not only centralizes monitoring of citizens and opposition groups to a few central IP addresses, but it indicates that they were trying to tear out the elements of the old online communications structures root and branch before the American exploited it.

Combined, the ISIS financial/personnel databases could be exploited by the United States not just for capturing or killing more senior ISIS members, but for a mission far broader and more important: it identified the national origin of every person in the group; where they were assigned to fight; how much they were paid; who were their parents, grandparents, and next of kin; who were their wives, children and slaves' names and dates of birth; as well as their level of loyalty and the rewards and punishments they received. Perhaps the greatest jewel in the crown was the mobile phone numbers, Twitter handles, Facebook accounts, and other social media links. Especially exciting for America's intelligence managers and operatives, whether on the ground or in the US, including the NSA, CIA, DIA, and others, all of these data points would give the precise locations of where ISIS-authorized mobile phones were being used and who used them.

The keys to the caliphate gave America the ability to determine who could be blackmailed or turned into a double agent, or to mark their most loyal commanders for death by Hellfire missile or JAM bomb. ISIS's own obsession for detail and knowledge proved to be the base alloy for America to craft a near-perfect weapon for the Pentagon to kill whomever they pleased, whenever they pleased. For spies and drone operators, the prospects were bone-chillingly thrilling and were coldly being applied. Perhaps with the Abu Sayyaf raid, America had defeated ISIS long before the caliphate would physically fall.

Treasury of Terror

The "ISIS" fancied itself a nation. But even a self-proclaimed caliph needs a treasury, a general accounting office, and a social security administration. The RAND Corporation estimated in 2014 that ISIS ran a budget surplus that exceeded $2 billion per year from all sources of illicit revenue-generating activities, such as the sale of oil and stolen antiquities, taxes on members of other religions, and sex slavery.[2] This financial web worked outside of the formal global economies until cleansed by regional profiteers. In the ruins of their captured Iraqi and Syrian cities, ISIS cannot disburse money electronically from a bank network, so for both international and local disbursing they are using an archaic money transfer process used widely throughout the Middle East called Hawala.

Hawala is as old as informal banking. You deliver money to a trusted Hawala broker, and he uses his personal contacts and pre-positioned funds to deliver the same amount of money, in cash, to your contact in another city. It is considered complying with Islamic law for brokers to charge only a flat fee rather than interest. Billions of dollars pass through the Middle East and Europe this way annually with almost no paper trail. It was the fastest and most secure way for ISIS to move funds from Raqqa to Mosul, Aleppo, or Ramadi to its fighters and tribes without losing it to theft or airstrike. Spain's *El País* newspaper detailed the network supporting cash transfers to ISIS and al-Nusra Front to pay Spanish jihadists their monthly salaries using the system operating through entities like European *Hilal* butcher shops and phone banks.[3] *Newsweek* reported that this ancient system is done with almost no oversight from international banks. It's an honor system in which no records are kept by the transferees apart from a receipt.[4]

The significance of exploiting an ISIS financial/personnel database cannot be underestimated. As ISIS's de facto treasurer, Abu Sayyaf, as US intelligence agencies had extrapolated, had to maintain an off-line central database where the paper information from throughout the caliphate is entered into a computerized internal accounting program in order to report on and pay the fighters, finance businesses, build or repair infrastructure, buy weapons, influence tribes, or sell women and children.

Such a database would necessarily be complex even for a small group like ISIS but would not require a large data storage capacity. If the *New York Times* report is correct, then just four to seven terabytes of data recovered on the mission would be equal to the sum of data in the disk memories of eight to ten average laptops or external backup hard drives. That was more than enough power for the group's data entry and accounting needs.

This payment system with its information about people giving and receiving money can, thanks to ISIS's extreme paranoia about what those in the caliphate are doing daily, be cross-checked against their highly detailed internal security database on personnel. Any nexus between ISIS's financial payments, its personnel rosters, and the internal security data on its own people are Spy gold for counterterrorism operations.

OPERATION VAPORIZE

Within a year, the evidence became overwhelming that the keys to the caliphate were not only in US hands but were also being ruthlessly exploited. Within thirty days after the Abu Sayyaf mission, a massive US military campaign of targeted assassinations began with one goal—"vaporize" the top ISIS commanders and noteworthy killers featured in their propaganda.

First in the kill chain was a pair of Tunisians who were deeply entrenched ISIS terrorists and on the FBI Most Wanted terrorists list: the al-Harzi brothers. In mid-June 2015, Ali Awni al-Harzi was killed in Mosul by a US airstrike. He was believed to have been a liaison for ISIS elements in North Africa, notably Libya. Ali Harzi was also a person of interest in the investigation of the 2012 US Consulate attack in Benghazi that killed the US Ambassador Chris Stevens and three others. Two weeks later, his brother, the ISIS "Emir of Suicide bombers" Tariq al-Harzi, was killed by a drone strike at his remote compound south of Hasaka in the village of Ash Shaddadi, Syria. He was a Tunisian with a three-million-dollar bounty on his head. He developed ISIS's logistics network to transfer Libyan weapons into Syria and developed contacts for weapons to be transshipped outside of Syria and Iraq. It is believed his Tunisian connections may have played a role in the attacks that killed 30 British tourists in the June massacre at Sousse and 19 foreign tourists at Tunis's Bardo Museum in March.

Within days of these strikes, two more of the ISIS senior leadership, including Amer al-Rafdan, the former Emir of ISIS's Deir ez-Zor "state" where Abu Sayyaf had his secret compound, and an Iraqi named Abu Osama al-Iraqi, the former Govenor of Hasaka state, were killed. It is noteworthy that al-Rafdan was a former Syrian regime policeman who had joined al-Qaeda's al-Nusra Front and had been given ISIS management positions in the Kuniko oilfields and the Deir ez-Zor granaries before taking over control as ISIS's governor. According to the Syrian Observatory for Human Rights, both men were killed in a vehicle struck by a US drone.

Add to this toll Hafiz Saeed Khan, the former Taliban commander who swore his allegiance to ISIS and who took the title of Governor of Khorasan State. He was killed on almost the same date and at the same time as Tariq al-Harzi and the others. The coincidence was stunning, but not if put into information-warfare context. Khan would have been in communication with each of the four dead commanders. Their cyber connectivity sealed their doom.

Given this devastating breach of security, Abu Bakr al-Baghdadi (for however long he lives) was terribly worried—and he should have been. US intelligence collection, coupled with the exploitation of a vast amount of intelligence plucked from documents, computers, and mobile phones captured on the battlefield, has yielded details that opened up cyberspace and enabled those planning strikes against him and his associates more than a location—it has given them all there is to know about every member of ISIS in Iraq-Syria and all of their jihad zones or *wilayat*.

Intelligence on these fighters led to identifying those at the top of the chain of command. Senior ISIS Military Commander of Military forces in the caliphate, Omar al Shishani (a.k.a. "Omar the Chechen"), was literally "vaporized"—blown into human pink mist by the 2,000-pound JDAM bombs or Hellfire missiles. ISIS Senior military commander in Northern Syria, Abd al-Rahman

Mustafa al-Qaduli (aka "Hajji Imam")—vaporized. The Chief Accountant of the ISIS treasury, Muwaffaq Mustafa Mohammed al-Karmoush (aka "Abu Salah")—vaporized. Killed along with him were two deputies including the chief extortion operators Abu Maryam and Abu Rahman al-Tunisi. Mohammed Emwazi (a.k.a. "Jihadi John"), the most famous of the four British beheading executioners from ISIS videos—vaporized. In Libya, the throat-slitting commander who killed Egyptian and Ethiopian Christians by the seaside named Wissam Najm Abd Zayd al-Zubaydi (a.k.a. "Abu Nabil")—vaporized. The Syria planner for the Paris attacks that killed 130 people, Charaffe al-Mouadan—vaporized.

But one of the most wanted high-value targets was the number two Commander of ISIS and chief of external intelligence operations and propaganda—Taha Subhi Falaha, also known as Abu Mohammed al-Adnani. He received a lightning bolt from Olympus, vaporized by a drone strike. His death was quickly confirmed by ISIS.

A week after al-Adnani was killed, the United States killed his replacement. Wa'el Adil Hasan Salman al-Fayad, also known as Abu Muhammad Furqan, was killed in a strike on his house in Raqqa, Syria, on September 7, 2016.[5] He was identified as the Minister of Information and leader of the top propaganda wing, al-Furqan. He had been chosen by the advisory group called the Shura Council to replace al-Adnani.

The mass retribution against the entire ISIS senior leadership was so thoroughly devastating that the *New York Times* reported that the "Caliph" Abu Bakr al-Baghdadi had delegated his authority to suvivors in the ISIS Shura Islamic Advisory council. Baghdadi had to be aware that the keys to the cyber caliphate had put him at the top of the high-value target list and opened the doors to his demise. ISIS was being physically destroyed by the very asset it cherished the most—the Internet.

Of all of the extraordinary ISIS leaders killed, one lower-level figure was identified and targeted for elimination by the National

Security Agency and US Cyber Command. He typified the future of the ISIS fighter—the cyber warrior. That cyber fighter was Junaid Hussain. Hussain was a British citizen who started hacking when he was eleven years old and was known as Abu Hussain al-Britani. He rose up the ranks to become a highly visible and influential member of the Cyber jihad against the West. He was living in Raqqa, Syria, ISIS's capital, when he was tracked down by the US intelligence agencies—the Central Intelligence Agency (CIA) and the National Security Agency (NSA)—and British secret intelligence services MI-6 and the Government Communications Headquarters (GCHQ), the British NSA. These agencies combined forces, isolated his location through the Internet, his mobile phone calls, and location signals, and then killed him with the utmost precision by a Hellfire missile fired from a CIA Predator drone. Vaporized. Death at the hands of the infidels is a hotly desired feature in the ISIS system, not a bug. Good Jihadis who do their job are rewarded with martyrdom. The losers who did not die a glorious death must remain on earth and continue reporting to the next-level Emir. Hussein did his job and reached his reward.

For such a seemingly low-level operative, Junaid was the one of the commanders of the Virtual Jihad—the heart of ISIS's global cyber operations, including their hacking groups and their foot soldiers of the Cyber Caliphate Army. Hussein fought the jihad from behind a keyboard, not with a Kalashnikov assault rifle. The ISIS cyber groups were almost as responsible for the mayhem and bloodshed as any knife-wielding throat-slitter in the group. It was their network of cyber operations and recruiting activities that gave inspiration to tens of thousands all around the world by distributing their thousands of videos showing their mass murder, videos that helped to secure their allegiances to ISIS and helped ISIS plan attacks in the West without ever leaving home. Abu Hussain al-Britani was one of the virtual Emirs in the Cyber Caliphate.

Chapter 2

Understanding the Cyber Battlespace

The Internet by 2016 reached an enormous size by any stretch[1] of the imagination with units of storage being measured in zettabytes and pages estimated to be over seven billion and growing.[2] To give scale to this number, imagine your average one terabyte external hard drive and multiply that by one billion. One thousand terabytes become a petabyte, one thousand petabytes become an exabyte, and one thousand exabytes equals a zettabyte. According to the Internet giant Cisco Systems, by 2019, Internet traffic will reach two zetta-bytes of data transferred worldwide. With nearly three-and-a half billion users, there was a large haystack in which jihadists could hide their cyber needles as they recruited and planned operations.

```
ZETTABYTES=1000 Exabytes
 EXABYTES=1000 Petabytes
PETABYTES=1000 Terabytes
TERABYTES=1000 Gigabytes
GIGABYTES=1000 Megabytes
MEGABYTES=1000 Kilobytes
KILOBYTES=1000 Bytes
    1 Byte=8 bits
```

Figure 1: By 2016, the yearly traffic on the Internet amounted to over one zettabyte, which is equal to one billion terabytes of information according to Cisco Systems estimates.

The good news is that fighting the E-Jihadists doesn't require the entire space known as the Internet. Therefore, it is important to identify where terrorists currently operate, where they congregate, and to identify and neutralize the tools they use. The challenge is to beat them before they adapt by pushing them into manageable areas that can be monitored and where cyber weapons can destroy their safe harbors. To be most effective, it makes sense to map out the cyber terrain in question and determine the benefits and limitations of each sector.

Corralling terrorists online could be done by engaging in crackdowns on some platforms such as Twitter and Facebook but intentionally leaving open a platform that intelligence services could infiltrate or monitor. Their adversaries work to erode terrorist confidence in encryption, in large part, by issuing bogus warnings about security weaknesses in platforms in common use. By finding legitimate weaknesses in the hacker or communications tools employed by terrorists, intelligence agencies can exploit these vulnerabilities to track and disrupt ISIS operatives.

At the same time, intelligence agencies and private sector firms benefit from letting terrorists blithely continue to use what they consider invulnerable while allowing them to operate freely—for a time. When ISIS accounts were dropping off of Twitter as a result of takedown requests and internal account checks, some intelligence analysts were concerned when accounts they were tracking were suspended. For example, when Telegram accounts, the secure communications app, went dark for certain users, it closed a window that had been vital to communications intelligence (COMINT) collection. The consensus of those in the intelligence community was that cutting off information that could be garnered from any site should be done with discretion so that law enforcement and intelligence agency programs or operations would not be deprived of a significant flow of intercepts and information.

However, despite the enormous digital territory and huge number of Internet users, only a few users of what is called the

"Surface Web" are aware of or actively observe what goes on in quite a different layer of the Internet. The data stored in another layer are not accessible to the majority of users. This is called "The Deep Web," which is data traffic not picked up by the algorithms of search engines. Then, there is the "Dark Web," where sites are intentionally encrypted and usually accessed by someone knowledgeable about how to find and get onto such sites. Typically, these sites are engaging in forbidden activities ranging from drug sales to weapons or hitman transactions. In order to see the sites on the "Dark Web," a user must have a specialized browser like Tor, The Onion Router.

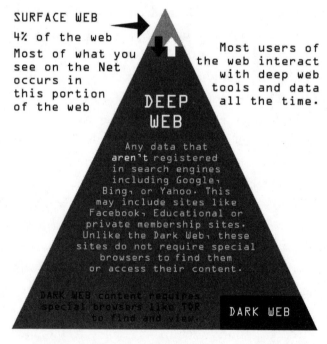

SURFACE WEB
4% of the web
Most of what you see on the Net occurs in this portion of the web

DEEP WEB

Most users of the web interact with deep web tools and data all the time.

Any data that aren't registered in search engines including Google, Bing, or Yahoo. This may include sites like Facebook, Educational or private membership sites. Unlike the Dark Web, these sites do not require special browsers to find them or access their content.

DARK WEB content requires special browsers like TOR to find and view.

DARK WEB

Figure 2: The layers of the web. (Source: TAPSTRI)

THE ABOVE AND BELOW

But most terrorist organizations communicate and recruit using the open Internet just like everyone else. Some terrorists have always used sites on both the "Surface Web" and the "Deep Web." If a nation-state engages in cyber intelligence operations (and has cyber attack capability), it makes sense to avoid trolling through all the online extremist postings, messages, etc.; you end up looking for a needle in an increasingly larger haystack. Cyber counterintelligence agencies should focus on shutting down portals that enable ISIS to spread their radical version of Islam and lure in new recruits. Everywhere. The Internet is (mostly) ubiquitous, accessible, and (with the exception of nations like China) it is "come one, come all." The global reach of the Internet is its strength; however, it is also its vulnerability, exploited by those who wish to use it to harm others. We are now well aware of the reach of how global intelligence agencies collect raw intelligence (thanks to people like Edward Snowden, the NSA contractor who defected to Russia). We are waging a war against terrorism on many fronts in the physical world, but the darkest of all is the cyber world—a shadow battlefield. The best way to look at this battlefield is to separate what activities occur in what regions. This distinction will allow appropriate and available resources to focus on targets and operations in each zone of activity. It will also identify special conditions and limitations on both ISIS and counter-ISIS forces alike.

To do this we will divide the web in three zones, the Surface Web, the Deep Web, and the Dark Web. Each of these zones has a set of conditions unto itself that obeys certain rules that are as true for the ISIS fanboy or operative as the counter operations crew.

Mainstream companies like Twitter, YouTube, and Facebook operate in the zone known as the "Surface Web." Though this is the area most seen by Internet users, it encompasses barely 4 percent of the data (usually in the form of pages or downloadable material) that make up the Internet. Instead, most of the data on the Internet is in the open expanse of the unindexed area known as the "Deep Web." Then there is some, but relatively little, activity in that level of the Internet, in which any exchange of data or communication always involves encryption. There are considerable resources for this, among them PGP (Pretty Good Privacy)—actually a pretty robust form of encryption. If you don't have a key, you can't open the door. What transpires in the Dark Web is available only to those who can run special programs like Freenet, I2P, or the browser most commonly associated with the "Dark Web" known as "Tor" or "The Onion Router." These pages cannot be found via search engines and are hidden behind layers of proxy servers that disguise the location of their elusive website ending with an "onion" address. Thus, setting up a strategy requires determining which zone you are going to approach to select targets.

Identifying terrorist locations on the Surface Web is a good place to start, since they are still quite prolific at posting their materials on Telegram and linking to sites like Archive.org, Just-Paste.it, Google drives, and dozens of free file sharing sites. In some cases, they still have blogs that appear briefly with links to videos and other materials loaded with either malware or ad revenue links.

THE SURFACE WEB

The "Surface Web" is available to any web user because of search engines that are accessed by conventional browsers. Search engines use programs to crawl the Internet to make note of pages, media, and other data and store the links for later recall. The method used to gather, parse, and store this information is called "indexing." In Surface Web, where the vast majority of us operate, our online content creation is indexed and searchable by Google and other search engines and essentially comprises the whole of what lay users would call the Internet. At over fifteen billion pages, the Surface Web is large and filled with most of the content you see day-to-day online. Most of what people consider the Internet is available in the Surface Web area, but it comprises only a small percentage of the web itself. However, the vast quantity of the web data is found in the Deep Web.

Over the first two years after the announcement of the Caliphate ISIS, there was first a flood of ISIS materials across the Surface Web, which made it easy to find their messages of death. Since then, just like their failing campaign to hold onto Iraq and Syria, they have struggled to maintain a position on the Surface Web. Using sites like WordPress and BlogSpot, for instance, ISIS could regularly post batches of video links for followers to share across the Net. Researchers and law enforcement regularly discover the sites and blogs and then file takedown requests. Postings on these and other sites (which will ultimately be shut down) reappear less frequently. The ISIS propaganda machine is responding to these blockages by using Telegram channels that publish the same inciting and often ghastly material. Thanks to Telegram, these ISIS sites are more easily hidden from view.

THE DEEP WEB

The second zone is the Deep Web, or the zone in which data fly below the search engine radar. Beneath the Surface Web, as if the greater part of an iceberg, is a world of data that isn't indexed but is accessible to browsers even if secured behind a login. When you move from the daylight of the Surface Web to the hidden caverns of the Deep or Dark Web, the rule becomes "Unless you are in the know, you don't know." If you don't know how to get there via Chrome, Explorer, Safari, etc., and if the site isn't found and indexed by Google, then most likely it is "deep web" material.

Most users of the Internet run into the Deep Web all the time if they log into websites that have usernames and passwords. An example of something found in the Deep Web would be a jihadist forum that requires a sign-in and doesn't appear in Google but is visible in Google Chrome or similar browser.

The activity of ISIS and related groups in the Deep Web is largely found in the forums that are intentionally hidden from Google and other search engines. Sometimes it is obvious that a website is seeking to avoid being found. Many forums and propaganda sites were installed a directory away from the root of the website. Example: ("website.com vs. "website.com/vb/"). It doesn't take much to prevent Google from searching a website or its contents. The most common way is a simple text often called "robot.txt" that simply tells the search engines to ignore the website and its contents.

Efforts are underway to map out the Deep Web including Memex, a Deep Web crawler used by law enforcement. There are privacy advocates who have expressed concern about using this method as a form of data mining, operations that would be illegal unless authorized by a search warrant. They are, indeed, disturbing when the "catch" trawled by its big and indiscriminating net includes innocent people.

According to some informed sources, there are five hundred times more pages in the Deep Web than in the Surface Web. There is no distinction between Deep Web and Surface Web when it comes to illicit activities. The chances of materials being discovered in searches are greater on the Surface Web than the Deep Web, but the Deep Web can be surveyed and mapped for terrorist activities by a combination of OSINT or Open Source Intelligence and HUMINT or human intelligence—information obtained by and from people. There is also no distinction between the Deep Web and the Surface Web when it comes to anonymity.

THE DARK WEB

Then there is the "Dark Web," sometimes known as the "Cipherspace," where users are required to use special browsers to access an array of websites including ones with illicit content that cater to a range of criminal, political, and social interests that are deliberately hidden from view. Not only can search engines like Google and Bing not discover and register these sites, they are only viewable through custom browsers like Tor (a.k.a. The Onion Router). Tor was developed in the 1990s by the United States Naval

Research Laboratory. In April 2016 in its French publication *Dar al-Islam,* ISIS warned that Tor was being used by its enemies. The article claimed that intelligence agencies had breached sites and put up honeypot sites to catch visitors. Some jihadis claimed the NSA was specifically targeting Tor users for surveillance. Other browsers that operate like Tor include I2P, Freenet, Subgraph OS, and Freepto.

Dark Web sites and forums still require user access in most cases, but there are some that still have ISIS/AQ-related news announcements or other bits of data that can help investigators put a larger picture together. Although the Deep Web is vastly larger in comparison to the Surface Web, the area of the Dark Web is significantly smaller than the Surface Web.

The Dark Web also provides plenty of opportunities to use anonymous currency like Bitcoin. Started in 2009 by an unidentified person who used the cover name Satoshi Nakamoto, Bitcoin is a decentralized digital virtual currency used online, especially in the Dark Web, to conduct transactions. Bitcoin is also the name given to the peer-to-peer financial network in which the currency operates. Because of the inability to track the movement of this currency, Bitcoin has been banned in several countries.

Bitcoin has been gaining traction in common markets. Dozens of businesses are opening up to the use of Bitcoin as currency. A few major businesses that accept Bitcoin as currency include Overstock.com, Subway, Home Depot, CVS, and Sears.[3] ISIS members have used it, as well. One was Virginia teenager, Ali Shukri Amin, known online by the name @AmreekiWitness. Amin was behind the publishing of a document and website attributed to the Islamic State that was soliciting donations of Bitcoins for the terror organization. He was arrested and sentenced to eleven years in prison in August 2015 on material support charges.[4]

Whereas sites on the Dark Web may be beyond the grasp of the average search engine, the US government hasn't simply given up and let the activities of online criminals elude their reach in the

Dark Web. In November 2014, international law enforcement knocked down hundreds of websites that had been engaged in various criminal activities ranging from drug sales and money laundering to the sale of weapons and illegal pornography. The alleged founder of Silk Road, an illicit Dark Web drug market, was arrested in San Francisco.[5] Along with Silk Road, two other drug sites named Hydra and Cloud 9 were busted in international seizures. The international effort was dubbed "Operation Onymous."[6]

During Operation Onymous, one site knocked off the Dark Web was purported to be an ISIS-affiliated financial donation site under (bc3nbr42tdnqamvs.onion) where contributions could be made via Bitcoins. Instead, it was a clone of the pro-ISIS American user's AmreekiWitness site. One blogger, Nik Cubrilovic, noted that the FBI knocked down several fake sites but missed the actual AmreekiWitness-operated site, which remained active for a period of time after the Operation Onymous effort had run its course.

DARK WEB SEARCH TOOLS

There have been programs introduced that search the Dark Web for information that law enforcement wants in its various investigations, ranging from drug cases, illegal pornography, and human trafficking to hired assassins and terrorism. One tool used for this is Memex, developed by the Defense Advanced Research Projects Agency (DARPA). As noted previously, Memex is a program that scours the web using crawlers that have been designed specifically to deal with the Dark Web. It is able to get past the conventional methods for avoiding search engines. One method is to place a simple text file on a website that tells Google's search engine bots to ignore the site. A key feature of Memex is that it also evades detection. Thus, if a site with terrorist materials is located by Memex, it doesn't leave behind any signs that it has searched the site.

Memex was specifically cited by a New York City District Attorney as being key to breaking several cases of human trafficking.[7] The software's design allows investigators to crawl beyond the Surface Web to areas that specialize in human trafficking, like prostitution sites, to aid in building perceivable patterns of activity.

Used against ISIS, a program like Memex can help identify networks under the Surface Web by searching the vast visual publications shared by ISIS or by engaging in crawls for specific terms associated with ISIS/AQ or related groups. Since groups like ISIS's CCA (Cyber Caliphate Army) have standardized the branding of their group, graphics, and related hacking hashtags, a search though the Deep Web for all locations with those graphics or phrases is a first option. What is required for a search to locate online depots for videos would be as simple as knowing the name of a release, having a related banner, or *wilayat* (the regional ISIS substates) information and conducting a search on for those specific items.

DEEP WEB VS. DARK WEB

While Dark Web sites elude detection by most search engines, what enables certain ones to distinguish the difference between Deep and Dark Web is how the pages are accessed. Deep Web sites can be accessed typically with any browser, but there may still be sign-in limits, and users must know how to get to content since, as noted earlier, it will not be listed in search engines like Google and Bing. In contrast, Dark Web sites are encrypted and only accessible via Tor or similar browsers. They are found via word of mouth. The difference between dealing with matter on the Deep Web and on the Dark Web comes down to how you detect and attack their communication centers.

Many assume that Dark Web means the user and activity are hidden and safe from prying eyes. There is a drawback to trying to use Tor in isolated sectors. To his misfortune, Harvard student Eldo Kim found out that Dark Web anonymity did not apply when he sent a bomb threat to the school in order to avoid a final examination. He supposed that he would send the threatening email message via Tor and that would help to anonymize his location and identity. What he didn't count on, though, was that Harvard was able to detect his usage because he was the *only* person using Tor on the network at the time. As a result, he was arrested, expelled from the school, and acquired a permanent criminal record.

Chapter 3

History of the Cyber Jihad

CYBER LITERACY SPARKED BY A LUST FOR PORNOGRAPHY

One of the more surprising features of ISIS fighters was their expansive street-level knowledge of modern Internet technology. In 2014, the average teenager had had years of hands-on experience using advanced mobile phone tools and applications. The reach and popularity of Facebook, as well as the free mobile phone Skype, led to the adoption of even more involved personal communications and social media apps like WhatsApp. WhatsApp was arguably the most popular online mobile phone app in the Eastern Hemisphere between 2010 and 2014, well before it moved to the United States.

This extreme depth of cyber knowledge by the youth in Europe, the Middle East, Asia, and South Asia was invaluable for al-Qaeda; its younger generation and fanboys would be crucial to the creation of ISIS. They knew how the Internet worked, how to reach and create groups of like-minded individuals, and how to avoid the national security services. Many of their countries had cyber security agencies that monitored every keystroke from a desktop computer but could not monitor every post or exchange of data on

Facebook or WhatsApp. Typically, pornography was the most transmitted data in these regions where sexual suppression was cultural. Then the gamers, kids playing Call of Duty and World of Warcraft, found they could communicate quickly, easily, and securely. Moreover, these young men could use WhatsApp to call girls or order the services of prostitutes—activities that their societies strictly prohibited. Some apps allowed them to share packages of porn, look at video streams, and easily transmit porn. The access to pornography and illicit materials was critical to the rise of the apps. Mobile phone porn was more circumspect than sitting in an Internet café trying to watch on a large screen. It was easier, cheaper, and safer to get porn on a cell phone than watching Russian and Italian live porn advertisement channels for pay-porn and cheaper than buying hacked subscription keys on the Hotbird or NileSat TV channels found in every home. For those rebelling against sexual suppression, these apps were a godsend.

Osama Bin Laden was said to have had a large stash of web pornography on his computer. So, needless to say, submission to Allah was not the full explanation of why their Internet recruiting and other activities became so pervasive and successful in spreading the messages promoting their version of what the Prophet demanded of believers. No, the spark that set off the flood of Internet activity was pornography.

Porn was not necessarily a forbidden fruit if it could lead to a greater good of spreading the ideology of al-Qaeda's *Takfirism*. Takfirism is the radical and un-Islamic act of declaring a Muslim an infidel. Though enjoying porn was often considered sinful amongst the more virtuous of the terrorists, the ubiquity of pathways to many things in the digital world provided ways for male Muslims to obtain a form of absolution by watching and listening to the proliferating online Imams, or preachers. That meant that sin could be counterbalanced by piety for every good Muslim who defied their parents, watched naked men or women writhe on the Internet, and enjoyed paying for chats with nude women in Romania. They would go to very popular websites like Quran.com and Islam.org to read passages from the Quran or ask a learned scholar if what they did was wrong. Everything would be forgiven by God once the message was received from a holy man stating that all indeed was forgiven. Since the early 1990s, al-Qaeda pioneered access to dealing with lust and forgiveness for it. The cyber salvation business boomed in the Middle East and South Asia with the explosion of commercial sites (pay-per-view or stream) on the World Wide Web by 1995. With it came masses of free porn. Al-Qaeda and its radical clerics saw that young men and women needed guidance to manage their virtues and excise vice from their lives. The industry of coming closer to God was not confined to Islam or even the Takfirist extreme, but they saw this as the gateway to gaining young followers who would buy into their redefinition of Islam as being corrupted by porn, western values, and the vice of money. In their rendering, the only absolution was to learn a new version of Islam that was fostered through blood, combat, and fighting like the immediate companions of the Prophet Muhammad did in the seventh century.

As early as 2003, al-Qaeda had mapped out cyberspace as a battlefront—a place where military operations, supplications to God, and showing feats of bravery would be broadcast for the world to see for free. Additionally, it would become a primary place of covert communications, logistics, trade, and recruitment.

For every one hundred young boys watching Pornhub.com, there would be one or two who could be recruited into their ranks. That meant potentially tens of thousands in the Middle East and South Asia alone. Offering them a virtuous life, a family, weapons of war, and a mission would give even the most restless losers a place in life. Al-Qaeda started this early. By the mid-1990s, radical clergy began transmitting data from underground mosques and groups to like-minded individuals using the Casio F91watch.

Soon after, they spread their message using VHS cassette tapes, soon followed by the DVD, then the digitally transferred mp3 audio clip. AQ became quite adept at adapting to new media for the transmission of its message. Most were innocuous, like lectures from extremist clerics, many of which sounded mainstream. But the 1996 video clip of the beheading of Russian Army soldier Yevgeny Rodionov was the first arguably globally disseminated jihadist extremist video that burned its way across cyberspace. In a video titled *Unknown Russian Soldier*, Rodionov's throat slitting was so popular in cyberspace that al-Qaeda would come to do it again as an organizational policy when it had the chance. In the years that followed the execution of Rodionov, al-Qaeda was harnessing the power of the web using encrypted communications, browsers that hid the IP address of the sender's location and steganography, and the embedding of encrypted messages into photographs. The 9/11 hijackers are believed to have used a variety of data transmission methodologies as well as face-to-face meetings and traditional tradecraft to communicate. They made the most spectacular media of all, the hijacking and mass murder of 2,977 people when they smashed their airplanes into the World Trade Center towers and the Pentagon.

Al-Qaeda's chance to match the video power of the Rodionov clip came when the American journalist Daniel Pearl was kidnapped in Karachi, Pakistan, in 2002. Working for the *Wall Street Journal*, he was abducted and personally beheaded on videotape, allegedly by Ahmed Omar Saeed Sheikh (though some investigations say Khaled Sheikh Mohammed, the 9/11 attack planner, confessed to the murder). The recording was coordinated by the mastermind of the Kenya and Tanzania bombings, Saif al-Adel. His video would be entitled *The Slaughter of the Spy-Journalist, the Jew Daniel Pearl*. It was one thing to fly airplanes into a skyscraper, but a more intimate horror, one that affected the watcher personally, was when they showed a man being slaughtered like a goat and then they held his bleeding head aloft.

When the US invasion of Iraq occurred, the newest group of al-Qaeda, Abu Musab al-Zarqawi's al-Qaeda in Iraq, quickly adopted and mastered the art of the video media blood spectacular. An American citizen and part-time drifter, Nick Berg, was kidnapped out of a hotel in Baghdad and personally beheaded by Zarqawi. His video was entitled *Abu Musab al-Zarqawi Slaughters an American.*

Al-Qaeda in Iraq would come to typify versions of what we call Terror Shock Value (TSV) video. Designed to shock, mortify, and instill absolute fear in its enemies, AQI mastered it between 2003 and 2011 against the US Army. They beheaded, eviscerated, shot hostages in the head, set people on fire, and showed helicopters being shot down and survivors being shot dead while their executioners laughed. It was *spectacle macabre* 24-7-365 in AQI's domain.

As we wrote in our treatise on jihadist groups, *Defeating ISIS*, any differences in their way of producing the shock media was significant between 2004 and the massacres of 2014:

> The huge difference in response between the 2004 execution of Nick Berg, for instance, and the death of James Foley ten years later, came by only adding a few changes to the original media style. The first change was to the venue. Zarqawi's' was in a basement and took the visage of a murdering trapped rat. ISIS subsequently conducted their murders outdoors in what they claimed was liberated land in a holy caliphate. They showed no fear of being caught or attacked from the air. The ISIS videos implied freedom to execute at will. The second change was that ISIS managed to get the victim to recite their message to the target audience, his people, and world leaders. The third change was to select a native speaker from the victim's region of the world. Using Mohammed Emwazi or "Jihadi John" to speak in English and carry out the beheadings had a powerful impact. Having him speak eloquent English and directly threaten the Western world caused a level of political emotional outrage that the murder of Nick Berg had not.[1]

By 2004, Osama Bin Laden himself would question the media value of these grisly productions. The transmission of them proved that the Western press would show almost anything. The more brutal the better. But a man who styled himself as following the teachings of the way of the Prophet Muhammad didn't believe that his group could continue to recruit with mayhem. Organized mass murder would be the most salient feature on the leading edge of his takeover of Islam. And he asked his deputy Ayman al-Zawahiri to keep killing the disbelivers, the *kufar*, but to tone down the videotaping of their beheadings.

But Zarqawi continued to make and distribute such horrific videos right up to his death. His successors in 2005, Abu Ayyub al-Masri and Abu Umar al-Baghdadi, kept up the production of combat videos, but beheadings were minimally displayed. When they died at the hands of the US Army Rangers and Iraqi Special Forces, their successor, Abu Bakr al-Baghdadi, a former US prisoner of war, would remember how successful Zarqawi had been and harnessed the newest forms of media to return to the good old days of blood spectacle. He would change the name of al-Qaeda in Iraq to the Islamic State of Iraq and create a new brand of horror at which God Himself would cringe.

CYBER BATTLESPACE FROM AL-QAEDA IN IRAQ TO THE ISLAMIC STATE OF IRAQ

By 2011, the web as battlefield became increasingly more important to both of the core missions of ISIS. The terror value was becoming a major part of the planning cycle and forecasting how the enemy forces would behave when they attacked. But manpower was key to implementing Abu Bakr al-Baghdadi's plans. More fighters were encouraged to come to Iraq, and, as the Syrian civil war started to spread, there were new battlefields to win. Cyberspace, al-Baghdadi was told, was America's gift to the Islamic State of Iraq's (and now the Levant or al-Sham or ISIS) global recruiting and communication structure. Fighters would not just come from around the world; they could stay at home while supporting, fundraising, and, eventually, carrying out operations to support a worldwide struggle. Iraq and Syria's jihad would be a global one directed through the virtual world of a laptop or mobile phone.

Terrorist groups have long known how to exploit all available technology options and continue to engage in overt and covert activity on the web using off-the-shelf but sophisticated tech gear—and the best off-the-shelf tool for communication in the world is the Internet. This allows organizations such as ISIS to project their power beyond physical borders. Al-Qaeda mouthpiece Ayman al-Zawahiri long has stated that he believes a large part of the violent *jihad* was going to be waged by skillfully using the media. Little did he know how right he would be.

Neither al-Qaeda nor ISIS pioneered harnessing jihadist warfare in the cyber information space. That honor would go to the Palestinians during the second Palestinian Intifada in 2000, or the al-Aqsa Intifada. This uprising in the Palestinian territories started with a visit to the holy Muslim temple mount by the former General Ariel Sharon. This sparked mass rioting and killings of both Palestinians and Israeli soldiers. In response, many Palestinians living abroad started attacking Israelis in cyberspace. They used relatively simple tools to deface Israeli government websites. The Israelis retaliated, and thus began the Electronic Intifada, which continues to this day. Anti-Israeli Lebanese Shiite Muslims of Hezbollah started their own cyber war offensive and called it the Cyber Intifada. However, these attacks were generally basic hacks that barely scratched the surface.

Al-Qaeda was watching and recognized the propaganda value of the cyber attacks through hacking as well as the importance of maintaining the secrecy and security of communication. But propaganda dissemination was going to be priority one.

Al-Qaeda quickly established a network of volunteers, both in their bases and around the Muslim world, to produce and distribute materials for the followers. AQ founded media centers including al-Fajr and As-Sahab ("the Clouds"), the Global Islamic Media

Front (GIMF), and an array of other media operations that fell under this umbrella organization. AQ used regional centers for more focused coverage in vital areas of activity. *Al-Malahim*, named after the Islamic book of Battles (Slaughter), was the media outlet for al-Qaeda of the Arabian Peninsula (AQAP) that started in the cities of Saudi Arabia and ended up in exile in Yemen. *Al-Andalus* or Andalusia, the home of the golden age of Islam, was the name of media outlet for al-Qaeda of the Islamic Maghreb (AQIM) in North Africa and the sub-Saharan Africans. Each of these organizations developed their own style of narrating the story of honorable jihadist war and romance—and their distribution networks did the rest. Other groups assisted with translation or distribution.

At one point around 2010, according to a report from the terrorism research group the Middle East Media Research Institute (MEMRI), the four main jihadist media networks were outperformed by al-Qaeda affiliates like the Global Islamic Media Front (GIMF). These affiliates are responsible for publishing propaganda and for developing some of al-Qaeda's messaging and encryption apps. But right behind them was the newcomer to the game, al-Furqan, the group run by Zarqawi's al-Qaeda organization in Iraq.[2]

Over the first decade of the twenty-first century, al-Qaeda learned, understood, and weaponized the power of releasing cyber chaos. The group made good use of this time. In 2007, al-Qaeda's global webmaster who went by the handle "Irhabi007" (Arabic for Terrorist 007), Younis Tsouli, a 23-year-old, Moroccan-born British man, was arrested and sentenced to 10 years in prison in the UK. Paying much less attention to his two accomplices, Tariq al-Daour and Waseem Mughal, the British media quickly dubbed Tsouli the "Jihadist James Bond." Tsouli and his partners distributed a wide range of AQ video murders, handbooks for making car bombs, and suicide explosive belts.[3] By 2012, al-Qaeda would make a public call for its own Palestinian E-Intifada-like global "Electronic Jihad."[4] Any al-Qaeda fanboy or E-Jihadist who could not make it to the global battlefield was to dedicate his efforts to disrupting the West's computer networks and systems from the comfort of his home.

The AQ hacking groups were and continue to be at best engaged what could be described as cyber graffiti. They deface websites and other low-level targets. The hacking tool kits they employed were simple, but they lacked organization, man power, and a history of scored victories. Al-Qaeda announced the establishment of the Electronic Jihad through a video. In the video, the main speaker discussed US cyber vulnerabilities and exhorted a "covert mujahideen"[5] to organize and launch cyber attacks against the United States and the West. In July of the same year, US officials confirmed there was evidence that al-Qaeda was seeking to recruit Arab members of the global cyber "hacktivist" group Anonymous in order to build an al-Qaeda hacker collective of their own.[6]

Al-Qaeda organized several different groups including the official AQ Electronic Jihad Organization (Tanzim Al Qaedat al-Jihad al-Electroniyya), led by Yahya al-Nemr (Jonathan the Lion), who was previously related to other amateur groups including the Iraqi Electronic Forces (Qwat al-electriniyaa al-Iraq), the Holy War Hackers Team (Team Al-Hackers Al-Mujahidin), and the al-Mareek Media Arm. He was an Iraqi who lived in Egypt and was last known to be living in Afghanistan. The extent of his operations involved simple defacements of websites.

Many of these al-Qaeda hacking and E-graffiti efforts were spearheaded by the young men who filled the ranks of al-Qaeda in Iraq. But another group would soon join them: the sons and daughters of the ex-Baathist Iraqis who lost their livelihoods after the fall of Saddam. They, too, knew how to use the web, their mobile phones, and the deepest parts of the Internet to send forth a message that would strike simultaneously with their military offensive to seize and capture both Iraq and Syria. They would become the electronic swords of the Islamic State of Iraq and al-Sham (ISIS). The Cyber soldiers of the Caliphate.

Chapter 4

The ISIS Cyber Hierarchy

We must spread our principles, not with words but with deeds, for this is the most popular, the most potent, and the most irresistible form of propaganda.

—*Mikhail Bakunin, 1870.*[1]

Propaganda by deed would be the byword for all of al-Qaeda in Iraq's (AQI) operations. The image of the fighters in the field presented as fearless and fighting under the protection of Allah was critical to sustaining the incoming flow of recruits that was crucial to breaking the American will to fight in Iraq. AQI would extend its entire range of jihad across the world by harnessing the power of media and the Internet. Videos showing training, planning, attacking, and ending the attack by slitting throats of all captives were going to play well across the media-hungry world. The more brutal the better.

Everyone in the world was familiar with al-Qaeda—primarily because of the 9/11 attacks and the media repeatedly showing two or three old photos of Bin Laden from the late 1990s or his deputy Dr. Ayman al-Zawahiri. However, al-Qaeda operations would only reach their pinnacle when al-Baghdadi took command.

In 2011, Abu Bakr al-Baghdadi was transitioning AQI's name and activities into the far more brutal and Iraqi-led Islamic State of Iraq and al-Sham (the Levant), or ISIS. His chief of intelligence, Haji Bakr, a former Iraqi Air Force counterintelligence officer, was also fully aware of the importance of mounting a digital offensive. In order for the future caliphate, the homeland of all Muslims without borders or class distinctions, to be established, the world must see what commitment and depth of heart must truly be like. Everything would be recorded, edited, made into the most rapturous propaganda, and then released via the Internet. Well before the caliphate was up and running, al-Qaeda and AQI's cyber communications and recruitment was well on its way.

The terrorist organizations in Iraq knew well how to conduct media operations, but it was imperative to use the fighters to create a media revolution. ISIS would stun the world by demonstrating its persistence and international presence through its media and Internet offensive. In order to do this, it had to substantially improve the professionalism of its preproduction, filming, and editing and ensure that distribution of its message would be effective well before it could go onto the web.

ISIS created Internet media teams compromised of imported news media and online developer talent. Many were experienced TV and radio news station technicians who likely had no choice but to assist in helping ISIS when their hometowns in Iraq or Syria, especially the cities of Raqqa and Mosul, were taken by force. Most were Sunni Muslims who fought or supported the ex-Saddamist insurgents who outfought the US Army, but when ISIS came along it offered the opportunity to join something bigger, in which their value as professional production staffs were honored and necessary.

The online media teams established their different identities by using names like al-Furqan, al-Hayat, or the various Wilayat Media Centers. But the cyber warriors, they were a different breed. They were shadowy groups of individuals who were hard to distinguish from the professionals. When hackers posted about the latest victims of their DDoS attacks, the problem for western intelligence services was to determine to which jihad entity they belonged. Were they even members of ISIS? The picture would remain muddied for a long time until they started to consolidate and form bands of hackers intent on rivaling the operations of the fighters in the field.

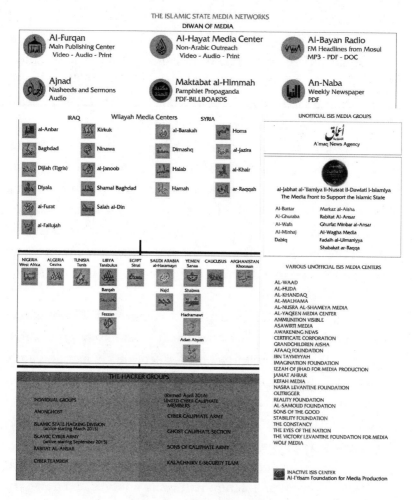

Figure 3: The ISIS Cyber Matrix.

ISIS power came from heeding lessons learned, exploiting the history, and acquired the manpower of both AQI and the ex-Saddam loyalists and forged them into five distinct operational units:

1. **THE MEDIA PROPAGATION TEAMS** included video and audio production, print/graphic, and propagating systems. They would disseminate the global message of the caliphate.

2. **THE CYBER COMMUNICATIONS SQUAD.** Those in a global network of activists and supporters outside of the caliphate and trusted members within would help set up both overt and secret communication channels on programs such as Telegram and WhatsApp. They would inform and educate the other members not in the caliphate on how to conduct operational security (OpSec) and work as the "Help Desk" to let trusted people gain access to the Caliphates databases.

3. **THE FUNCTIONARIES.** Routine operations of running a nation state would require computing power to conduct fund raising, using money provided by Islamic charities and through taxation, imposing licensing fees, bribes and extortion, as well as tracking combat operations and paying the fighters and those in logistical support units. The Adara or "administration" would account for everyone in the ISIS organization or under its thumb—this is the most valuable information in the organization because all of the real name data would be found within its databases. For those engaged in counterterrorism, this information was the keys to the kingdom.

4. **THE RECRUITER BROTHERS AND SISTERS.** They would reach out across the web and inspire tens of thousands of men and women to abandon their former lives and come to the caliphate to help establish the paradise that God himself commanded. Though hidden from view, the "sisters" of the cyber jihad had a profound role in enticing both women and men to come to the caliphate.

5. **THE HACKERS.** The smallest unit and the one with the broadest range. A small band of "E-Jihadist" volunteers

would be tasked to bring about their own "Cyber Jihad" by attacking the West on all electronic media. These would be the most technically savvy members within the caliphate; they would also handle the volunteers in cyberspace.

THE MEDIA PROPAGATION TEAMS

Terrorism by media has long required an effective stream from the production level to the user level to get the most shock for your efforts. From the days of cassettes and pamphlets passed among believers to the videos dropped off to Al Jazeera in hopes of immediately hitting the airwaves, jihadists of the past knew they had to use a range of available media conduits to disseminate their message whether internal or external. If you are going to hide your message and restrict access to members only, you still need an effective network to spread the word without being detected by an adversary. If detected, vital information could fall into the hands of adversaries. ISIS engages in both internal and external messaging.

The standard consumer gadget-to-media technology curve has led to a tremendous jump in access to powerful creation, editing, and production tools for media that puts professional level results into the hands of the owners of computers, smartphones, and tablets. In addition, sophisticated encryption methods were not at the forefront of public conversation but were in play well before the Edward Snowden case. The ability to make a professional-looking video today is in the hands of amateurs, and ISIS has a distinct ambition to use these tools for low-to no-cost campaigns.

Over the years, jihadist production houses have sought to simultaneously disseminate materials and maintain message control. There has long been a tendency in jihadist groups to attempt to maintain both secrecy and brand quality and recognition at the same time. Before ISIS, there were media groups that maintained an official outlet for their related terrorist groups via websites or forums. After two years of ISIS presence in the jihadist media world, there have been increased demands to remove all content associated with ISIS from the Internet. This has had a direct effect on the recycling nature of ISIS media websites where domain names have begun to cease resembling their media center because of the risk of being detected.

THE ISIS MEDIA COUNCIL

From the beginning of ISIS's days as al-Qaeda in Iraq (AQI), there has been a leader of the media wing who helped call the shots and support the leadership with a controlled messaging campaign directed at unbelievers that projected strength and prophetic destiny. This role was as critical to the organization as any military operation in the field. To bolster that role, they established a wide range of media councils and regional media centers. The cabinet member position for the ISIS media is led by an "Emir" or prince.

From AQI to ISI to ISIS, the group has maintained a consistent structure with roles for both Minister of Information and Spokesman for the organization. Under al-Zarqawi, the AQI organizational mouthpiece was Abu Maysara al-Iraqi. Under Abu Ayyub al-Masri, the first ISI spokesman, Abu Muhammad Mashhadani, would handle the spokesman duties until his capture in 2007. And under Abu Bakr al-Baghdadi, the first ISIS spokesman would be Abu Muhammed al-Adnani.

First Spokesman Emir for al-Qaeda in Iraq (AQI)
Abu Maysara al-Iraqi (2004–2007)—*Killed March 2007*

The first spokesman for the organization that would become ISIS was Abu Maysara al-Iraqi. When ISIS was still in its infancy, Abu Maysara's name popped up in web forums like Muntada al-Ansar to promote the latest utterances of the then-leader of AQI, Abu

Musab al-Zarqawi.[2] To get into these forums, one had to be vetted, and the entry was password protected. Abu Maysara was a Syrian and, in addition to his media work, had many other job responsibilities. He had been captured by Coalition forces on November 29, 2004. He was identified by the US Army as "Muhammad Wasim Abdullah Halabi." He was held at Badush prison until freed in the mass prison break in March 2007. His freedom didn't last long; he was killed on November 17, 2007, just northeast of Samarra. Coalition forces started a massive campaign to hunt down and kill all AQI media sources, and Maysara was target number one. According to the Pentagon, his body was positively identified by DNA. Maysara was also living in a technological setting quite different from the ones Islamic State fighters encountered, since he had access to mobile phones and Internet. Twitter, YouTube, and other media sharing sites were not available yet, so the spokesperson for Zarqawi turned to YouSendIt to share files online.[3]

First Minister of Information for al-Qaeda in Iraq (AQI)
Muharib Abdul Latif al-Jubouri—*Killed May 2007*

Named the al-Qaeda in Iraq Minister of Information, Muharib Abdul Latif al-Jubouri was responsible for the al-Qaeda in Iraq propaganda releases. He was also noted for a role in the kidnapping of Jill Carroll, an American journalist, in 2006, and American peace activist Tom Fox in November 2005.

Al-Jubouri was killed along with four others near the Camp Taji military base north of Baghdad. The predawn raid was a part of Operation Rat Trap. Six other workers were arrested. His death was announced by Maj. Gen. William Caldwell on May 4, 2007,[4] and was celebrated as martyrdom by forums linked to AQI. After his death there was speculation about whether he was secretly "Abu Omar al-Baghdadi," the leader of AQI who was in fact later killed on April 18, 2010, in Tikrit, Iraq.

First Spokesman Emir for Islamic State in Iraq (ISI)
Khalid Abdul Fatah Da'ud Mahmud al-Mashhadani[5]
(a.k.a. Abu Zayd al-Mashhadani, Abu Muhammad al-Mashhadani,
and Abu Shahid)

With a long history in jihadist groups including time as leader
of Ansar al-Sunna, al-Mashhadani was the first Minister of
Information after the process that transformed AQI into ISI
in 2006.[6] A very trusted agent of Osama Bin Laden, he was
close to the interim joint AQI leader, Abu Ayyub al-Masri. In
this capacity, he was responsible not only for media responsibilities, but he was a liaison officer between AQI and the leaders of al-Qaeda in Afghanistan. Al-Mashhadani was captured
in a raid in Mosul in July 2007. Coalition forces had specially
targeted the media centers for months before the raid. A few
months later, coalition forces arrested a Saudi video editor
with special effects skills and a computer graphics artist. Navy
Rear Adm. Gregory Smith explained the mission: "Since the
surge began, we've uncovered eight separate al-Qaeda media
offices and cells, have captured or killed 24 al-Qaeda propaganda cell members, and have discovered 23 terabytes of information."[7]

In July 2007, the reported mass haul of AQI media materials
came after a raid in Samarra found a fully functioning film studio
that was capable of mass producing CDs, DVDs, posters, pamphlets, and web materials. The raid found a dozen computers, 65
hard drives, hundreds of CDs, and 18 thumb drives.[8]

First ISIS Minister of Information
Abu Mohammad al-Furqan—*Killed September 2016*
Wa'el Adel Hasan Salman al-Fayad
Head of al-Furqan—Senior Shura Council member
a.k.a. Dr. Wa'el al-Rawi, Dr. Wa'el Adel Hussain

Known as "Dr. Wa'el," he was one of the more elusive ISIS figures, yet he was responsible for the creation and publication of thousands of videos, mp3s, pdfs, and the system that projected weaponized media to the world. He was the head of al-Furqan, the first and main ISIS media house, as well as al-Hayat, the non-Arabic ISIS outlet, and was a board member of Amaq News Agency.[9] He also played a role in the publication of the weekly newsletter *an-Naba*.

He was chosen by the Shura Council to be the replacement for Abu Muhammad al-Adnani. He worked closely with Abu Muhammad al-Adnani, who was killed just nine days before. The Pentagon announced on September 16[10] that Wa'el was killed on September 7, 2016, in Raqqa. Though the news of this death took over a week to travel to the West, it was noted the next day, September 8, 2016, by Abu Musab al-Zarqawi's mentor, Syrian Salafist scholar, Abu Muhammad al-Maqdisi, who confirmed Dr. Wa'el was dead. The trail of whether and when these players had been killed or captured is a long and confused one. After al-Rawi's death, Craig Whiteside of the Naval War College noted that it was the third time the United States had killed both the spokesman and media emir for ISIS at the same time. The first was when Abu Maysara and an unnamed media emir were captured. In 2007, Muharib and Mashhadani were killed. In 2016, it was al-Adnani first, then Dr. Wa'el a week later.[11]

Figure 4: Abu Al-Atheer al-Absi as seen in al-Furqan video. (Source: TAPSTRI)

First ISIS Emir of Media
Abu al-Atheer Amr al-Absi—*Killed March 2016*

Amr al-Absi was the emir of ISIS media until his death in 2016 by a US drone attack. Al-Absi rose through the ranks in Syria's early civil war battles. He was a core member in the establishment of the caliphate. It was al-Absi who helped bring Omar al-Shishani (Omar the Chechen), the black-bearded Chechen warlord, to support Abu Bakr al-Baghdadi. Some have suggested it was al-Absi who put the idea in al-Baghdadi's head to declare the caliphate.[12]

Amr al-Absi and his older brother, Firas al-Absi, were well-established members of the jihadist cadre before the announcement of the caliphate. Firas al-Absi had been known to Abu Musab al-Zarqawi since 2000, since the al-Absi brothers were prominent in the Syrian town of Aleppo. The older brother, Firas, was the founder of the ISIS advisory council, or "Majlis Shura Dawlat al Islam." His group was also involved in kidnappings, and eventually Amr came to be known as "kidnapper in chief" by both the United States and Britain.[13] Amr al-Absi would eventually become the Emir of the media. Under his authority, ISIS personnel in the media efforts turned to recruiting online volunteers from the region and also ones in North Africa to engage in an online offensive that was preparing to seize an opportunity. In an attempt to gather as many fighters to the cause as possible, the campaign presented images of a victorious group that was vibrant and active. They knew that fighters under al-Qaeda influence were restless for results, so they crafted the image necessary to recruit over 10,000 fighters from around the world.

Firas was killed in August 2012 by the Salafist group al-Farouq Battalion over territorial disputes and because he was extorting payments from those seeking access trade routes along the northern Syria border with Turkey.[14] The younger brother took over the group, and under his guidance the group would become a major component to the ISIS campaign to seize land in Syria and Iraq in the summer of 2014. The younger brother went on to become the Emir of Halab. In September 2014, he also became a designated terrorist under Executive Order 13224. He was featured once in a video from the al-Furqan series called *Messages from the Land of Epics*, which also featured the former Chechen military Emir Omar al-Shishani. In the video, you can watch al-Absi and al-Shishani plan an attack on Assad's 66th Brigade. He, too, was killed in an airstrike on March 3, 2016, by the Syrian Air Force.

First ISIS Official Spokesman
Abu Muhammad al-Adnani— *Killed August 2016*

Perhaps the only man in a position that rivals that of the caliph, Abu Bakr al-Baghdadi, was his mouthpiece, the official spokesperson. From 2006, the announcement of the transition from al-Qaeda in Iraq into the Islamic State of Iraq (ISIS) was handled by Abu Abdullah Moharib Abdul Latif al-Jubouri. He was also alleged to have been part of the kidnapping of American journalist Jill Carroll. He held this position until his death on May 3, 2007.

All of the transitional AQI members were good at their jobs, but they tended to have a short shelf life. The spokesman and media Emir for the Islamic State would most recently be held by one of the oldest and wiliest of the Old Guard, Abu Muhammad al-Adnani. Adnani was the voice of ISIS until his death was announced on August 30, 2016.[15] His real name was Taha Subhi Falaha.[16] Born in the Idlib town of Binnish, he had been an active jihadi and a prominent figure in the organization's lineage from Zarqawi's leadership until the present day and was reportedly personally involved with the selection of elements of the ISIS media campaign, including having control over what got released. This was confirmed by Harry Sarfo, the German documentarian who went to Syria and was featured in an August 2015 video shot in Palmyra, who said al-Adnani personally picks out videos that are to be released.[17]

Figure 5: Abu Muhammad al-Adnani.
(Source: TAPSTRI)

The announcement of al-Adnani's death was of no small consequence. It was al-Adnani who announced the caliphate had been restored for the first time since the fall of the Ottomans in 1924. It was al-Adnani who announced that Abu Bakr al-Baghdadi would be the new Caliph Ibrahim as a rightful descendent of the Prophet Muhammad.

Adnani had a role much larger than simply being a spokesman. According to reporting by *New York Times* reporter Rukmini Callimachi, Adnani was in charge of a secret organization within ISIS known as the "al-Amni" or "Security," a group that was a dual-purpose intelligence cell used to spy on ISIS members and conduct covert operations outside of Syria and Iraq.[18]

Adnani was killed in Aleppo on August 30, 2016. The announcement of his death on that same day came first from the Amaq News Agency before an official notice of his death was released by an ISIS official. Telegram channels posted photos of him for days. The *an-Naba* newsletter featured his death in their first release after his death a day later. Videos from Al-Battar and other memorials followed. ISIS had lost its voice in another round of defeats by the coalition of nations.

Figure 6: The AMAQ news agency delivers the news that the ISIS mouthpiece has been silenced. (Source: TAPSTRI).

In September, ISIS launched a new multilingual web magazine called *Rumiyah* through their al-Hayat Media Center. It was released the day after al-Adnani was killed, yet he was on the cover and in the first and last pages. No replacement for al-Adnani was announced by the group in the subsequent weeks.

Figure 7: The official notice from ISIS of the death of spokesman Abu Muhammad al-Adnani. (Source: TAPSTRI)

Chapter 5

The ISIS Cyber Fighters

THE WEBSITES AND WEB FORUMS

For the longest time, the locations for jihadist activity online, before the creation of social media sites or Telegram channels, were the standard website or web forums. Though they became rarer after increased pressure to eliminate terrorist propaganda from the Net, there were still standard run-of-the-mill terrorist websites found on file hosting servers. The jihadist media operatives also built a standard set of tools from stand-alone pages to CMS (content management systems) like WordPress, Joomla, PHPNuke, etc., to simplify the website construction for all.

The history of al-Qaeda and ISIS would not be complete without mentioning their online web forums. It is as much a standard weapon for them as the AK-47 assault rifle. Used to post lectures, graphics, and eventually videos, these sites have served as the backbone of jihadist propaganda for over 20 years. They were often hosted with small, random web hosting companies often without the knowledge of their hosts. Whether the sites were used for posting the latest sermons, mission reports, martyrdom celebrations, or the occasional speech by terrorist VIPs, the forums of al-Qaeda and video posting sites of ISIS roamed the frontier of cyberspace until ISIS came along. Because of the overt savagery of their terrorism spectacles, the managers of the Internet's hosting spaces have routinely removed ISIS materials from their servers. Though full-blown stand-alone websites still pop up in announcements of momentous events, deaths, and other administration or news, their names are getting more and more obscure.

In order to evade detection, the site creators would sometimes build the sites away from the base or "root directory" of the website. Instead, they would install them in a secondary folder to throw off undesired detection. Often the folder used was named "vb," e.g., the "alfidaa.biz" site was found at "alfidaa.biz/vb/." But by the middle of 2016, website forums related to ISIS were using domain names that show little resemblance to the topic of ISIS. For example, the URL "gavlikop529.ml" was published mid-July 2016 for a very popular site that has bounced around the Surface and Dark Webs for nearly two years since the announcement of ISIS's caliphate.

In many situations, the reason a website location disappears is related to a high-profile media clip that draws people to search out the origin. For instance, the Muntada al-Ansar website was being hosted on a server in Malaysia until the Nick Berg video was posted, and the server company shut the servers down entirely to prevent any further propagation of the video from their servers. The small server company stated it had no knowledge that a terrorist organization was using the server space in this manner.

There was a point at which posting videos and discussions was a frequent pattern of the online ISIS community; but increasingly, with the repeated takedowns of materials on WordPress, Tumblr, and other platforms, those efforts have been driven into Telegram feeds, and some remain in Twitter form. There are also Facebook groups that are occasionally identified as originating from ISIS and taken down.

Figure 8: Screenshot of the Ansar al-Mujahideen Forum's "Jihaad [sic] Related Media" thread. (Source: TAPSTRI)

Shumukh al-Islam (The Pride of Islam)

There have been many notable forums for jihadist activities over the decades. One of the most notable ones is the Shumukh al-Islam forum, created by Nabil Amdouni in 2007.[1] A prime resource for more than just propaganda materials, the forum was a hub for all types of conversations in the jihadist world.

Amdouni, a Tunisian, worked for Shumukh al-Islam under the pseudonym "Abu Ayman." He was arrested in July 2012 in Toulon and sentenced to eight years in prison, a sentence that was affirmed on appeal in April 2016. He stated he regrets his participation in militant life and that he has undergone a change in prison.[2] Shumukh al-Islam had the official nod from al-Fajr media and was a chief outlet for any official materials under al-Qaeda. An ideal portal for sharing secrecy tools with terrorists, Al-Fajr used the forum to publish the release of its encryption program Amn al-Mujahid in December 2013.[3]

The forum was a very popular portal for jihadist media that was approved by both ISIS and al-Qaeda. There were posts that were encrypted, discussions on tactics, strategies, fundraising, and a steady flow of recruiting. Amdouni admitted to helping facilitate people going to Yemen.

As a gateway for jihad, the forum led from merely playing a role undercover for ISIS media to actually engaging in fighting for some. A Moroccan ISIS defector who was a media operative for ISIS spoke to the *Washington Post* under the name "Abu Hajer." He said that before he became involved in ISIS video productions, he had been an administrator of Shumukh[4] after a decade of being active in various militant forums. Analyst for Flashpoint Partners, Laith Alkhouri, estimated the forum had around 15,000 members at the time of its being disrupted in July 2016.

The security of the forum came under scrutiny when a hacker hit an administrator of the forum with a "spearphishing" attack. Spearphishing is a method used to trick a specific person to clicking on a link inside of a false email full of malware attachments or with links to malware on a secret server. Abu Alaaina Khorasani was the site administrator targeted in the attack. The hacker threatened the administrators of the forum with releasing information on *their* information if they didn't make him a technical leader or Tech Commander.[5] The correspondence was revealed by an independent researcher who operates under the Twitter handle "Switched" with a link to a Pastebin page. Whether he was a real ISIS player or a bold intelligence officer remains unknown.

Al-Minbar

Another very well-known forum for jihadist traffic was "al-Minbar Al-Jihad Al-I'lami." Al-Minbar did not require a password to read posts, but in order to interact with the forum's site, users had to register. Hosted at alplatformmedia.com, the forum was often called al-Platform forum instead of al-Minbar. Like many forum communities, users posted like-minded materials—but this one focused on calls for violence against governments, officials, and other prime "enemy" targets—as well as innocent citizens

Isdarat

Known for its publications of ISIS official and unofficial videos, Isdarat was one of the most prolific video sites that supports the ISIS video propaganda flow. Its URLs varied on a regular basis due to takedowns. Likewise, its Twitter channel rarely remained up for very long. Its Telegram channel was more like a chatroom than other ISIS channels that are simply broadcasting channels.

Figure 9: Logo from the Isdarat Telegram Channel. (Source: TAPSTRI)

Figure 10: Isdarat doesn't last long on the web, whether it's Twitter or Facebook.
(Source: TAPSTRI)

THE TELEGRAM REVOLUTION

Telegram burst on the scene in the second half of 2015 after the announcement about the use of the app in the Paris attack operations in November 2015.

Telegram is a secure, encrypted chat, audio, and file sharing program for mobile phones that quickly became the preferred ISIS communications application. In September 2015, ISIS added the ability to create channels, which changed the app from simply a secret messaging app to a massive hidden forum platform ripe with content from the world's active terrorist organizations. Multitudes of groups post in channels that are outside the scrutiny of Google and other search engines. Yet if you sign in on the phone app or via Telegram's website today, you'll find not only ISIS, AQ, and other terrorist channels, but a wide range of conversations.

The file-server-based channels hosting chats and postings are fine-tuned to different functions, ranging from video publications to the latest rant on how the medieval scholar Ibn Taymiyyah interpreted a Quran passage or the online trolls of Online Da'wah, who seek out Facebook and Twitter posts and invade the posts with comments in favor of ISIS. A "troll" is, among other things, a deliberately ill-intentioned or malignant abuser of the Internet.

Typically, these Online Da'wah attacks are indistinguishable from any other political bickering found on Facebook or Twitter except that the Online Da'wah campaigners are explicitly being sent there to troll on behalf of ISIS.

These Telegram channels are popular and effectively inform no differently from a stand-alone website. Analysts and journalists are able to quickly find these channels by followers who share Join Chat links that help restore access to channels that either deleted themselves or were deleted by Telegram. However, there are many channels that are closely monitored by their administrators and quickly ban users they suspect of being spies.

TWITTER

In 2014, the territory that ISIS invaded along with Iraq and Syria was Twitter.

Twitter is a short posting program that allows the user to send messages of a maximum of 140 characters. If a graphic is included, it decreases to 125 characters.

Figure 11: ISIS fanboys hijacked the Twitter logo.

With millions of accounts, the system quickly became the go-to place for the followers of ISIS to recruit, propagandize, and rejoice in the twenty-first-century way. The use of Twitter by ISIS ranged from low-end chatter about the latest releases or news to specific contacts posted in publications like "Hijrah to the Islamic State," which advised getting in touch with a member known as @Abuzakariyyahls.[6] In February 2016, Twitter published a post stating that it had suspended "over 125,000" accounts that were "primarily related to ISIS." In response, ISIS slowed their usage of Twitter and urged followers to use the encrypted app messenger Surespot to communicate.[7]

The Case of Jalil ibn Ameer Aziz, Colonel Shami

Fifty-seven Twitter accounts to his name. On June 29, 2014, Aziz issued his bay'ah to al-Baghdadi via Twitter under @AnsarUmmah. From these accounts, he frequently posted violent comments, including the repeated "#KillAllKufar" under his @AnsuralUmmah8 account, or a threat to decapitate President Obama under his account @Colonel_Shami on January 29, 2015.[8] He was quick to post about the Chapel Hill shooting of three Muslim students under his @abubritani3 account, stating "#usa will pay for #Chapel-HillShooting we will make sure you don't live in peace" on February 11, 2015. He added, "This martyrdom will be a spark that awaken the sleeping lions in America, let their blood watered the side of jihad #ChapelHillShooting." He chimed in on the March 2015 release of Military Personnel info by an ISIS group called the Islamic State Hacking Group with a few retweets.

The Case of Bilal Abood

Former U.S. military translator Bilal Abood of Mesquite, TX, on June 19, 2014, pledged his bay'āt via Twitter under "ibn_alislaam," and he had created an account associated with a Hotmail account, albaghdady_1978@hotmail.com. He had a penchant for passing on tweets for the Islamic State, which eventually caught up with him. He then later lied about his pledge to the FBI when they asked. As a result of his actions, he was sentenced to four years in federal prison for making false statements.[9]

FACEBOOK

There are dozens of cases of ISIS radicalization and recruitment that involve the use of Facebook as both messenger and platform for ideas. The use of these tools shows up in many of the cases in the United States including cases in which suspects befriended under-cover agents and shared elaborate plans to travel to fight or launch attacks with a complete stranger that could be and was law enforcement.

Real ISIS agents on one side of recruitment and real FBI agents on the other side of conversations with targets of investigation show what a tangled world the indoctrinated subject was engaged in either to go to Syria or to engage in lone wolf attacks. Yet, this cautionary tale didn't stop dozens of people who have already been arrested and prosecuted on material support charges.

ISIS was very aware of the utility of Facebook in recruiting potential followers and aims specific campaigns to disrupt posts most often related to Middle East or the Muslim world. The goal was to both recruit for ISIS and to shame Muslims into joining ISIS as part of their religious obligation.

Case Study: Alexander Ciccolo

In July 2015, Alexander Ciccolo,[10] an American from Boston who fancied himself a jihadi named "Ali the American," dreamt of becoming an honored holy warrior. But his dream came to a halt after he planned an attack on a local bar.[11] Ciccolo was once a peacenik who protested against nuclear power plants. He was now willing to kill in the name of the Islamic State.[12] On Facebook, Ciccolo operated under the name "Ali Al-Amriki" until he changed it to "Ali NoSisters Al Amriki."[13] Another example is the son of a police captain who had multiple profiles on Facebook. He sought to attack using the same explosives employed by the Boston Marathon bombers, the Tsarnaev brothers. However, he intended to livestream the event on the Internet so the entire world could see his mass murder in real time.

Ciccolo used his profiles on Facebook to express his desire to kill others and die as a martyr. He would applaud attacks like the Sousse beach attack in Tunisia in June 2015 that killed 38 tourists, mainly from Britain. In addition to his hateful ISIS views, Ciccolo had expressed the desire to wear a Nazi outfit to school and said that he considered Hitler "so bright and beautiful."

Eventually, Ciccolo was arrested after an undercover sting in which an informant sold him four guns; he intended to use them to kill innocent civilians. He was prohibited from possessing a firearm due to a previous conviction. Ciccolo's goal was to attack a university outside of his state. A federal grand jury indicted him in July 2016 on material support charges, attempting to use a weapon of mass destruction (the pressure cooker bomb), illegal firearms possession (due to a previous conviction), and assault with a deadly weapon for attacking a nurse with a pen.[14]

Facebook Live Video Streaming

In June 2016, an attack on a police officer Jean-Baptiste Salvaing and his partner was announced in a live stream by their killer, Larossi Abbala, who used a new Facebook feature launched in spring of 2016 to stream video. In the video, he expressed his support for ISIS and loyalty to al-Baghdadi while pondering what to do with the three-year-old son who may have witnessed the entire event. Authorities said Abbala had other targets including high profile TV personalities.[15]

TUMBLR

Like Facebook, Tumblr is a photo posting and microblogging program that can allow the jihadi fanboy or fangirl to build up a social circle that engages in its exclamation of hopes and desires to join the fight against the unbelievers. With an overwhelming number of posts devoted to porn, Tumblr was a perfect place to hide pro-ISIS images. Tumblr also acts like a diary, and for a period of time many ISIS followers shared their fantastical stories of making *Hijrah*, or yearning to go to the caliphate, on Tumblr.

Diary of a Muhajirah—"Umm Layth"

Aqsa Mahmood, a resident of Glasgow, was a medical student who traveled to Syria in November 2013. The daughter of Pakistani immigrants to the UK, Mahmood took to Tumblr to express her views as an ISIS bride. Posting under the name "Umm Layth," she posted enthusiastic comments about attacks attributed to ISIS on her blog, fatubalilghuraba.tumblr.com.[16]

Beginning in January 2013, Mahmood posted on Tumblr until September 2015. Her most noted post was a checklist of "musthave" items for women traveling to Syria. Not only did she have advice about what bras and undergarments you could wear, but she had advice for the ladies to "avoid searching things from your home Wi-Fi and devices you plan to bring" and "don't download anything that could cause suspicion." Her post on what to bring said to only bring Android operating system phones, and "No Apple" devices because ISIS did not trust them.[17] She was suspected of having a hand in recruiting Amira Abase, Shamima Begum, and Kadiza Sultana, three teen British girls who left to go to Syria in February 2015.[18] Most of them would die there.

The Story of Terrence McNeil—"Abu Fil"

Terrence Joseph McNeil, a twenty-five-year-old Akron, Ohio, hospital worker, was arrested and charged with over one hundred counts of soliciting violence and threatening military personnel when he posted the names of over one hundred military personnel and threatened to have them killed. He was an avid user of Tumblr and posted on June 12, 2015, "If you mean the Islamic State I have stated many times that I do support them." McNeil would most often post to Tumblr as "Abu-fil" at abu-fil.tumblr.com. He shared this URL via Twitter to another user, "@bint_crackeriya abu-fil.tumblr.com my Tumblr."[19] McNeil posted to Tumblr that he would go to ISIS's caliphate (Dar al-Islam, land of Islam) or attack at home (Dar al-Kuffer, land of the unclean) in his post, which stated, "Hijrah from dar al kufr to dar al islam or jihad in dar al kufr" to Tumblr under his "Abu-fil" account. In April 21, 2015, he stated, "No American citizen was safe, fisabilillah [In the path of Allah] they are all valid target." He followed up with another threat on July 7, 2015: "Too many homicidal thoughts,"Abu-fil. He openly celebrated the attack by Muhammad Youssef Abdulazeez, the killer at a US Navy & Marine Corps recruiting office, in Chattanooga, Tennessee, on July 16, 2015.

MULTILINGUAL MEDIA

The beauty of the ISIS media and cyber effort is that it lends itself to broad availability internationally but can also focus on regions that might easily be overlooked. Using regional distinctions to divide the digital terrain into more manageable target zones and areas of responsibility gave ISIS the ability to optimize resources.

ISIS wasn't the first terrorist organization to explore the need for multilingual tool sets but it has become the most engaged. The organization has expanded its publications into over 28 languages, including French, German, Spanish, Portuguese, Russian, Bosnian, Bengali, Turkish, and Indonesian. It has openly sought to recruit from around the world, so it has produced many key releases in multiple languages. The primary outlets that produce such material have been al-Furqan and the more specialized unit al-Hayat Media Center. However, it is not uncommon for videos to come from one of the *wilayat* releases, especially out of Aleppo, where there have been releases aimed from foreign fighters to their respective countries of origin.

Figure 12: The al-Furqan video And Wretched Is That Which They Bought *features a child executioner along with Sabri Essid, stepbrother of Mohamed Merah, the Toulouse, France, attacker. (Source: TAPSTRI)*

A particularly shocking al-Furqan video was released on March 10, 2015. It was aimed at Israel and used a French-speaking fighter, accompanied by a child who killed a man ISIS accused of being "a

Mossad spy," Muhammad Musallam. The roughly thirteen-minute video titled *And Wretched Is That Which They Bought* [*Purchased*] features a forced confession from Musallam before the fighter identified as Sabri Essid.[20] He and the young executioner are pictured with Musallam in a field. The well-known al-Furqan video ends with the child executing Musallam with a gunshot through the head.

Figure 13: A video out of ar-Raqqa, Syria, titled You will be disappointed and humiliated, oh Russians! *aims its threats in Russian from an undisclosed location in Syria before executing an alleged FSB officer. (Source: TAPSTRI)*

The Wilayat ar-Raqqa video release called *You will be disappointed and humiliated, oh Russians!* and released in December 2015 featured a Russian executioner beheading a man who identifies himself as Khasiev Magomid, a Chechen from Grozy.[21] The video begins with a forced confession where Magomid claims he has been working for the Russian FSB intelligence service. He confesses that his mission was to collect intelligence on Russians who had gone to Syria. Chechen leader Ramzan Kadyrov issued a denial of the validity of Magomid's confession but also warned that there would be consequences for his death.[22]

Knowing how much effort ISIS aims at each region can give you some insight into development patterns in attacks and resource allocation. "Messages to the Maghreb," calling for focusing on Morocco, Algeria, and Tunisia, was released in early 2016.

THE HIJRI CALENDAR

Figure 14: Hijri Calendar.

Another facet of the battlefield with ISIS was keeping up with differing calendars. When it comes to matching up "claims of responsibility" graphics or al-Bayan radio releases, ISIS observes the hijri calendar it releases every month. All the metrics videos released by ISIS through al-Janoub and through al-Sayna are also noted according to their hijri month and hijri year. But by mid-2016, Amaq News agency began to add conventional calendar dates to its releases. Previously there were often no notifications in their graphics of dates associated with events.

Chapter 6

Software of the Global Jihad

As average Internet users around the world know, online web tools are very useful—particularly for ISIS operatives and fanboys. In many ways their behavior on these websites, social media, and apps was not unlike the average Internet user sharing the latest news or music clip or video with her friends. But in a very distinct way, the ISIS/AQ followers are using the tools for ongoing operations, to celebrate perceived victories, or to recruit and train members.

The use of tools by ISIS/AQ and other groups was largely dictated by the perceived security of any particular tool from detection or interference by counteroperations, including those carried out by law enforcement or the military. Frequently updated OpSec postings by ISIS on various channels and pasting websites cover not only cell phone security, but discussions about the perceived security of the apps or social media outlets recommended and used by terrorist groups. There are Telegram channels like the *Horizon (Afaaq)* channel dedicated to the lone discussion of cyber security for the terrorist user. The channels associated with the Cyber Caliphate Army are often filled with up-to-date tech posts from American or European tech sites and their discussion on technology.

Security was and still is a major concern for terrorist groups, which work hard to stay well informed about which apps will help them elude law enforcement and intelligence agencies. Similarly, activist groups stuck in Syria between Assad and ISIS uses many of these apps to avoid detection by both ISIS and the Assad forces. But the opposition to ISIS mounts counteroperations that seek not only to detect but also intercept or interrupt the communications among operation organizers, recruiters, and end users.

One effort that ISIS employs consistently is devoted to maintaining a level of operational security that at least successfully eludes the surveillance of intelligence services. Many cases before the US courts showed that the suspects were given specific instructions on phone purchases, messaging systems, emailing, and destroying traces of activities.

Take, for instance, the case of Jalil Ibn Ameer Aziz in Harrisburg, Pennsylvania. In the complaint, it is alleged that Aziz told his coconspirator to switch to a "US-based messaging application that allows for encrypted communications." Also, upon starting on his way to Syria, Aziz told his conspirator to wipe "pro IS materials" from his laptop. Another example is the Hendricks case related to the Garland, Texas, attack, where strenuous efforts were made to direct others to specific messaging apps and to advise operatives and sympathizers about how to use an anonymizing app.

For all the work these ISIS channels or posts put into advising followers on how to avoid detection, many cases in the United States and Europe show that the end users were not always so savvy at executing the advice.

In addressing the security skills of terrorists, CIA Director John Brennan spoke at the Center for Strategic and International Studies (CSIS) in November 2015 and said:

> But I must say that there has been a significant increase in the operational security of a number of these operatives and terrorist networks as they have gone to school on what it is that they need

to do in order to keep their activities concealed from the authorities.[1]

The constant endeavor to track terrorists using their communication tools involves more than simply trying to crack the encryption of their phone and devices or figuring out which social media platform ISIS prefers for the moment. It also involves looking at the metadata that are produced—the raw digital fingerprint and location information, knowing the flaws and slipups of terrorists using these tools, and knowing the trends that the groups or members themselves recommend and why.

END-TO-END ENCRYPTED MESSAGING APPS

End-to-End messaging apps are often cited as a key tool in ISIS planning and recruiting. ISIS used a range of messaging apps that were largely determined by perceived security and limited often to free downloads for Android devices.

Telegram

Figure 15: Telegram Logo.

Released in August of 2013, Telegram was the most popular end-to-end messenger for ISIS, and by the summer of 2016, Telegram had become the leading app for mass proliferation of ISIS media and announcements.

Telegram added "channels" to its app usage in September 2014, and with this came a burst of ISIS related "channels"[2] and a spectrum of channels catering to different groups within the jihadist world, from ISIS and al-Qaeda to more nationalistic groups like the Taliban using these channels. Channels are accessed as "open join" options in some cases, whereby anyone can participate and/or by special invite or "short term join" option in others. The channels post a wide array of propaganda and chatter about any number of events in the ongoing war on the apostates and unbelievers. This may be slide shows and videos from official ISIS media or the various satellite groups like Amaq News Agency or shout-outs announcing that a Twitter channel is back up after deletion.

Developed by Nikolai and Pavel Durov, the app features "secret chat." According to its founder, "The No. 1 reason for me to support and help launch Telegram was to build a means of communication that can't be accessed by the Russian security agencies, so I can talk about it for hours."[3] As of February 2016, Telegram user count hit 100 million users.[4] One example of the effect of this growth of users is Najim Laachroui, who was a suspected accomplice in the March 2016 attack on the Brussels airport. He was alleged to have used Telegram to plan the operation with Syrian-based ISIS operatives. He had turned to Syrian allies to help test explosives he could use in attacks in France. Had authorities been able to intercept these messages, they might also have learned the discussed plans to attack a soccer championship or that he and colleagues were living in three separate safe houses.[5]

He maintained communication with Abu Ahmed, an ISIS commander in Syria, via Telegram. He used the app to report to Abu Ahmed that they had lost their AK-47 ammunition in the March 15, 2016, raids in Belgium. In addition, investigators found his laptop and recovered more data including audio and texts.

Around the world, not much has been done to limit ISIS's use of Telegram. Iran is notorious for controlling Internet usage by most of those in the population. The Iranian government has cracked down on Telegram users, arresting over 100 group administrators and charging them with "immoral content" propagation.[6]

After the Paris attack in November 2015, ISIS began encouraging its followers to shift to using Telegram as a preferred messaging app. The claim of responsibility for the attacks was posted on channels related to ISIS. In the subsequent months, it would become common for analysts and news media outlets to turn to ISIS-related Telegram channels and media to keep up with claims of responsibility.

When it came to dealing with ISIS on their channels, Telegram stated to ProPublica that it had taken down more than 660 public ISIS channels as of July 2016.[7]

To back up its claim that it was maintaining security, Telegram launched a contest in early 2014 to invite hackers to break its encryption with a $200,000 Bitcoin prize for the hacker who could break their encryption and intercept a message in a "secret email" published by Telegram "backer" Pavel Durov.[8] By March 1, 2014, no winners were announced, and the contest was relaunched with a larger Bitcoin prize of $300,000. By the end of the contest in February 2015, there were no winners.[9]

ISIS issues warnings about channels and users who might be posing as ISIS members but instead turn out to be law enforcement seeking to discover the identities of the pro-ISIS users.[10]

In late November 2015, Sony Mobile Communications consultant Ola Flisbäck discovered metadata being displayed by the Telegram app that allowed for observing the activity of users mainly visible when using a "third party client such as vysheng's CLI client" to see and display the data. He pointed out that by observing the metadata you can "make guesses about who's talking to who" as well as data from other users the "victim" had in common with the "attacker."[11] Additionally, the targeted user or "victim" is not notified when they are added to the "attacker" contact list, and the "attacker" will receive subsequent metadata from the target. Thus an attacker can possibly ferret out the "target" by comparing contacts.

In February 2015, Zuk Avraham discovered he could see portions of texts by dumping the process memory and examining the "data-at-rest" information instead of the "data-in-transit" results.[12] In doing so, he was able to see portions of his test messages including the deleted messages.

WhatsApp

Released in January 2010, WhatsApp is another end-to-end encrypted messenger app owned by Facebook. The result of an effort by Brian Acton and Jan Koum, WhatsApp was created in February 2009. First it started as an app that showed if the user was online before becoming a messaging app. Facebook purchased the company on February 19, 2014, for $19 billion. In late August of 2016, it was announced that metadata from WhatsApp would be shared with Facebook.[13]

WhatsApp claimed as of February 1, 2016, it had over one billion people using its messaging app worldwide.[14]

The app features Instant Messaging with end-to-end encryption. In addition to text, it is capable of sending photos, audio messages, and pdf documents, so there is a metadata record still stored that includes phone numbers and timestamps that can be used to build a picture of communications between parties.

For example, in April 2015, Milanese police heard a Moroccan receive instructions to "Blow yourself up, O Lion" via a secret wiretap of his WhatsApp communications app. Abderrahim Moutaharrik was arrested when he used an Indonesian phone with WhatsApp after the audio messages from Mohamed Koraichi had been detected by Italian police.[15] He was preparing to attack a synagogue in Milan. He had planned to leave with his wife Salma Bencharki to go to Syria.[16] In a ProPublica article called "ISIS via WhatsApp, Blow yourself up o Lion," an unnamed FBI official said, "Then you'll see one of them says: 'OK, reach out to me on WhatsApp.' At that point, we can't do anything."[17]

WhatsApp was banned in Brazil, which kicked off around ninety-three million Brazilians after the Facebook-owned company refused to comply with court orders to turn over messages in drug cases. Facebook responded by stating that they could not help because the messages weren't stored and are encrypted.[18]

Bangladesh temporarily blocked access to WhatsApp along with Twitter, Facebook, Messenger, Tango, and Viber in November 2015.[19] The crackdown came in conjunction with the announcement of a death penalty sentence handed down to members of the political opposition, leading some to suggest that this had been done to stifle the reaction of supporters of the two men sentenced to die.

In March 2014, Bas Bosschert wrote a post on his blog revealing how to retrieve messages by stealing the database file and by intercepting it as it was being written to the SD card. The blog post went viral, according to Bosschert. Additional security issues arose including vulnerability to malware links and the ability to track a targeted user with a program no longer available on the web called WhatsSpy. WhatsSpy allowed the application user to track a target including their "online/offline status," "profile pictures," "status messages," and "privacy settings."[20]

Signal

Released in July 2014, Signal is a free end-to-end communication app with encryption that works on both Android and iPhone.[21] It is sometimes known as the "preferred" or "favorite" messaging app of Edward Snowden. In addition to texting, it supports voice calls.

In the hands of ISIS, Signal proved to be too tempting not to break apart and exploit for development. Indian officials say that ISIS member Abu Anas said he discovered Signal as an alternative to possibly monitored apps like WhatsApp, Facebook, and Instagram.[22] He was tasked to reverse engineer the open-source app and develop an ISIS communication app based on the popular app.

Wickr

Released in December 2014, Wickr is an end-to-end encryption messenger based in San Francisco started by a group of security and privacy experts as a project in 2012. This app features automatic expiration of messages. Just like the famed spy lore of self-destructing messages, Wickr messages can be set to expire in minutes or days. This messaging app has been mentioned as one of the safest by ISIS supporters. For example, Australian Jake Bilardi, a teen who joined ISIS, directed would-be recruits to contact him via Wickr in a Telegram posting.[23] Frequently, when news reports come out about the security of well-known apps like WhatsApp, lesser-known apps like Wickr become the fallback favorite for a period of time. Wickr gets high marks for its ability to erase messages.

Surespot

Surespot is an open-source app that features end-to-end encrypted instant messaging for both the Apple iOS and Android. It is capable of texting and sending images and voice messages. It is capable of "multiple identities" on the same device. Like Wickr, it is capable of message destruction.

The ISIS publication "Hijrah to the Islamic States" repeatedly references Surespot for its security. For instance, in a list of Twitter accounts to contact for recruiting, they advise contacting them via Surespot: "These people live in the Islamic State. They have Surespot and other private messaging apps." And "The Brothers on Twitter share their Surespot and Kik Messenger accounts."

For example, when British teenagers Shamima Begum, Kadiza Sultana, and Amira Abase disappeared, investigators combed over all their web communications. In time, they found that the girls had been lured by ISIS to come to Syria. In tracking their path to Syria, they found that the girls had initially talked on Twitter before they were told to move the conversation to Surespot.[24]

Australian Mohamed Elomar headed to Syria and became infamous for a picture showing him holding up the heads of two dead Syrians; that got him banned from Twitter.[25] A former boxer from Australia, Elomar became a fiery social media character taking to Twitter with suggestions "get an AK47" or "How to make C4" and for his followers to contact him on Surespot.[26] His evil life ended in a drone strike in Syria.

Threema

Released in December 2012, this Swiss-made messenger features end-to-end encryption and can send multimedia, voice messages, and other files. It ranks a six out seven in its "Secure Messaging Scorecard" by the Electronic Frontier Foundation. When Edward Snowden came forward and discussed NSA surveillance in 2013 and after Facebook bought WhatsApp in 2014, Martin Blatter, the CEO of Threema, stated to *Business Insider* that the company saw a doubling of downloads in Threema "overnight."[27] According to Threema, "messages media are stored" up to fourteen days if not delivered on servers or are deleted when delivered, "whichever happens first."[28] However, Threema is not free. There are versions that have posted on terrorist websites, but without a source of the free file, the OpSec (operational security) would be risky.

In late January 2016, the Cyber Caliphate notified its followers to move to Threema. The *Times of India* stated that the suicide squad that took hostages at the Holey Artisan Bakery in Dhaka, Bangladesh, on July 1, 2016, was sending messages via Threema to ISIS's al-Amaq agency.[29]

Figure 16: Afaaq Electronic Foundation recommended messenger Threema in JustPasteIt graphic.[30]

Silent Circle

Released in October 2011, SilentCircle was named by ISIS as a preferred app. Alarmed, the developers changed the app to increase the accountability of those who used it. Silent Circle, which was cofounded by former Navy Seal Mike Janke, works with both government and private intelligence agencies.[31]

Viber

Viber is a voice-over-IP and instant messaging app designed for Android and iPhone. It allows users to call or text for free via Wi-Fi connection. In an interview with Richard Engel, jailed former ISIS fighter Ahmad Rashidi stated that ISIS would frequently use Viber and WhatsApp to communicate with people in Europe. He also noted that ISIS fighters didn't use cell phones but preferred to use laptop apps.[32]

Bangladesh temporarily blocked access to Viber in November 2015 as well as over a half-dozen other social media companies.[33]

Viber was also used to pass the bad news back to the families of fighters. New Zealander Karolina Dam's autistic son Lukas went to fight for the Islamic State in May 2014. By December 2014, Lukas was no longer responding to his mother via Viber. A month passed before she received a response from someone else who had Lukas's phone. "Can you handle some bad news?" the text read. "Yeah, honey," she responded to the text. "Your son is in bits and pieces. This is what Denmark USA has done to him. I know it's hard, but it's true."[34] The most interesting component was not that he was dead but that ISIS kept his mobile phone and continued to use his Viber account after his death as a form of operational security.

Skype

One of the most widely used communication apps in the world is Skype, now owned by Microsoft. It provides video and voice services via smartphones, laptops, and desktops and the service is free. Founded in 2003, it has become so synonymous with video chatting that it is used as verb. However, the communication system isn't particularly secure, as revealed in several security reviews including one in 2013 by *Ars Technica* aided by Ashkan Soltani where messages specifically sent to test the encryption were easily detected.[35]

This was not lost on law enforcement. Maria Giulia Sergio, once an Italian Catholic, married a Muslim from Albania. In 2014, she went to Syria from her home in Inzago outside of Milan with her husband to join ISIS. She used Skype to communicate with her husband and her family.[36] "When we behead someone, I say we because I too am part of the Islamic State, when we take such action, we are obeying the sharia," she said via Skype.[37] She remained determined to convince her father, mother, and sister to convert to Islam and come to Syria. Eventually they relented, but before they could make their journey to Syria, Italian police arrested them. The authorities had been monitoring the Skype communications for weeks.[38]

American ISIS recruit Shannon Conley used Skype to communicate with an unnamed thirty-two-year-old Tunisian who "claimed to be in Syria fighting on behalf of ISIS," according to the complaint filed against Conley. She even asked her father to bless her upcoming marriage to the Tunisian and permission to go to Syria. The father declined. After her arrest at the airport, her residence was searched, and the agents found CDs and DVDs that were marked "Anwar al-Awlaki."[39] British ISIS predator Ahmed Canter tried to lure a Canadian TV reporter from Global News via Skype after she went undercover as a fifteen-year-old. He messaged her via Twitter first before moving on to Skype videos.[40]

In a similar story, a French reporter had an encounter with an ISIS recruiter using the name Abu Bilel. Shortly after talking to her on Facebook, he suggested, "We should talk over Skype." Using a pseudonym of "Melodie," she had created a full Skype profile to talk with this person. She informed her editor and included a colleague in the process. Abu Bilel skyped her from his car.[41]

OTHER WEB TOOLS

Not all web apps and tools fit neatly into the communications or social media categories. Many facilitate the ability to have the messages sent securely using encryption, and some give the sender the ability to hide from detection or tracking.

TrueCrypt

TrueCrypt is a program for Windows, MAC OS, and Linux that is used to encrypt files. The program's support not only ended, but on the Sourceforge page (the developers used for the software), a warning was published that said, "Using TrueCrypt is not secure as it may contain unfixed security issues."[42]

Returning fighters claimed that when they were dispatched for attacks, they were given thumb drives with a series of programs to avoid their being traced, one of which was TrueCrypt.[43] Why did ISIS choose this tool if it has such security issues? In an exposé on NSA's capabilities, the German news site *Spiegel* said the Snowden document dump revealed that NSA had "major" problems cracking TrueCrypt. How does a program that NSA has trouble cracking get described by its developers as having "unfixed security issues"? The reason for that may never be known.

Tor Browser

Tor is a free browser used both to surf the Surface Web with an increased amount of anonymous protection and to access websites found on the Dark Web, sometimes known as the Tor network.[44] To anonymize the user traffic, the Tor browser starts by sending out a request to the Tor network directory. The directory supplies the computer with the appropriate location, yet the information between both the requesting party and the host is anonymized. To do so, the network is designed to pass the requests across a series of random computers around the globe until the destination is reached. The process repeats in reverse, disguising the hosting server to the recipient. As each request passes to the next computer, the Internet Protocol address of the last computer is stripped away like an onion layer and replaced with the current relay computer's IP. This effect is like peeling an onion back layer after layer, thus The Onion Routing or Tor.

T.A.I.L.S.—The Amnesic Incognito Live System

This Linux-like operating system (OS) was often cited as the preferred system of Edward Snowden, journalists Glenn Greenwald, and ISIS. Booted per session from a USB stick or DVD, the OS was geared for privacy. The OS does not write to hard disc, which decreases the chances that logs and data can be recovered for forensic examination and decreases vulnerability to malware. The OS can be used on a computer with a conventional OS but will leave no trace of the TAILS activities.

The system comes preloaded and ready to work on both the Tor and the I2P networks and is loaded with an array of encrypted tools for encrypted messaging, password generators and managers, metadata cleaners, and more. Its base browser is Tor.[45]

The NSA has said it was concerned about TAILS and combination usage with other encryption that prevents their ability to scoop data from these users. Developers have reported that the agency has been pushing for backdoors that would allow intelligence or law enforcement access.[46] TAILS 2.0 was released in January 2016.

Jihadist Developed and Distributed Apps

Jihadist terrorists did not always trust the source applications that were popularly used, particularly after the Edward Snowden revelations that revealed that NSA was working with many software developers. Based on this mistrust, they often attempted to write their own programs to encrypt and transmit secret communications.

Mujahedeen Secrets

Al-Qaeda began publishing encryption tools in 2007 when its media group, the "Global Islamic Media Front" or GIMF, released an encryption program for use on Windows known as "Asrar al-Mujahideen," sometimes called "Mujahedeen Secrets." Used in conjunction with email, the program would allow operatives and supporters to encrypt their messages, including the ability to create a private key. It was updated to Version 2.0 in 2008. Al Qaeda would later release a segment in the first edition of AQAP's *Inspire* magazine called "How To Use Ansar al-Mujahideen: Sending & Receiving Encrypted Messages" that showed how to operate the program.[47]

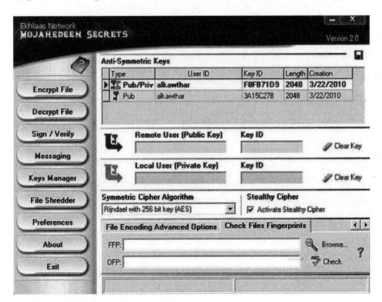

Figure 17: Screenshot of Mujahedeen Secrets 2.0 from Inspire magazine #1
(Source: TAPSTRI)

The program, intended to be used off a USB flash drive, allowed users to "Generate keys" in the "Keys Manager," which creates public and private keys. Just like the key to your home or your car, a digital key is personal and in this case is used to confirm your identity in encrypted messages. When messages are sent and received, if the key's line matches up, the messages will decrypt and contents can be read. The public key is sent to the associated contact, who returns a copy of their public key. Al-Qaeda of the Arabian Peninsula (AQAP) even published a copy of its public key in the same first edition of *Inspire* magazine.

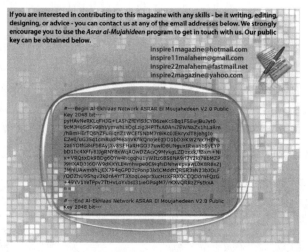

Figure 18-Encryption Key published in last pages of Inspire magazine #1.
(Source: TAPSTRI)

Morton Storm, the Danish double agent who worked alongside the late terrorist Anwar al-Awlaki, said he was shown how to use the program by al-Awlaki himself. The information he decrypted from al-Awlaki was later passed on to the CIA.[48]

Tashfeer al Jawwal

Like its predecessor, Mujahedeen Secrets, al-Qaeda's Global Islamic Media Front (GIMF) group released an encryption app for

Android Mobile in September 2013 through the jihadist forums. The group claimed it was the "first Islamic encryption software for mobiles."[49] However, al-Qaeda didn't demonstrate any new ability to encrypt. They used existing Twofish encryption designed by master American cryptographer Bruce Schneier and the "Twofish" team in 1998.[50] In releasing the program, GIMF published tutorials on how to use the program in Arabic, English, Indonesian, and Urdu.[51]

Asrar al-Dardashah

On February 6, 2013, al-Qaeda's GIMF released an encryption plugin for the instant messenger Pidgin using RSA 2048 encryption.[52]

Amn al-Mujahid

On December 10, 2013, one of al-Qaeda's groups, the al-Fajr Technical Committee, released a Windows program called Amn al-Mujahid or the "Security of the Mujahid" program in addition to a 28-page manual.[53] In June of 2014, they released a version as an Android app. Again, like the other al-Qaeda creations, the encryption relied up Twofish encryption.

ENTER THE ISIS APPS

By 2013, ISIS was developing apps to meet its desired encryption, communication, and indoctrination needs. Notably, the Amaq News Agency and al-Bayan radio apps were often promoted as a way to follow the latest events in the terror organization.

Asrar al-Gurabaa

On November 27, 2013, ISIS launched the asrar006.com site. The Asrar (Secrets, in Arabic) site was used as a web-based encryption tool created by ISIS developers found via the Tor site.[54] In December

2013, the AQ-friendly GIMF group released a statement saying the app was "suspicious and source is not trusted."[55]

Figure 19: Amaq Banner. (Source: TAPSTRI)

Amaq News Agency

The Amaq News Agency released an app to feature its headlines for ISIS followers. By using it, you will never miss news of key events, or you can monitor publications and learn about ISIS leaders killed in action. It is designed for use on Android phones.

Figure 20: Al Bayan Banner. (Source: TAPSTRI)

Al-Bayan Radio

Known as an FM radio signal station on 92.5, al-Bayan radio delivers its version of the headlines from around the Islamic State from Mosul, Iraq. The group released a new Android app via Telegram and links to Archive.org in early February 2016. The file was released as BayanRadio.apk.

Figure 21: Huroof Banner. (Source: TAPSTRI)

Huroof

An Android app aimed at teaching children Arabic, it is loaded with Jihadist propaganda including AK47 symbols, ammunition, tanks, and more. Released through al-Bayan, Huroff was published on Telegram channels in May 2016.

THE ISIS HELP DESK

In November 2015, the news broke of an ISIS Help Desk designed to help supporters of the terrorist organization use their gadgets and Internet tools with 24/7 support. However, there was no Help Desk, as NBC and others reported. Instead, the concept was a media misunderstanding of information given to them by Dr. Aaron Brantly of the West Point Combating Terrorism Center (CTC).[56] He had briefed them that ISIS was indeed working to train potential recruits on how to safely navigate the web for both coming to Syria and for operations around the world.

Figure 22: Afaaq Banner. (Source: TAPSTRI)

THE AFAAQ ELECTRONIC FOUNDATION

On January 30, 2016, a new Telegram channel appeared accompanied by a Twitter channel under the name Afaaq Electronic Foundation, sometimes known by the English word Electronic Horizon (Afaaq) Foundation. According to an unnamed "security specialist" in an article for *The Hill*, EHF comes after a fusion of groups including "Information Security" and "Islamic State Technician."[57]

Another addition to the misconception that ISIS had a notion of an ISIS "help desk" was the publication circulated on JustPasteIt without attribution to the legitimate Kuwaiti security firm who developed it for training materials in 2014. Called the "ISIS OPSEC Manual" by *Wired* initially, it was in fact created to help journalists operating in sensitive regions by Abdullah al-Ali of the Cyberkov firm. Following the news of this connection, a small war of words broke out over Twitter between parts of the group Anonymous and the CEO of Cyberkov. Anonymous threatened the firm with DDoS attacks on the company website if it did not remove a post written about Anonymous and affiliated group GhostSec.[58]

ISIS Responds to the Encryption Battle

If you take a look at the published reactions from ISIS/AQ, you can see that, from just after the headlines hit about Edward Snowden's intelligence leak, the ISIS operational security section (OpSec) sent out advice and reactions showing they were clearly paying attention and not only making adjustments but also making progress in learning better ways to hide and to obscure their intended covert activities.

The AQ Global Islamic Media Front (GIMF) said, "Take your precautions, especially in the midst of the rapidly developing news about the cooperation of global companies with the international intelligence agencies, in the detection of data exchanged over smartphones."[59] It was also pitching its new encryption app Tashfeer al-Jawwal, which was released just after the Snowden leaks.[60] When the Afaaq Electronic Foundation was announced in January

30, 2016, it specifically noted the Snowden leaks as a reason jihadists should ramp up their own security. There is little guessing about whether ISIS, al-Qaeda, and other threats to the United States benefited from the leaks—the releases were of great value to their understanding of US operations.

At one end, there are those who advocate forcing tech giants to release skeleton keys to government agencies so that under court order they can retrieve data on a target without interference from the tech company protesting, "but the data is encrypted." This "backdoor" technology has been criticized for several reasons, among them the fact that once you make such a choice, you have to consider that backdoor now exists for *everyone* including nefarious actors. At the other end, after the San Bernardino case, Apple CEO Tim Cook made this clear—such a backdoor would be for good guys and bad guys.[61]

Chapter 7

Jihadi Cyber Warfare Units

The Internet is populated with plenty of individuals and groups who may know its tools better than the average user. Some of these tools are highly sought after by criminal and terrorist organizations worldwide. ISIS and al-Qaeda have long sought and used skilled individuals to exploit those recruits who have experience and determination to use the Internet's information systems and tools to their advantage. These groups have learned how to weaponize the Internet's social media networks and have effectively spread terror as they employed horrific images in their propaganda, thereby earning them a reputation of being a bloodthirsty, savage death cult. But their hackers are at best a nuisance; they lack the coordination of state actor organizations like the Cyber Bears of Russia, the Pandas of China, or the Kittens of Iran. This doesn't mean they should be taken lightly, though.

The reason for the sophistication of many jihadists has less to do with genius than intent. In examining the nearly one hundred cases in the United States and dozens of cases in Europe, we clearly saw that ISIS fanboys and operatives alike often make huge mistakes as they navigate their way to and from Syria or plan a local operation. Many of these unforced errors can and will occur in their use of the Internet or other communication devices.

To determine how to defend against their efforts, it helps to identify the groups and individuals who comprise the ISIS cyber media force. Each group's efforts require unique examination of their objectives, resources, and threat capability. Each group may have overlapping members in various roles as ISIS picks from the total skill base of fighters and then exploits their skills wherever it sees fit.

While many of these roles can be filled by overlapping person-nel, it is clear there are people who function solely to publish information on phone security and communications. There are operatives who focus mostly on setting up Twitter or Facebook pages. These intermediaries perform the function of keeping com-munications flowing around the caliphate.

The Horizon channel (aka the Afaaq Electronic Foundation) on Telegram frequently posts the latest information on secure com-munications. Launching their Telegram channel in January 2016, the group frequently posts up-to-the-minute, timely suggestions on phone hardware and suggested apps for communication and encryption.

THE ONLINE JIHADI GROUPS

There were several hacking teams under ISIS who engaged in defacements and DOS attacks. These groups sprung from exist-ing hacker communities, including the famous hacker group Anonymous. Equipped with a desire to create chaos and fear, these groups mostly swapped home pages with ISIS banners and slogans. This "capture-the-flag"-style campaign was common until the groups turned to publishing "kill lists" drawn from already available information or lists stolen by other hackers who had real skills to do so.

AnonGhost—#anonghost

Launched as a pro-Palestinian effort, AnonGhost became one of the members in the loose affiliations that comprise the ISIS hacker groups. AnonGhost detached from Anonymous after the #OpISIS campaign that followed the Charlie Hebdo attacks in Paris in January 2015. The Anonymous campaign vowed to knock down all ISIS content from the web regardless of Twitter, Facebook, or stand-alone websites.

AnonGhost was founded by a hacker named "Mauritania Attacker"[1] as an offshoot of a cyber group called "Teamr00t." Teamr00t was focused on pro-Palestinian/anti-Israel hacking campaigns, according to a Twitter channel associated with the group that was active between June 2012 and December 12, 2012.[2] After years of inactivity, another channel for Teamr00t emerged in January 2016. Teamr00t was responsible for approximately 163 attacks, of which 141 were defacing attacks.

Figure 23: Flyer circulated by AnonGhost before the #OpPetrol attacks in 2013.

The hacker known as "Mauritania Attacker" claimed that virus maker Farid Essabar of Morocco, a.k.a. "Diablo," virus writer behind the Zotob worm in 2005, was the one and only hacker he admired. His alleged identity was "Moulaye Ahmed Ould Ahmed

Semane" from Nouakchot, Mauritania, according to a rival group known as the Ghost Squad Hackers.[3]

In April 2013, AnonGhost launched attacks as part of the campaign "OpIsrael," which aimed to strike Israeli-affiliated sites with Distributed Denial of Service (DDoS) and defacing website attacks. Its other campaigns included "#OpUSA" and "#OpPetrol." The OpUSA came with an official video for the campaign on YouTube and resulted in hundreds of sites being defaced. Despite the hassle, though, no serious breaches occurred. The announcement of #OpPetrol threatened attacks on 12 countries by both Anonymous and AnonGhost. Like the previous operation, an official video of the campaign was published. The 3:20 video threatened that the multinational effort would begin on June 20, 2013. Later in November of 2013, AnonGhost claims attacks against Total, the oil company. As proof of the hack, the group released emails and passwords of company employees to a pastebin.com url.[4]

According to posts on a Cyber Caliphate Army's Telegram channel, AnonGhost merged with CCA in January 2016.[5] This was later disputed in another post by members who objected. The resulting split in the group resulted in two groups, the Ghost Caliphate who went with CCA and the Ghost Squad Hackers.

A group of hackers who used to be aligned with AnonGhost went in another direction when members like Mauritania Attacker expressed their support for ISIS. As mentioned previously, this group, known as Ghost Squad Hackers, GSH, was a pro-Palestinian hacking group led by its founder who went by "s1ege," which is hacker dialect for "siege." After the split with AnonGhost, Ghost Squad members started outing AnonGhost members, including the leader, Mauritania Attacker.[6] But by the end of August 2016, according to both of their twitter channels, the two groups had made peace and were once again focused on attacking Israeli cyber targets.

According to an interview with "Sec4Track," the members are international and live in Mauritania, Morocco, Malaysia, Indonesia, Tunisia, US, and Ireland, to name a few:[7]

The founder and administrator was "Mauritania" Attacker." Other members' cyber street names are "Virusa Worm"— "SpitFir3"—"ManSyk3z"—"Deto Beiber"—"BL4ckc0d1n6"—"Dr. SaM!M_008"—"Sky Lion"—"Kais Patron"—"Ian Surgent"— "B0o3nAs"—" Gbs Aremiey"—Mr Domoz"—"RetnOHack"— "Tak Dikenal"—"Chahid inj3ctor"—"b3ta"—"Rehber Khan" —"AnonxoxTN"—"Spec Tre"—"PsyferR"—"Raka 3r00t"—"Gh0st_ 3xp10!t"—"PirateX"—"Kopra1337"—"Bl4ck jorozz"—"Riad Spamer" —'VirUs AsEr AlrOoh"—"Younes Lmaghribi"—"Zaky"—"joker inside"—"AreTheIS."

Figure 24: CCA Mask Gazwa Reloaded Graphic. (Source: TAPSTRI)

Cyber Caliphate Army—#cybercaliphate

The name perhaps most associated with ISIS hacking groups was the Cyber Caliphate Army, which was led by hacker Junaid Hussain until his death in August 2015. After years of his work with TeaMpOisoN, Junaid Hussain took his hacking experience and joined ISIS. He had served time for hacking into Tony Blair's emails through his advisor's account. Once he had reached Syria, he started to recruit both hackers and fighters alike. He had built up an extensive set of hacker contacts before establishing CCA, but his extreme views and joining ISIS guaranteed that many of his former hacker friends weren't going to join him in his new pursuits.

Figure 25: Cyber Caliphate Army members published on a page that was hijacked.
(Source: TAPSTRI)

After Junaid's death, he was reportedly replaced by a Bangladeshi web developer named Siful Haque Sujan. Sujan inherited Hussain's role after his death but didn't hold it for long. By December 10, 2015, Sujan was killed in Raqqa, like his predecessor.

CCA Cyber Caliphate Army—Decentralized in 2016

Figure 28: CCA Abu Hussain Graphic. (Source: TAPSTRI)

The group divided into four divisions, according to CCA postings.

CCA was known for its defacing attacks. There are members named by the group as "Eng Caliphate," "Dr. Caliphate," "Cyber Caliphate," "Lion Caliphate," "Damar Caliphate," and "Ghost Caliphate."

Figure 26: Ghost Caliphate Graphic. (Source: TAPSTRI)

Ghost Caliphate Section

According the members of the Ghost Security Hackers (GSH) group, Ghost Caliphate members are former AnonGhost members who chose to join ISIS. Though the GSH initially rebelled against CCA, a peace agreement was reached months later.

Sons Caliphate Army (SCA)

Figure 27: SCA Graphic. (Source: TAPSTRI)

This subgroup to the Cyber Caliphate Army was first mentioned in a post by CCA in January 2016. The group released a video called "Flames of Ansar," which claimed credit for hackings on Facebook and Twitter accounts. They also threatened the founders of these companies, Mark Zuckerberg and Jack Dorsey, if they didn't stop removing ISIS accounts from their systems.

Kalachnikov E-Security Team (KTN)

Figure 29: Kalachnikov E-Security Team Graphic. (Source: TAPSTRI)

This group's efforts are focused mainly on tech security advisory posts on Telegram. However, they have conducted or assisted in defacing hacks. The group shares overlapping members with the Cyber TeamRox group. The CTR group launched a Telegram page on March 3, 2016, and renamed it Kalachnikov E-Security Team on March 16, 2016. They later affirmed the connection by denying ties to a Telegram channel and reminding users that "We only have this channel here and the kalachnikov one" in a post on their Facebook page.

Identified members: f@ng, Zeehaxor, AlW4S, Adarius, Dr Avatar.

CCA Telegram Information

In the period between the relaunch of a CCA telegram channel on July 16, 2016, and August 23, 2016, 812 members had joined a channel. This number doesn't distinguish between CCA members, intel organizations, fanboys, or curious bystanders. It is possible there are only a handful of CCA members and 700 to 810 watchers and fanboys, many of whom are also researchers' intelligence community onlookers.[8]

First, the channel was delivered almost entirely in English with occasional bits of Arabic. The channel's profile page has "جيش قناة الخلافة الالكتروني الرسمية CCA" or the "Official Channel of the Electronic Caliphate Army CCA" on Description and an icon set of a hooded figure against a coded background. "Caliphate Cyber Army-Information not available-location/Unknown" is written in English again instead of in Arabic.

CCA frequently reposts from the United Cyber Caliphate, its self-claimed umbrella affiliation group established in April 2016. They also send out links to Telegram affiliates that often expire within just a few hours, some in a matter of minutes. If you don't join those channels before the moderator closes the group, you'll miss out and have to watch for another invite.

CCA's channel frequently posts variations of imagery derived from several video-style graphic arts packages ranging from overtones of the game Halo to variations on the balaclava image à la Jihadi John, a.k.a. Mohammed Emwazi, the British executioner from the ISIS videos. They use these styles to trumpet their four core groups, "GHOST," "CCA," "SCA," and "KNT."

"Ghost" appears to be made up of AnonGhost people who went over to ISIS. SCA, the Sons of Caliphate Army, is known for its twenty-five-minute video aimed at Mark Zuckerberg and Jack Dorsey, *Flames of Ansar*, in which it claims to have compromised the content of 10,000 Facebook accounts and over 5,000 Twitter channels. The video was the first threat of this level against social media companies in response to their crackdown on militant profiles and postings. Twitter's position on the matter was summed up by its spokesman: "We condemn the use of Twitter to promote terrorism."[9]

One of those campaigns stamped July 16, 2016, was labeled "'Central Military District'—russia hacked," accompanied by a graphic of an ISIS fighter from Russia who was previously featured in an execution video from Raqqa called *You will be disappointed and humiliated, oh Russians*! CCA claims to have hacked a Russian Army base database in Arabic first, then English, and then Russian and under the banner of "united cyber caliphate" (all lower case) and without relinking from the UCC Telegram channel as they do in other examples. The file was released in "kmz" format. Following that post, CCA released another kmz file with information on "American civilian and military" claiming to be lifted from US military databases.

CCA posted "#Wanted to be killed Massachusetts #US" along with a young man with an ISIS flag in front of the White House with the bottom caption "The End Is Near Soon" in English. In another post, CCA said the next target listed in the campaign was "Government employees data Rhode Island #USA."

CCA was challenged on whether their data releases were previously stolen by others or a result of combing publicly available information, even if you had to look it up with a bit of effort. They reacted in one Telegram graphic written in English, "they are lying when they tell you 'The DATA are all #public' and 'No-Your systems failed to hide it and that is the true [*sic*]'". Yet the data released in some cases were clearly obtained by others.[10]

But there is something of a clownish aspect to many of these groups when you watch them long enough. An example of this is their meme mockery of the deployment of the *Charles de Gaulle* aircraft carrier by putting a stuffed cow on the deck and again in English, "Charles de Gaulle-Cows carrior," and in very small print "UCC media."

If you forget they are serious about at least terrorizing people, they post graphics of attack metrics or graphics that show methods of killing, including icons for "Remmed [*sic*] them," "stab them," "shoot them," "throw them" with a picture of a pile of stones, "intoxicate them," "hit them" with a pic of a stick, and, strangely, "SCREEM [*sic*] THEM" with an icon of two people with lines indicating yelling from one to the other. The "Remmed them" graphic was circled in one because of the Nice, France, killing on July 14, 2016. As the other graphics passed, they used the same overall imagery but light up each icon as events transpired, almost as if they comprised a checklist of methods. The footer of the graphic stated, "Instructions to individual wolves-Kill them" and specifically tagged by the Cyber Caliphate. The post itself with the graphic stated, "Mission has been completed waiting #next and #UCC."

The "Gazwa" campaign was launched with the "We Will Kill You All" banner and "We are watching you, our ideas are sophisticated. Our systems you cannot under estimate. Islamic state wins." CCA seeks often to project abilities beyond its cannon of self-credited attacks. In their graphics and videos, they also seek to convey proof of their competence, which begs the question, how competent are they ultimately? If Junaid Hussain's first claim to fame was to hack the email of Tony Blair, it's an accomplishment that falls far below the expectations of even the finest hackers.

Despite the tremendous brutality of their campaign videos and the quality of their social media campaign, their hacking skills leave much to be desired in a Grade A terrorist organization. Consider, for instance, that they couldn't seem to hack Google but did get "earned media" that published their names anyway because they did successfully hack a company's site that used Google in the name, AddGoogleOnline.com.[11]

In August of 2016, a man identified as Othman Zebn Nayef was arrested by Kuwaiti authorities on suspicion of working with ISIS. Once arrested, he confessed to working with CCA. Authorities said they also captured other suspects related to a case in Iraq and Jordan but did not specify their relationship with Nayef.[12]

Most of what has been learned about CCA's operation comes from their overall postings, graphic messages, efficacy of attacks, depth of attacks, and their demeanor while conducting these operations in a semipublic manner. The group continues posting threats and self-aggrandizing graphics, all designed to encourage its members to wreak havoc on the *kufar*.

Figure 30: United Cyber Caliphate Graphic. (Source: TAPSTRI)

UNITED CYBER CALIPHATE (UCC)—UNITED APRIL 2016

In March 2016, the groups associated with CCA announced that they would be uniting under the new banner, The United Cyber Caliphate. The group was comprised of "Cyber Caliphate Army," "Ghost Caliphate Section," "Sons of Caliphate Army,"and "Kalachnikov E-Security."

UCC has been claiming data releases since naming itself on April 5, 2016. Each of these data dumps was usually accompanied by a demand of lone wolf attacks on the targets listed. On April 10, 2016, UCC defaced sites as part of its #KillCrusaders campaign. The countries affected by these attacks were the US, Chile, China, France, Malaysia, and Mexico. On April 18, 2016, the group launched its "#Gazwa: Reloaded," which claims to have released information on ten thousand personal accounts in a breach. A few days later, on April 21, 2016, the group released a list of names of people in New York with "We Want Them Dead" as its banner. On April 24, 2016, the group released a list of names from US State Department staff with "Wanted to be killed" as its banner. Later, on June 7, 2016, the group released another "Kill List" with 8,318 names from 21 countries. The post indicated the list of people should be killed as "revenge for Muslims." Then again on June 21, 2016, they repeated the effort with a list of names from the United States, Canada, Australia, UK, and others. This "kill list" contained 4,681 names.

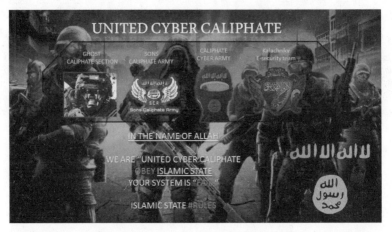

Figure 31: United Cyber Caliphate Telegram graphic. (Source: TAPSTRI)

Figure 32: United Cyber Caliphate Gazwa Reloaded Telegram Graphic.

Islamic State Hacking Division (ISHD)

The Islamic State Hacking Division started its operations in early 2015 under the leadership of CCA leader Junaid Hussain. Like CCA, their attacks are mainly defacing or DDoS attacks. They were largely active between March 2015 and August 2015 and then went dormant after the death by airstrike of their leader, Junaid Hussain, in August 2015. The only hack attributed after that date came in May 2016 with a leak post aimed at 76 drone operators.

Figure 33: ISHD hacking screenshot. (Source: TAPSTRI)

March 23, 2015: ISHD releases names of 100 military personnel.
April 13, 2015: ISHD attacks and defaces two bios on Huffington Post.
April 15, 2015: ISHD hacks an Egyptian radio station Nogoum FM's Twitter account and uses it to post ProISIS messages.
June 1, 2015: ISHD hacks Italian military servers.
August 11, 2015: ISHD releases a list of 1,500 US military and government workers. The list originated with Kosovo hacker Ardi Ferizi, a.k.a. "The3Dir3ctory," who was later charged with stealing the data in October 2015.
September 11, 2015: ISHD releases a "Kill list" of 100 American military personnel on a JustPasteIt post. The posts included photos, names, addresses, and service branches.

May 2, 2016: ISHD releases a list with the names of 76 drone operators.[13] After the leak was released, the group proclaimed under the ISHD tag:

> *Peace be Upon The One Who Follows True Guidance*
> *O Crusaders, as you continue your aggression towards the Islamic State and your bombing campaign against the Muslims, know that we are in your emails and computer systems, watching and recording your every move, we have your names and addresses, we are in your emails and social media accounts, we are extracting confidential data and passing on your personal information to the soldiers of the Khalifah, who soon, with the permission of Allah, will strike at your necks in your own lands! So wait; we too are waiting.*
>
> *-Islamic State Hacking Division*

Figure 34: ICA members graphic. (Source: TAPSTRI)

Islamic Cyber Army—#IslamicCyberArmy

Started in September 10, 2015, ICA was part of a series of fall campaigns of cyberattacks starting with #AmericaUnderHacks. At the opening of the campaign, ICA released a video titled *We Are Back In America*. The group launched attacks up to late November 2015 under a series of hashtags ending with "underhacks." The hashtags were filed under #AmericaUnderHacks, #SaudiUnderHacks,

#RussiaUnderHacks, #IsraelUnderHacks, #FranceUnderHacks, and #IranUnderHacks. By November, the group moved to its final hashtag, #WorldUnderAttacks.

The names of the hackers were announced in the September video with a listing of nine members. The members included "Syria Virus," the leader of the group; "Hcer Arkani" (identified as a member of the Kalachnikov team); "Abo 7OZYFA"; "Abu al-Qasam"; "Cyber," sometimes listed as Ciber and may have joined CCA; "Hacker Alomar," also known as "HaCKeR AldMaR" and who appears to have joined the Rabitat al-Ansar group; "ENG ISIS," who later joined CCA; "DR ISIS," who later joined CCA; and "SKWO 808."

Rabitat al-Ansar (Union of Supporters)

Previously, Rabitat al-Ansar was known for its work with "The Media Front for Support to the Islamic State," which included a batch of other ISIS media groups including al-Battar, al-Ghuraba, al-Wafa, al-Minhaj, and others. In this capacity, the group predominantly included reposting media releases for the Islamic State.

They claimed to have turned to hacking in 2015 after being focused on propaganda campaigns including hashtag campaigns. They were part of the #WeWillBurnUSAgain campaign starting April 8, 2015, which was announced days earlier. They were part of the #CalamityWillBefallUS campaign starting June 25, 2014. On June 25, 2014, it was the "Warning the American people" tag, and on August 22, 2014, the group chimed in with #StevensHeadinObamasHands as the world waited to hear what would happen to the American captive.

April 10, 2015: The group posts claims of data hack on 2000+ Americans, Canadians, and others on JustPasteIt. (The info had already been breached elsewhere.)[14]

May 11, 2015: Rabitat al-Ansar posts link to video on Twitter called *Message to America: from the Earth to the Digital World*. The video threatens to hit the United States with cyber war.[15]

July 13, 2015: Hacker Aldmar, a division of the Rabitat group, claimed to be involved in the American Visa and Master Card data breaches in July 2015.[16]

September 4, 2015: Hacker Aldmar issued threat to attack banks and US government on September 11, 2015. "Hacker Aldmar" was specifically named in an FBI warning to banks.

Cyber TeamRox

CTR is a group of pro-ISIS hackers who are very active at website defacings and claimed data breaches. For instance, on March 11, 2016, the group listed information on the employees of LaSalle and Purdue Universities. This group appears to have spring out of the Kalachnikov team under the CCA banner. On March 2016, the CTR group launched their Telegram feed then a few weeks later changed the page's name to "Kalachnikov E-Security Team."

Figure 35: Hacked by Cyber TeamRox. (Source: TAPSTRI)

The CTR hacking group was led by "Zeeshan Ali," a.k.a. "Zeeshan Haxor," and members have overlapped from other groups. Known mostly for defacing websites, CTR's members are "K3L0TEX," "Zeeshan Haxor," "Harith101," "D@rkCoder," "MrGhost," "Ctr_ Def4c3r," "Phr34ky Dump," "CrYpt0," "Kara dzx," "Clinkz48," "Aisoulu," "ph4nt0m," "M1S74KE," and "Dr. Neox (Achraf)."

Examination of the ISIS Cyber Attacks

In light of the skill sets demonstrated by hackers for the Islamic State including those of its former leader, Junaid Hussain, a review of the hacks by the various pro-ISIS hacker groups yields a narrow range of methods used and shows a lack of coordination of any master strategy and likely lacks a qualified leader who is well placed in the ISIS military command structure. A list of their attacks from the early days of their operations shows an interest in defacing websites and replacing them with banners praising the Islamic State. This effort would likely only benefit the aims of the propaganda wing of the organization. As the groups moved toward the formation of the United Cyber Caliphate, the emphasis shifted to announcing data breaches around the world in order to instill fear of targeted attacks. "We Want Them Dead" or "Wanted To Be Killed" was often tagged on the releases. Similar to the defacings, this strategy is a propaganda-based strategy.

AnonGhost Hacks

This group is most commonly known for defacing websites. By examining a range of attacks from 2014 to 2016, one can see that AnonGhost predominantly engages in posting propaganda pages that replace the site owner's home page. Targets have included Duke University, Sky News, subdomains of the U.S. Air Force, a Turkish government site, and hundreds of private enterprise sites. In November 2014, the group claimed to have hacked over 100 government sites.

After the attacks in Paris on the Charlie Hebdo offices in January 2015, AnonGhost launched attacks on hundreds of French websites. The French government confirmed that hundreds of websites had been coming under attack with defacings. The hackers dubbed the action "Operation France."

Islamic State Hackers Division (ISHD) Hacks

March 23, 2015-September 2015: The Islamic State Hackers Division is credited with a handful of notable data dumps, starting in early 2015 with the claimed leak of the names of one hundred military personnel. Later in August of 2015, ISHD also put out a list it claimed leaked the personal information of 1,500 U.S. service members and government workers. A month later on the four-teenth anniversary of the September 11 attacks, ISHD released a list of one hundred U.S. military personnel on a JustPaste post with their names, addresses, branches of service, and photos. They then announced the post on Twitter.

The group claimed to be behind the data breach of ten Italian army personnel in June 2015.

After a period of silence of nearly a year, the group reappeared on May 2, 2016, with the previously cited post claiming to iden-tify 76 drone operators for the US military. Additionally, the group has engaged in a few attacks that vary from the data breaches including defacing bios at Huffington Post in April 2015 to seizing the Twitter account of an Egyptian Radio station a few days later. **May 2, 2016:** ISHD releases a list with the names of 76 drone operators.

Islamic Cyber Army (ICA) Hacks—active September 9–November 24, 2015

The ICA group engaged in operations that included defacings and data dumps. Working in a brief window of just over three months, the group performed many of its ops under a variation of #under-hacks headers. They began by defacing British websites and threats to release private information from the breaches on September 11, 2015. The same day, they claimed to have information on FBI employees and NASA to make public. At the same time, they were committing defacing attacks under #AmericaUnderHacks and threatening to release information on military members.

The ICA group shifted its attention to Britain later in Septem-ber 2015, with threats to release information on Army personnel, and engaged in more defacings. They ended the month with threats aimed at Saudi Arabia with a campaign announced to hack the royal kingdom under #SaudiUnderHacks.

In October 2015, ICA turned its sites on Russia, Israel, and France. In each case, there were more defacements and threats of releasing information, each time stepping up the call for lone wolf attacks on names released. On October 14, 2015, the group released a list purported to contain members of Israel's Mossad.

In the final month of its appearance on the cyber stage, ICA focused its aims on Iran and defaced sites in early November 2015 along with threats of releasing information on government personnel under the hashtag #IranUnderHacks. They finished out November 2015 with a campaign under #WorldUnderAttacks, which included releasing a list of over 270,000 Twitter account details, French government personnel data, and a list claiming to be made up of United States DOD, FBI, CIA, and NSA officials.

Figure 36: CyberCaliphate JesuISIS graphic. (Source: TAPSTRI)

Cyber Caliphate Army (CCA) Hacks

Like its colleague groups, CCA has engaged in site defacings and data dumps, which are used to terrorize citizens, government personnel, and military members. Beginning in December 2014 and again in January 2015, CCA hit the scene seizing control of the website of the *Albuquerque Journal* newspaper and its social media page. They did the same to WBOC NewsPlex's twitter page January 2015. But it really got attention on January 12, 2015, when the United States military's CENTCOM Twitter and YouTube sites were replaced with the CyberCaliphate banner and icon.

The group frequently makes lofty claims about penetrating the systems of the United States government. In January 2015, CCA announced that it had breached an FBI database and stolen documents. No evidence was released to support the claim. Again in November 2015, it released 36 names it claimed were US Military. It did the same thing again days later on December 11, 2015, releasing 160 names. It claimed that there were seven hundred more to come. On December 17, 2015, the group claimed to have hacked the U.S. National Guard, Andrews Air Force Base, and NASA. In January 2016 came a list of supposed U.S. Air Force names. On June 14, 2016, came two posts with lists of DOD and U.S. Air Force names with a call for lone wolf attacks. In December 2015, the group targeted US Senator Harry Reid's associates with calls for lone wolf attacks.

Non-US targets of the group have included data releases aimed at France, Russia, Israel, Saudi Arabia, India, and Bangladesh. Defacing of websites around the world have included targets in Saudi Arabia, Russia, Iran, India, France, UK, Spain, and Greece.

United Cyber Caliphate (UCC) Hacks

After April 4, 2016, when four groups merged to form the United Cyber Caliphate, there was a series of website defacings and data breaches claimed by the new combined group. Starting with sites defaced in the United States, China, Chile, France, Malaysia, and Mexico under the tag #KillCrusaders, UCC became a very active group that stepped up the operations by coordinating the efforts of the existing four cells.

The group largely publishes data claimed to be material for "Kill Lists" and has focused on several US government agencies including US military personnel and the US State Department. UCC has also aimed its sights at US regional law enforcement and private citizens as it did on April 21, 2016, when it released the 3,600 names of New York citizens with "We Want Them Dead" attached.

They released three large data dumps in April and June of 2016 with a total of more than twenty-two thousand names from around the world. The names were released with instructions by the group to engage in lone wolf attacks on the individuals listed as "revenge for Muslims."

Outside of the United States, the targets have included 19 Australian websites on April 14, 2016, and the Saudi Ministry of Defense on April 22, 2016, claiming they would release information on over eighteen thousand employees. In June 2016, they defaced sites in Brazil and India. The same month they focused their sites on Canada with data dumps released as "Kill Lists." In July 2016, they claimed they would leak the information on twenty thousand Suez Canal personnel.

In addition to citizen and government or military personnel releases, UCC has released satellite images of U.S. air force bases with emphasis that the bases are "used by the US military." The Google earth graphics were posted to their Telegram channel in July of 2016.

There are two types of activities these groups mainly engage in—defacings and data dumps. There is little posted by the groups themselves or others on how they are acquiring their data, yet we do know they engage in passing on data already breached by others from the case of the Kosovar hacker Ardit Ferizi, member of the Kosova Hacker's Security Group, who was arrested and sentenced to 20 years in September 2016. Ferizi gave data that had been stolen by other sources to the hacker Junaid Hussain, who in turn published the data as an original hack. Hussain posted on August 11, 2015, that he had US military and government names in a 30-page document.

Are the Dumps PSYOPS?

One researcher on the topic examined the data dumps and concluded that many records were the result of copycat dumps. Troy Hunt runs the website "Have I been pwned?" or HIBP, which is described as a free source to investigate if you've been the victim of a breach. He assessed the data presented in several of the ISIS data dumps and concluded that it came from multiple locations and that it was not likely that the information came from a lone breach. He concluded that many records were culled into another database system, which resulted in inconsistent data structures and both duplicate and altered records.[17]

Russian Hackers: The Two False Flags

One of the most infamous attacks attributed to the Cyber Caliphate occurred on April 8, 2015, when the French television station TV5 Monde found that its website had been hacked by the dreaded Islamic State. A new graphic posted with the phrase "Je suIS IS" had replaced its Twitter page, as had been done in the CENTCOM attacks. However, this attack was going to be far worse than a simple defacing. Hackers were able to get into the station's internal networks and began shutting down the digital broadcast system. The staff indicated that all the systems began to collapse in a very organized manner. This included the station's admin systems and emails. They were dead in the water for three hours just after 10:00 p.m.

For days there was increasing media speculation about the ability of the Islamic State to seize a television station, which, for many news program anchors, was a reason to treat the event as terrorism itself. Yet, it turns out that event wasn't exactly as it was being presented or even received. Further examination of the malware used to damage the system had left a trail for forensic firms to flush out the nature of the attack, and this one left bear marks. Months after the attack on the station, several firms concluded the attack had all the signs of a Russian operation.

Similarly, months before this attack, the Warsaw Stock Exchange in Poland had come under fire with a seizure of credentials for brokers in the exchange. In that case, the victims at first believed that the threat came from the Islamic State in retaliation for Polish troops in the coalition attacking the terrorist group. The dump of data on Pastbin said that CCA had hacked the economic institution.[18]

In both cases, the footprints on the digital trail indicated these were not jihadist tracks but those of the Russian hackers associated with the malware known as APT28. Advanced Persistent Threats or APT is a term given to malware found to have been made with the intent of being a determined, well-organized, and developed and intentional goal. In this case, the APT28 is associated with Russian intelligence and has been found in a series of attacks around the world including attacks on Russian adversaries in Ukraine, Georgia, and the United States. In the summer of 2016, the use of APTs came to highlight because of a breach of the Democratic National Committee's data.

The evidence used to link the malware in the TV5Monde, Warsaw Stock Market, DNC, and other, related attacks is based on metadata left by the malware, including using the same command-and-control server to steal the data from targeted machines. The coding of the malware has been tracked by several leading cyber security firms including Trend Micro, FireEye (Mandiant), Symantec, and Crowdstrike.

The Russian intelligence hack on TV5 in France was part of the sophisticated global propaganda campaign. That they chose to mimic and blame the attack on the Cyber Caliphate Army shows that their usage of "false flag" operations has enhanced the image of the ISIS cyber terrorists. Many people still blame ISIS for an operation that only the Russian version of NSA could have performed.

THE AL-QAEDA HACKERS

Although al-Qaeda has issued communications indicating it was starting a cyber war on the West, the few groups working for al-Qaeda lack manpower, track record, and, based on their listed attacks, a strong skill set. Two teams are commonly identified as al-Qaeda hacker groups, the al-Qaeda Hacker Team and the official group al-Qaeda Electronic. Here are the basic overviews of the two groups:

Al-Qaeda Electronic

PROFILES:

Al Qaeda al-Jihad al-Electroniyya[19]
Al Qaeda Electronic Army (AQEA)
Al Qaeda Electronic Cyber Army (AQECA)
Under command of Yahya al-Nemr (Emir)[20]
facebook.com/mujahed.yahyanemr

Deputy: Mahmud al-Adnani[21]
Deputy: Qatada al-Sainawi[22]—Announced July 6, 2015, on al-Mareek Media
Spokesman: Abu Obeida Saidi
Head of Funding: Moaaz al-Tikriti—Announced July 6, 2015, on al-Mareek Media
The group was announced January 20, 2015, in video release from al-Mareek, the official media arm of the group.

Al-Mareek Media Arm

Twitter account
Created March 2015
Kandahar, Afghanistan
مؤسسة المعارك
@almaarek_media
"الحساب الرسمي لمؤسسة المعارك للإنتاج الإعلامي التابعة لقاعدة الجهاد الإلكترونية | The Official Account of al-Mareek Media
Last Tweet, July 1, 2016

LEADERS

Yahya al-Nemr

Yahya al-Nemr may have been born in Tirkrit, Iraq. He lived in ar-Rish and in Kandahar, Afghanistan. He conducted over three hundred defacements between October 2013 and May 2014.[23]

He was active on Aljyyosh.com, a defacing mirroring site.

Yahya al-Nemr's Facebook page.

Figure 37: Yahya al-Nemr posted an announcement calling for his arrest by CENTCOM to his Facebook page. (Source: TAPSTRI)

Yahya al-Nemr's other groups:
"Forces Iraq Electronic" (FIE)

Nemr served as commander for FIE.

Active: January 6–April 2014. They defaced over 94 sites.[24]

Members: "SWAT Ghost Baghdad," Commander of special operations; "Abu al-Mashakl," attorney general; "Lion Diyala," Commander of Intelligence; "Prince Hacker," spokesman.

January 4, 2014—FIE's first post on Facebook.

March 24, 2014—Members SWAT Ghost Baghdad and "Al Qaisi" booted from FIE.[25]

Other FIE members included Sakar al-Karada, Ali al-Kaabi, and "!-_*YaSSeR*_-!"

AEI's Eric Liu noted that FIE made lofty false claims of responsibility, whereas AQE's outlet, al-Mareek, does not indicate a variation of seriousness during al-Nemr's transition from FIE to AQE.

"Team AlHackers AlMujahidin"

Members: Yahya al-Nemr operating under name "Yahya al-Saddami", "Abu al-Mashakl," "Alwaawi al-Malik," "Ahtrafi."

Figure 38: Hacked by Team al-Hackers al-Mujahidin. (Source: TAPSTRI)

AL-QAEDA ELECTRONIC ON SOCIAL MEDIA

AQE had a YouTube video that was suspended. It reportedly hosted hacking lessons including working with remote access tool, njRAT. The Twitter account set up for AQE (alqaeda_11_9) has been suspended.

Al-Qaeda Electronic Hacks

May 2015—Attacks Egyptian news outlet.

June 29, 2015—Threatens US Economy in defacement.

July 3, 2015—AQE defaces 22 British sites.

July 7, 2015—AQE targets Edicot, French software company.

July 14, 2015—ACE defaces Austrian sites and claims it hacks French sports club website.

October 7, 2015—The extremist media tracking site MEMRI reports AQ took over Russian websites in "Website Kristen Russia Hacked." The user name was Izza Mujahid, who used the hashtags #OpSaveSyria, #OpRussia, and #Mujahidn_Cyber_Army.

March 2, 2016—ACE hackers claim to have struck the Indian Railway's Railnet page. The hack affected the Bhusawal division of the Central Railway's Personnel Department. The message posted was attributed to Maulana Aasim Umar, AQIS Emir.[26] ""Why is there no storm in your ocean? A message for Muslims of India from Maulana Aasim Umar (May Allah protect him)." This phrase first appeared in 2013 video of Umar. An 11-page document of the speech circulates online.

April 20, 2016—ACE starts defacing sites in multiple countries including France, Russia, Greece, and the United States.

March 17, 2016—ACE defaces Iranian websites.

Figure 39: Al-Qaeda posts this graphic to hacked Websites. (Source: TAPSTRI)

The Al-Qaeda HaCKeR TeaM (AQHT)

Figure 40: Al-Qaeda Hacker Team Twitter Logo. (Source: TAPSTRI)

AQHT Hacks

On March 1, 2013, the AQHT hacked the Washington State Community College website by al-Qaeda hacker Team & TKL, an unidentified member of the Palestinian Gaza Hacker Team. The home page was defaced, replaced with a picture of OBL, and signed: "Hacked by al-Qaeda Hacker Team&TKL."[27]

Figure 41: We Are All Usama Page —Image posted to WSCC site by Al-Qaeda Hacker Team. (Source: TAPSTRI)

On March 3, 2013, the AQHT struck the town website for Wanatah, Indiana.[28]

I swear by Allah, who raised the heavens with no pillars, America and who lives in America will never enjoy security until we live it practically in Palestine and until all the infidel forces leave the Peninsula of Muhammad.

The al-Qaeda Hacker Team's twitter channel was active starting August 31, 2013. The group attacked a Pizza Hut of India site on August 31, 2013.

Figure 42: AQ Hacker Team—Tweet 1. (Source: TAPSTRI)

They lasted on Twitter for six days. The last tweet came on September 6, 2013, one week after the page was launched. They posted mostly about a few hacks but found time to joke about the CIA and conspiracy theories.

Figure 43: AQ Hacker Team—Tweet 2. (Source: TAPSTRI)

Al-Qaeda Cyber Affiliates

In March, 2013, The Tunisian Cyber Army was a small unidentified group that claimed coordination with AQEA, al-Qaeda Electronic Army, in hacking US government sites. They also claimed assistance from Chinese hackers.[29] They claimed to have attacked the Pentagon and released the statement "Thanks to Allah, the al-Qaeda digital [team], in collaboration with us [i.e., TCA], succeeded in striking America [with] a painful blow against the Pentagon."[30]

Date	Notifier	H	M	R	L	★	Domain	OS	View
2014/05/16	Al-Qaeda HaCKeR TeaM					★	covertlab.stanford.edu/subpage...	Linux	mirror
2014/05/09	Al-Qaeda HaCKeR TeaM	H				★	congregation.chapel.duke.edu	Linux	mirror
2013/06/17	Al-Qaeda HaCKeR TeaM	H				★	www.mosports.gov.mm	Win 2008	mirror
2013/06/10	Al-Qaeda HaCKeR TeaM	H					insurance.olivetcollege.edu	Win 2008	mirror
2013/06/10	Al-Qaeda HaCKeR TeaM	H					nglc.sln.suny.edu	Unknown	mirror
2013/06/10	Al-Qaeda HaCKeR TeaM						www.iipm.edu/casestudies/	Win 2008	mirror
2013/06/06	Al-Qaeda HaCKeR TeaM	H	M				www.teachnw.com	IRIX	mirror
2013/06/06	Al-Qaeda HaCKeR TeaM	H		R			www.wscc.edu	Win 2008	mirror
2013/06/06	Al-Qaeda HaCKeR TeaM	H		R		★	www.centerline.gov	Unknown	mirror
2013/03/04	Al-Qaeda HaCKeR TeaM			R			www.kepler.edu/home/	Linux	mirror
2013/03/04	Al-Qaeda HaCKeR TeaM	H					www.irl.ucf.edu	Linux	mirror
2013/03/04	Al-Qaeda HaCKeR TeaM		M				easy4.udg.edu/easyinnova/	Linux	mirror
2013/03/04	Al-Qaeda HaCKeR TeaM	H					cisco.dnet.clark.edu	Linux	mirror
2013/03/04	Al-Qaeda HaCKeR TeaM	H					www.iie.org.vt.edu	Linux	mirror
2013/03/04	Al-Qaeda HaCKeR TeaM	H	M				www.ise.org.vt.edu	Linux	mirror
2013/03/01	Al-Qaeda HaCKeR TeaM	H					www.easyinnova.com	Linux	mirror
2013/03/01	Al-Qaeda HaCKeR TeaM	H	M			★	www.wanatah-in.gov	Linux	mirror

1

Figure 44: Zone H list of Al Hacker Team Hacks. (Source: TAPSTRI)

Chapter 8

The Hackers, Wannabees & Fembots

There was legitimate reason to pay attention to the activities of groups like the Cyber Caliphate Army. They lead almost daily actions against companies, government agencies, and individuals that compromise privacy interests, erode trust in account security, and keep law enforcement busy with assets. On a small scale, the disruptions to businesses can be financially burdensome or even devastating. In many cases, sites can be reset if they have normal server backups running.

Thus far, the known hackers related to ISIS have launched limited types of attacks and with a skill set far below that of nation state-level actors like the Russian intelligence and criminal hacking crews behind dozens of spearphishing and cyber espionage attacks across Europe and on the Democratic National Committee in the 2016 election. The skill sets of the nation state hackers require some things the ISIS hackers do not seem to have in their tool kit: finances and institutional brainpower. Although ISIS may pay its cyber attackers a good wage on caliphate scale, that doesn't constitute the financial and institutional power you'll find in Russian intelligence services like the FSB or GRU, who have redundant manpower, attack history, and brainpower resources.

Based on observing the daily postings from the Cyber Caliphate Army and its allies the Kalashnikov-e channel, United Cyber Caliphate Channel on Telegram, and the listed hackings associated with these groups on Zone-H.com (a website dedicated to announced website intrusions) and other resources, the cyber Jihadis did not represent a significant online threat as of late summer 2016. Mostly these groups are focused on "capture the flag"-style campaigns where they hack websites and mark them up with their propaganda. They most often result in a homepage replaced with ISIS friendly messages. For a sense of perspective, Junaid Hussain, leading member until his death by airstrike mentioned earlier, was busted for breaking into Tony Blair's email through his advisor Katy Kay's account rather than doing something substantially destructive, such as taking down the London power grid. This doesn't rule out the possibility of advances in coordination if given the opportunity to try.

Figure 45: Junaid Hussain. (Source: TAPSTRI)

Killing a Cyber Emir—Junaid Hussain

There are few individuals in the ISIS cyber ranks who get named, but one person stands out for his part in developing the cyber activities under the black banner. His name was Junaid Hussain, also known by his long time handle, "TriCk." Born in 1994, he was raised in a Pakistani family in Birmingham England. Junaid had developed a reputation for his skills as a hacker early on. He was even once called "the Best in the UK" in an interview from 2012. In the interview, Hussain states he started hacking when he was eleven years old out of revenge for being hacked on a console game system.[1]

His efforts were assisted by a hacking group known as "TeaMp0isoN" (Team Poison) long before he joined ISIS in 2008. He popped up on the radar in January 2011 after Facebook announced that unauthorized postings had occurred due to a bug in its system. Team Poison was credited with exploiting the Facebook bug after they posted a late New Year's Eve post stating, "On the evening of the 31st of December 2010 (New Year's Eve), TeaM P0isoN and ZCompany Hacking Crew will clean up Facebook."[2]

Years later, Hussain would move in a more extreme direction. He said in an interview with Softpedia that he became political at age fifteen when he had been "watching videos of children getting killed in countries like Kashmir and Palestine."[3] He had built up a reputation and clout in the hacker collective Anonymous's world despite his comments that often insulted his western peers. He stated that TeaMpOisoN was akin to "Internet Guerilla Warfare," while Anonymous is equivalent to the "peaceful protesting, camping on the street." He also criticized their efforts that resulted in hacking random sites as "useless" and ineffective.

A key entry in the 2012 Softpedia interview with Hussain exposed his arrogance about being caught. He stated, "My real identity doesn't exist online—and no I don't fear getting caught."[4] Yet, get caught is exactly what happened to Hussain after he hacked the gmail account of Tony Blair advisor Katy Kay. After he posted about the hack and began baiting law enforcement with prank phone calls, Hussain was arrested April 12, 2012, and sentenced to six months in jail.[5]

As the Islamic State rose to power in Iraq and Syria, Hussain changed his path from hacktivist in the wild to cyberjihadist. He adopted the Islamic honorific name or *kunya* of Abu Hussain al-Britani (Father of Hussain, the Britain) and hit Twitter with a penchant for maximizing the use of the 140-character platform. In 2013, Hussain left England for Syria to join ISIS.

His skills were immediately recognized, and he was not sent to the front line or made a suicide bomber. Hussain was assigned to grow the ISIS hacker command but was unable to convince his former allies on the Internet to join him. While he was able to gain followers as a hacktivist when fighting the oppression of people in Palestine and the Indian/Pakistan Kashmir, the extreme nature of ISIS put a barrier between him and former hacking peers, which ultimately prevented the cyber groups he formed from becoming a formidable force.

By the time Junaid reached Syria he was married to a British convert to Islam named Sally Jones. Jones, a mother of two, was a former punk rock guitarist now going under the name, "Umm Hussain Britanya." Hussain was treated very well by ISIS because they counted on him to empower their cyber capabilities. Sally Jones would herself become a major ISIS female recruiter who would become famous for her exhortations for Brits and Americans to attack their fellow citizens.

Hussain often acted as a facilitator for recruiting and was in contact with numerous Americans who were later arrested or killed. One of his disciples was the American Munir Abulkader of Ohio. Abdulkader was a twenty-one-year-old Eritrean-American who was arrested for planning firebomb and AK-47 gun attacks on police officers and military. While in communication with Hussein, Abdulkader was encouraged to stay in the United States and fight as a lone wolf.

On May 3, 2015, two gunmen—Elton Simpson, an African-American, and Nadir Soofi, an American of Pakistani parents—armed themselves and drove from Phoenix, Arizona, to Garland, Texas. Simpson was well known to the FBI as a wannabe jihadi who had been arrested and imprisoned for attempting to travel to

Syria and Somalia. The two had driven to Texas with three AK-47 rifles and handguns with the intent to attack the First Annual Muhammad Art Exhibit and Contest. Internationally known anti-Muslim speakers Pamela Geller and Dutchman Geert Wilders were present, as well as a massive law enforcement presence. A few minutes before the attack, Simpson and Soofi tweeted under the hashtag #texasattack, "The bro with me and myself have given *baya* (oath of loyalty) to Amirul Mu'mineen (Prince of Holy Warriors). May Allah accept us as mujahideen. Make dua." This was a direct call to giving their fealty to Abu Bakr al-Baghdadi, caliph of ISIS.[6] Simpson had been in communications with Junaid Hussain before he was arrested while trying to go to Syria and had served as an al-Qaeda recruiter for the Somali al-Shabaab militia. After they were killed, Junaid Hussein tweeted, "Allau Akbar," in response to their *bay'āt* and deaths.

Great effort went into tracking and killing Hussain by US intelligence. As noted previously, he was finally killed in Syria outside of Raqqa on August 24, 2015, after a secret technique that UK intelligence developed to hack his mobile phone's software and give away his location. The drone waiting overhead verified him and put a Hellfire missile into the car he was travelling in. He was replaced by Bangladeshi hacker Siful Haque Sujan.

THE WANNABE—SIFUL HAQUE SUJAN

After the death of Junaid Hussain, Siful Haque Sujan, a Bangladeshi web developer, took over the operations previously run by Hussain. Sujan lived in Rhydyfelin near Pontypridd in Wales for six years.[7] He had immigrated to the UK in 2003 from Bangladesh. In England, he became the CEO of Ibacs IT Solutions LTD, a web development and e-commerce company, from November 2006 until his departure.

The thirty-one-year-old developer had studied systems engineering at the University of Glamorgan. According to his LinkedIn account, he graduated from Oxford Mission High school in 1999 and attended ALD College from 1999 to 2001. Afterwards trained at Trinity College in London from 2004 to 2006 and University of South Wales from 2007 to 2008.

In 2016, his Linkedin profile says: "Currently working on worldwide joint ventures and expansion of my businesses . . . I am an IT graduate and an entrepreneur from Cardiff, South Wales. Some of my ventures including iBacs Limited (Bangladesh), iBacs IT Solutions LTD (UK), iBacsTel Electronics LTD (UK), iBacs Trade International (UK), British Jordanian Company for E-Commerce (Jordan), iBacs Limited Jordan (Jordan) and so on. My expertise are [*sic*] in IT and Telecommunication and I enjoy designing IT systems. In iBacs, we have designed various IT systems including real estate, food portal, social networking, job portal and many more. I am privileged to work with some extra ordinary people who made it all happen."[8]

When he joined ISIS, he adopted the kunya or honorific name of Abu Khalid al-Bengali.[9] Like other ISIS recruits, according to his associates in the UK, he never appeared to have shown signs of radicalization. He traveled to Syria in July 2014 after he was denied a visa a few months earlier. He told friends he was headed back to Bangladesh.[10]

Although he replaced Hussein, he clearly did not learn the lesson of the lethality of the Internet. He, too, was killed near Raqqa on December 10, 2015, just 90 days after the death of Junaid Hussain. In the Pentagon briefing by Col Steve Warren, Sujan was called a "key link" in ISIS cyber operations.[11] He was married to Saima Aketer Mutka, 28, who is believed to be in Syria with his three children.[12]

After his death, UK authorities revealed that Sujan had been involved in money laundering and he had been sending money to Bangladesh and Syria. He sent £333,000 or approximately $425,000 to his father. His brother, Ahsanul Haque Galib, age fifteen, and his father, Abul Hasanat, age seventy, were arrested in

Dhaka. Sujan sent £500 to a fifteen-year-old girl to marry him and travel to Syria. Authorities arrested his associate, Abdul Samad. The company director was arrested, as well.

Figure 46: Rashid Kassim appears in Wilayat Nineveh video before executing captive.

THE TELEGRAM RECRUITER—RASHID KASSIM

Rashid Kassim, a.k.a. Ibn Qassim, was born around 1987 in France. He was radicalized under the influence of a Salafist imam in Rouanne, Loire, and worked there in a childcare center in a Muslim community.[13] Like some jihadists from the west, Kassim considered himself a rapper; at one point, he released two songs called "I'm a Terrorist" and "Rap Attack."[14] He was fired for trying to teach the children to be jihadists. The other members of the mosque found him to be too extreme and obsessed. He had traveled to Algeria before he decided to travel to Egypt in 2012 with his wife and child. From there he went on to Syria and Iraq to join the Islamic State. In May 2015, French authorities were notified that Kassim and his wife had left France. This set off an investigation into their whereabouts.

Kassim was active in using social media to recruit. He opened a Facebook page and pretended to be a girl under the name Nicole

Ambrosia.[15] He used Telegram to lure other children to fight for the terror organization in France. Kassim ran a Telegram channel that passed out advice to fighters. He posted once that he was unable to be active on social media due to injury: "The only reason that I have time to do all this is that I was wounded."[16] In September 2016, an announcement came that intelligence agencies gained access to Kassim's Telegram account. *Le Monde* broke the story. Kassim was known for talking about random topics including vampires, freemasons, hell, evolution, and the Holocaust.

Arrests and disrupted plots

Kassim has been at the center of many events and had been orchestrating the activities of attackers. His Telegram messages gave him away and led to the arrest of ten teenagers in a month. A flurry of arrests took place after investigators reviewed the Telegram chats. The arrests included a nineteen-year-old from Hauts-de-Seine, a twenty-three-year-old from Lyon, a sixteen-year-old from Melun on August 4, 2016, and an eighteen-year-old from Clermont-Ferrand.

He was responsible for setting three fifteen-year-old boys on a course to strike at Paris with stabbing attacks. On September 8, 2016, a teenage boy who had been in contact with Kassim was arrested. On September 10, another teen was arrested in Paris after authorities discovered that he was involved in a planned stabbing. He, too, had been in contact with Kassim. On September 14, an Egyptian teen was arrested in Paris after planning an attack with Kassim via Telegram.[17]

Kassim and the Larossi Abballa Attack

Larossi Abballa murdered Jean Baptist Savaing, a police officer, and his wife, officer Jessica Schneider, on July 13, 2016, in their Paris-area home before livestreaming a message to the world via Facebook. After Abballa killed Savaing, he quoted Kassim in his live message. Investigators said Abballa was a member of the Telegram channel run by Kassim.[18]

Murder of priest in Saint-Étienne-du-Rouvray

Days later, two teens from Rouen murdered a priest in Saint-Éti-enne-du-Rouvray by slitting his throat after chatting with Kassim via Telegram. He was implicated in attacks on officers in Magnan-ville in June 2016.

Failed Car Bomb Attack

On September 4, he attempted to pull off a failed remote control attack from Syria by detonating a Peugeot near Notre Dame Cathe-dral. To pull off the plot, he gave instructions to Ines Madani, a nine-teen-year-old girl, with her friends Amel Sakaou, Ornella Gilligman, and Sarah Hervouet. He instructed them to "fill a car with gas cylinders, sprinkle petrol in it, and park in a busy street . . . *BOOM*" The plot failed after the ignition by cigarette malfunctioned. The cigarette went out. A police officer was stabbed during the arrest of one of the women.

Of the four women charged in the plot, Sarah Hervouet was a former girlfriend of both Larossi Abballa, the Paris killer of the police officer, and Adel Kermiche, murderer of the eighty-year-old priest of Rouen.[19] Despite the failed attack, Kassim still hit Tele-gram to celebrate the women and use it as an example to shame men into acting. "Where are the brothers?" he asked.[20]

Appearance in Nineveh video

Kassim appeared in a Wilayat Nineveh release called *Their Alliance and Terror*, a 7:18 video applauding the 2016 Bastille Day attack in Nice by Mohamed Lahouaiej-Bouhlel and Larossi Abballa. Kassim was featured in the video, which showed him beheading an accused spy. He also issues threats to France with calls for lone wolf attacks or "*terrorisme de proximité.*"

THE CASE OF PEANUT BUTTER AND JELLY

In 2001, before the attacks on the United States, Ahmad Abousamra, born in France in 1981, and his friend Terek Mehanna were visiting with an unnamed friend of Mehanna's. According to court filings in the case, the three discussed going to training camps before September 11, 2001. The son of a Boston-area doctor, Abousamra was a Syrian-American who was born in France before moving to the Boston area. He graduated from Northeastern University and became very proficient with computers.

In 2002, Daniel Maldonado, born in New Hampshire in 1983, met Abousamra, who introduced him to Mehanna. They watched jihadist videos on VHS tapes at Mehanna's home or downloaded video clips from the web according to Mehanna's friend, who had watched the videos with them and known Mehanna for almost 20 years. The videos featured grievance segments on Bosnia and Palestine before ending with the noble story of victory by the mujahideen.

Years later, the unnamed friend would purchase tickets for the three to go to Yemen. They would watch jihadist videos to get psyched up about their journey. The trip was a failure, though. The important people that Mehanna wanted to see were either in jail or on hajj.

Abousamra left the United States in 2004 to go fight in Iraq against US forces and returned in 2006. He was questioned by FBI's Joint Terrorism Task Force (JTTF) in 2006. He then went to Syria in 2006. The unnamed friend of Terek Mehanna began to cooperate with the JTTF that same year.

Maldonado had moved his family to Egypt in November 2005. After the move, he began work as an IT administrator for a forum called "Islamic Networking." Omar Hammami (a.k.a. Abu Mansur al-Amriki), an American who travelled to Somalia to fight with al-Shabaab, was one of the people who would join that discussion forum under the name "al-Mizzi." He would later join Hammami in Somalia to train with the al-Qaeda-backed al-Shabaab terror group. Hammami, an active recruiter and propagandist, was killed in a village raid in Somalia. Maldonado was arrested by Kenyan authorities in February 2007 along the border with Somalia. After his family lived in Somalia for a period of time, they fled to Kenya, but it was too late for his wife, who died of malaria. He was the first US citizen charged with support for terrorism related to Somalia. He pled guilty in April 2007 and received a sentence of ten years.

Ahmad Abousamra was accused by the US government of being involved in the social media campaign of ISIS.[21] There was no explanation given about his role or evidence of this activity. He was regarded as important because he was an an American with computer skills. Al-Arabiya referred to him as "an expert in film-making, an ISIS documentary film maker."[22] Patrick Pool, how-ever, characterized him as a "Top ISIS media propagandist official" involved in beheading videos.[23] ISIS has never acknowledged his presence in any releases either official or unofficial.

Later unconfirmed rumors claimed he died in a Syrian air-strike.[24] He had been charged along with Terek Mehanna in 2009 related to a plot to attack in Boston on a shopping mall and planned attacks on Condoleeza Rice and John Ashcroft. He was listed as one of the FBI's Most Wanted with a $50,000 reward.

The group of friends would discuss their plans with secret codes, including Mehanna discussing the use of encryption in communi-cations with an associate in order to evade surveillance. Together they would use phrases as code for terrorist activity. Example: "pea-nut butter," "peanut butter and jelly," or "PB&J"—all meant "jihad." In order to get good at "peanut butter and jelly" they would need to go to "culinary school" or training camps.[25] According to the criminal complaint, Maldonado made up the phrase "culinary school," thinking that it would be understood by Mehanna. Mehanna acknowledged that he understood the meaning.

THE FEMBOTS OF JIHAD

If one were to sit down and watch the hundreds of hours of videos and dedicate hundreds of more hours to going through photo slide shows, you would be hard-pressed to see a woman in any of it. You might occasionally see a hijab-covered girl among children in a few rare scenes or in a few that are meant to show off ISIS education. But the life of women in the caliphate is essentially absent from their propaganda. There are no official releases that feature women. But there was one unofficial video made by the al-Khanssaa Brigade, a "female policing brigade," that was notable in that it features Sally Jones, widow of Junaid Hussain. Despite their absence in jihad imagery, women are vital to the online ISIS effort to thrive. Their number one mission is to recruit other young women, from any nation or faith, to come to the caliphate so they can serve as "jihadi brides" for soon-to-be-dead fighters of the cult of death.[26]

"Women of the Islamic State" was a manifesto published by the al-Khanssaa Brigade in January 2015 and translated by the Quilliam Foundation, a London-based counterextremism think tank. The foundation contends that it was "a piece of propaganda aimed at busting myths and recruiting supporters," but aimed at women in the Gulf region rather than Westerners. It touches upon anti-Western sentiment and discusses what a woman's role should be—which was mainly taking care of her husband and children. "It is always preferable for a woman to remain hidden and veiled, to maintain society from behind this veil," the manifesto reads. "This, which is always the most difficult role, is akin to that of a director, the most important person in a media production, who is behind the scenes organizing."[27] The manifesto also condemned the wide range of fashions and beauty practices as the work of the devil, or Iblis.[28] The analysis by the Quilliam Foundation notes that the fact that it hadn't been translated into other languages, including English, as past propaganda has been, means "it will have been deemed ineffective—perhaps even counterintuitive—in achieving its propagandistic aims with a Western audience."[29]

The Punk Rock Jihadist Sally Jones

Sally Jones was the poster girl for the al-Khansaa manifesto. Jones was born in Kent, England, and, before becoming a jihadi bride, was a punk guitarist in a band called *Krunch*. She met Hussain online. Years later she'd be married to a British terrorist, raising her son in Syria and being known as the "Punk Rocker Jihadi." She's also been known as Umm Hussain Britanya and tweeted under the handle @ UmmHussain102 for a while. She went from playing shows in the south of England to appearing in a video of the al-Khanssaa Brigade and issuing threats via Twitter. She has extensively tweeted a range of posts including: "You Christians all need beheading with a nice blunt knife and stuck on the railings at raqqa [*sic*] . . . Come here I'll do it for you." Then there were her veiled threats in May 2016 with comments about avoiding Central London in June and July "especially by Tube." She has changed her named to Sakinah Hussain.[30]

In September 2015, the U.S. Department of State designated Jones a "Specially Designated Global Terrorist." "Jones and Hussain targeted American military personnel through publication of a 'hit list' online to encourage 'lone offender attacks,'" the State Department wrote. "Jones has used social media to recruit women to join ISIL. In August 2015, Jones encouraged individuals aspiring to conduct attacks in Britain by offering guidance on how to construct homemade bombs."[31]

A propaganda video released August 26, 2016, showed five young boys murdering a group of Kurdish prisoners; one of the boys has been identified as Jones's eleven-year-old son, called Abu Abdullah al-Britani in the video.[32]

As Jones demonstrates, there is no stereotypical terrorist, male or female. FBI Director James Comey said as much in the aftermath of the 2015 San Bernardino shootings, in which husband and wife Syed Rizwan Farook and Tashfeen Malik killed 14 and seriously injured 22 in a terrorist attack. The attack was said to be Islamic State-inspired—Malik allegedly posted a pledge to ISIS on Facebook just before the attack—although no terror groups have been directly linked to the attack.[33] "The challenge of our efforts to try and find and redirect people is that it is a wide spectrum of folks," Comey said. "It isn't a particular demographic or geography. It's about people seeking meaning in their lives in a misguided way."[34]

In a 2015 report, a London-based think tank, the Institute for Strategic Dialogue, writes there has been an "unprecedented surge in female recruits to the terrorist organization Islamic State," with figures at the time estimating at least 550 Western women had flocked to ISIS.[35]

Research from a range of experts shows that the women who wind up traveling to Syria or Iraq to join ISIS have a complex range of reasons to do so. The pressures vary from the cultural stress of fitting in as a Muslim in non-Muslim countries to seeking adventure and believing in the honor of marrying and having the children of a "martyr." According to the Institute for Strategic Dialogue, the reasons women join ISIS go far beyond the concept of the "jihadi bride." "Push" factors include "1. Feeling isolated socially and/or culturally, including questioning one's identity and uncertainty of belonging within a Western culture. 2 Feeling that the international Muslim community as a whole was being violently persecuted. 3. An anger, sadness and/or frustration over a perceived lack of international action in response to this persecution." "Pull" factors include "1. Idealistic goals of religious duty and building a utopian 'caliphate state.' 2. Belonging and sisterhood. 3. Romanticisation of the experience."[36]

The report continues: "ISIS has increased its female-focused efforts, writing manifestos directly for women, directing sections of its online magazine publications Dabiq to the 'sisters of the Islamic State' and allowing women to have a voice within their recruitment strategy—albeit via social media." The Western girls and women who move to Syria and join ISIS are then used to recruit more Western women particularly to fill the sexual desires of fighters. "You have French girls messaging French girls and American girls messaging American girls," Mia Bloom, professor at Georgia State University and author of *Bombshell: Women and Terrorism* told *Marie Claire*. "It helps with relating, finding common ground. It makes it feel more like the recruiter is just like you, a friend."[37]

"The group creates propaganda that specifically targets women, and sells them a different message from the one sold to men (though both are told it's their religious obligation to join the Islamic State)," Kate Storey writes in *Marie Claire*. "Men are marketed the chance to prove their faith by joining the fight; women are marketed the idea of sisterhood and the opportunity to marry a jihadi fighter, thus supporting the cause by raising the next generation of militants."[38]

Katrin Bennhold writes in the *New York Times*:

Social media has allowed the group's followers to directly target young women, reaching them in the privacy of their bedrooms with propaganda that borrows from Western pop culture—images of jihadists in the sunset and messages of empowerment. A recent post linked to an Islamic State account paraphrased a popular L'Oréal makeup ad next to the image of a girl in a head scarf: "COVERed GIRL. Because I'm worth it."[39]

Umm Isa al-Amrikiah—The First ISIS Feminist

Someone blogging under the name Umm Isa al Amrikiah (*Mother of Issa, the American*) posted her first message on her Telegram channel in mid-January 2016. A post on her channel, published by *News Corp Australia Network*, gave some insight into why she created the channel. It read:

"This channel is dedicated to everyone who wishes to do Hijrah to the blessed land of Sham (Syria) . . . I will be posting daily reminders, pictures of Sham, short articles and general information about my life here in Sham . . . I am a married sister so all brothers will be directed to the Beast who married me on his telegram."[40]

Over twelve thousand users followed her channel. Among other things, she wrote about men and women she believed were not following the religion as strictly as they should be. In one post, she railed against the men who were sending her messages. "My account is for sisters only, so unless you menstruate do not message me . . . And anyone who messages me will be forwarded to my husband and will be dealt with accordingly." In another, she criticized women for posting pictures of themselves on social media. "Are you a Hijabi or a Hoejabi?" she wrote. "Hijabi: A Muslimah who is fully covered head to toe, as her Lord commanded. Hoejabi: A hybrid between a whore and a hijabi. A creature somewhat confused whether she belongs in this camp or that." She continued, "If you look pretty or cute in the hijab then know that you're doing something wrong." She also posted a graphic that read, "Hijabi selfies everywhere. Duck lips, shaped eyebrows & a cake face is not Hijab."[41]

The messages, however, went far beyond simply calling out what she saw as improper behavior or lack of a strict adherence to the customs of the Islamic State. Umm Isa was also used to doing ideological recruiting and propagandizing for lone wolf murder:

Who out there will get u and kill the kuffars in the west? Who wants to sacrifice himself for the sake of Allah subhana wa ta'ala? Get off your couches and do something instead of spending 24/7 on social media. You think you are doing something good by posting some ahadith and verses of the Quran while your brothers are out in the cold dark night facing the enemies? You cry out on social media "I want sharia" "I want to make hijrah" yet you are doing nothing about it. You are not a man, just a male.[42]

In another post, she wrote, "Allhamdulilah finally got my Hizam (suicide belt) today. May Allah subhana wa ta'ala grant me the opportunity to use it soon, to grant me the honor to sacrifice my self for Him, for his deen (to kill the kuffars). May Allah wa ta'ala grant us all shahadah Ameen."[43]

When her end came, it became clear that "Umm Isa al Amrikiah" was not even American. She was identified as Australian national

Shadi Jabar Khalil Mohammad. She traveled to Syria at age twenty, one day before her younger brother, Farhad, shot and killed a man outside of an Australian police station in October 2015. She married a Sudanese man, Abu Sa'ad al-Sudani, whose nickname was "The Beast of Islam." Both Mohammad and her husband were killed in April 22, 2016, by a US air strike in Syria. Cindy Wockner writing for *News Corp Australia Network* noted that in her seven months in Syria "she had risen to what would appear to be senior ranks within the propaganda arm."[44] Pentagon press secretary Peter Cook told reporters, "The death of al-Sudani and Shadi remove influential ISIL recruiters and extremists who actively sought to harm Western interests and further disrupts and degrades ISIL's ability to plot external attacks."[45]

Few details about specific threats have been disclosed, but Cook said there was "an effort specifically to target Western interests."[46] "Al-Sudani was involved in planning attacks against the United States, Canada, and the United Kingdom," Cook said. "Both al-Sudani and his wife were active in recruiting foreign fighters in efforts to inspire attacks against Western interests."[47]

Keonna Thomas—The Young Lioness

Keonna Thomas was a thirty-year-old mom in Philadelphia who according to US officials wished to travel to Syria and die for ISIS. She was served with a search warrant two days before her scheduled March 27, 2015, flight to Barcelona.[48] On April 3, she was arrested and charged with knowingly attempting to provide support to a foreign terrorist organization. The criminal complaint against her alleged she had researched "indirect routes" to Turkey, which the complaint states was "known to be the most common and most direct transit point for individuals traveling from locations in Europe who are seeking to enter Syria and join ISIL," according to the complaint.[49]

Thomas, who also went by the names "Fatayat Al-Khilafah" and "Young Lioness," frequently communicated with two alleged fighters, one of whom claimed to be in Somalia and one in Syria.

The criminal complaint against her cited several instances of her apparent ISIS support on social media. On August 18, 2013, she retweeted a graphic of a young armed boy in camouflage with the caption: "Ask yourselves, while this young man is holding magazines for the Islamic state, what are you doing for it? #ISIS." On April 27, 2014, she tweeted: "I would prefer the *shahada* [martyrdom] of being in the bodies of green birds." On December 2, 2014, she tweeted: "If we truly knew the realities . . . we all would be rushing to join our brothers in the front lines pray ALLAH accept us as *shuhada* [*sic*; martyrs]," according to an affidavit by the FBI special agent investigating the case.[50]

Hoda Muthana

Hoda Muthana was a twenty-year-old college student studying business at the University of Alabama before she ran away to Syria to join ISIS. She traveled to Syria in November 2014 and married Australian jihadist Suhan Abdul Rahman just one month after arriving. Rahman was killed shortly after by an airstrike. Ellie Hall of BuzzFeed, who originally reported Muthana's story, wrote about an alleged interaction between Hoda and her father, Mohammed, after he sent her a message urging her to come home:

"I'm not going to come back," he read from his phone. "This is the right place for me to live and I am really ready to die, to meet my God as a true Muslim." Hoda denies that she told her father she was "ready" to die. "I told him that I'm obeying Allah and if that means sacrificing everything, then I will," she said.[51]

Mohammed said that in the year and a half leading up to her departure, she had actually been immersing herself more and more in her religious life. He said that at the time he was proud of his daughter. "Hoda's newfound dedication to her faith was a source of pride to her father, particularly her commitment to memorizing the Qur'an," Hall writes.[52] What he didn't know, however, was that her increased focus on her Muslim faith was all part of her radical plan to join ISIS.

Emilie Konig

Emilie Konig was from Brittany, France. She supported a French Islamist group from Nantes known as Forsane Alizza, or Knights of Pride, which has since dissolved. Konig had two children she abandoned to go to Syria in 2012. Just as it did with Sally Jones, the US State Department designated Konig as a Specially Designated Global Terrorist. "While in Syria, Konig directed individuals in France to attack French government institutions," the State Department press release reads. "In a video posted on May 31, 2013, Konig was shown training with weapons in Syria."[53] The magazine *Paris Match* reported that in one propaganda video, she appeals directly to her own children to not forget that they are Muslims.[54] *Le Monde* reported Konig was active on social networks since 2012 and has called for attacks in France.[55]

Aqsa Mahmood

Aqsa Mahmood was nineteen years old when she left Glasgow, Scotland, bound for Syria in November 2013. Mahmood was one of many women who had begun to recruit other young women to join ISIS. Ellie Hall of *BuzzFeed* writes, "The women of ISIS appear to have established networks across social media platforms, which they use to connect with one another and recruit other women."[56] Kimiko de Freytas-Tamura writes in the *New York Times* that Mahmood "acts as a virtual den mother offering sometimes stern advice to peers who would follow in her footsteps."[57] Hall wrote that the women of ISIS use the messaging app KiK to communicate with those seriously considering making hijrah, the journey to the Islamic State.[58]

The Daily Beast writes Mahmood has been "highly active on Twitter and on her blog trying to persuade would-be 'sisters' in Europe and the United States to travel to the Middle East to help ISIS establish its extremist vision of a militant Islamic utopia."[59]

Mahmood allegedly communicated with one of the three British schoolgirls who left their homes in Bethnal Green, London, to join ISIS in Syria. Kadiza Sultana, Shamima Begum, and Amira Abase were fifteen when they ran away to Raqqa.

Mahmood also went by the name Umm Layth, which translates "Mother of the Lion." In a series of Tumblr posts that she titles "Diary of a Muhajirah," Mahmood gives insight into her transition into life in Syria and offers tips to other Westerners considering doing the same. "Muhajirah" translates literally as "immigrant" and "is used to refer to women who have travelled to the lands controlled by Islamic State," according to the Quilliam Foundation.[60] In an April 2014 post, she writes:

> For the winter you will most likely need a good pair of boots and a thick warm coat. The winters here are freezing, trust me I'm from North of Britain and even still I found it cold. You can find shampoos soaps and other female necessities here, so do not stress if you think you will be experiencing some cavewomen life here. *Alhumdulilaah* [praise be to Allah] I have experienced far too much luxury than I was expecting. Deen wise please do remember to bring all your Kitaabs and download as many pdfs as you can on your tablets and mobiles (Be careful to not make them too Jihadi as you also have to tie your camel - and all precations must be taken not to bait yourself out. *Wallahi* [I swear to Allah] these *Kuffar* [derogatory Arabic term for non-Muslims] and *Munafiqeen* [derogatory term for religious hypocrites] will do anything to cause the Muslimeen harm. But they plot and plan however Allah is the best of Planners).[61]

She also writes about the difficulty of separating from her family and tries to counteract the image of the typical ISIS recruit she says the media portrays. In a September 2014 post, she wrote:

> The media at first used to claim that the ones running away to join the Jihad as being unsuccessful, didn't have a future and from broke down families etc. But that is far from the truth. Most sis-

ters I have come across have been in university studying courses with many promising paths, with big, happy families and friends and everything in the Dunyah to persuade one to stay behind and enjoy the luxury. If we had stayed behind, we could have been blessed with it all from a relaxing and comfortable life and lots of money.[62]

Nine British Students, Nine Online Recruiters

In March 2015, it was reported that nine British students who had been studying medicine in Sudan traveled to Syria, allegedly to work as medics in the Islamic State. Four women were among the group: Lena Maumoon Abdulqadir, Abdul Qadir, Nada Sami Kader, and Rowan Kamal Zine El Abidine. A second group from the same school—Khartoum's University of Medical Sciences and Technology—later joined with the earlier group. It was alleged the students had been radicalized and recruited to help ISIS by Mohammed Fakhri al-Khabass, a British student who ran the school's Islamic Cultural Association. By June, he had allegedly gotten sixteen of his classmates to join ISIS as medics.

Turkish lawmaker Mehmet Ali Ediboglu told the *Observer*, which originally reported on the story, that he and the families of the students believed they had been "brainwashed" into joining the Islamic State as medics. "Let's not forget about the fact that they are doctors," Ediboglu told the *Observer*. "They went there to help, not to fight."[63] One student from the original group, Ahmed Sami Khider, appeared in an ISIS propaganda video two months after his arrival in Syria. "Dear brothers and sisters, we as Muslims and as doctors have a great responsibility," the BBC reports Khider as saying. "All you are doing is sitting in the West in the comfort of your homes. Use your skills and come here."[64]

Asia Siddiqui and Noelle Velentzas

Asia Siddiqui and Noelle Velentzas of Queens, New York, were arrested in April 2015 for allegedly conspiring to use a weapon of mass destruction in the U.S. The two former roommates, age 31 and 28, respectively, at the time of arrest, were "conspiring to prepare an explosive device to be detonated in a terrorist attack in the United States," according to a complaint filed in U.S. District Court in the Eastern District of New York. Stephanie Clifford writes in the *New York Times*, "Ms. Siddiqui had been communicating with al-Qaeda in the Arabian Peninsula, and Ms. Velentzas had watched violent videos made by the Islamic State, also known as ISIS, the complaint says."[65]

The *New York Times* writes: "When agents arrested the women at their apartments on Thursday, they found 'three propane gas tanks, soldering tools, pipes, a pressure cooker, fertilizer, flux, detailed handwritten notes on the recipes for bomb making, and extensive jihadist literature' along with 'two machetes and two daggers,' prosecutors said. 'The women also had instructions on how to turn propane tanks into bombs,' the government said."[66]

An affidavit given by an FBI special agent investigating the case reads:

In 2013, the UC met with VELENTZAS on multiple occasions. During these meetings, which were not recorded, VELENTZAS expressed violent jihadist ideology and an interest in terrorism. For example, VELENTZAS praised the attacks of September 11, 2001 and stated that being a martyr through a suicide attack guarantees entrance into heaven. According to VELENTZAS, a suicide bomber does not take her life; she gives her life in the name of Allah."[67]

Of Siddiqui, the agent wrote:

In or about 2009, SIDDIQUI wrote a poem that was published in a magazine called *Jihad Recollections*, which was a predecessor of *Inspire*. I have obtained a copy of the poem, which is called "Take Me to the Lands Where the Eyes Are Cooled." The poem calls for its readers to engage in violent jihad and to destroy enemies of Islam. For example, SIDDIQUI wrote that she "drop[s] bombs" as she swings on a hammock and "[h]it[s] cloud nine with the smell of turpentine, nations wiped clean of filthy shrines." She also wrote that she "taste[s] the Truth through fists and slit throats" and that there is "[n]o excuse to sit back and wait - for the skies rain martyrdom."[68]

The affidavit continues that Velentzas expressed a "preference for attacking military or government targets, rather than civilian targets." It also chronicles several incidents that occurred during an undercover investigation:

VELENTZAS pulled a knife from her bra and demonstrated how to stab someone to show SIDDIQUI and the UC what she would do if attacked. VELENTZAS added, "Why we can't be some real bad bitches?" and stated that people needed to refer to them as "citizens of the Islamic State."[69]

Chapter 9

Jihadi Murder & Cyber Media

In a truly shocking scene, a journalist named James Foley was executed by beheading with a bayonet by the British terrorist Mohammed Emwazi, a.k.a. Jihadi John on August 19, 2014. The video included a direct taunt to the American president, Barack Obama, by the Londoner wearing all black. The shock resulted in coverage that frequently obsessed with the "Hollywood style" production of the video they were now covering. Shot in High Definition (HD), the propaganda videos of ISIS grabbed the attention they sought by using better quality cameras, editing skills, and, most important, a clear narrative. ISIS videos said the caliphate was here and anyone who got in their way would be beheaded.

In 2004, AQI leader Abu Musab al-Zarqawi killed Nicholas Berg the same way; it was captured on a grainy tape in a Sony handycam video. It was shuttled to the web by his associates, including Abu Maysara, the first AQI information minister. Within the first twenty-four hours of the Berg video being uploaded from London to al-ansar.biz in Malaysia, it was downloaded more than a half-million times. US authorities had previously tracked this website from other locations including Alexandria, Egypt. Abu Maysara had to adapt how to post the Nick Berg video. Due to limitations at the time, AQI's efforts to publish the video ran into file-size limitations in emails, user access issues in Yahoo, and limited footprint on the web for jihadist forums. He was, however, able to find a file sharing site called YouSendIt, which allowed the user to send out links to anyone on the web.[1] This model of propagation was adopted by ISIS. Tease the video through small clips or still images on Twitter, drop it into a file sharing folder, and let the world download it from the site. What AQI had pioneered, ISIS had perfected. Tens of millions of downloads occurred after the James Foley video, and the caliphate harnessed the chariot of visual media to spread their message of fear.

THE ISIS VIDEO MEDIA STRUCTURE

ISIS official videos have specific logos and styling that are very distinctive and bear the stylistic signature of the regional and central branches. The head production house was al-Furqan Media. The second tier outlets are focused on messaging across the entire ISIS region or beyond, as if the message comes from a central government. They include *an-Naba*, a weekly newspaper; Maktabat al-Himmah, a publications center that releases printed publications; and al-Hayat Media, the outward bound messaging voice for ISIS. Al-Hayat Media serves to broadcast the ISIS message beyond the regions under the caliphate's control and beyond the Arabic language audience. There are also the regional centers divided by Wilayah, or states. Each of these centers has their own logo and graphic presentation style. For instance, Wilayah Dijlah videos use a 3D intro that shows their logo appearing from water to emphasize its association with the Tigris. Each center may focus on presenting the events in the allocated region they cover or may be turned to speak against an enemy. In a few cases, many regional centers were used to send unified messages to a particular ISIS region or a potential ISIS affiliate. "Messages for the Maghreb [Western North Africa]" were sent from across the ISIS regional centers to incite action in Morocco, Tunisia, and Algeria. In other cases, "Messages to Somalia" releases came in early October 2015 as the terrorist group Al-Shabaab was caught in contemplation on joining ISIS or remaining in its loyalty to al-Qaeda. The ISIS messages were aimed to persuade the group to swear an oath of loyalty or Ba'yat to the Caliph Abu Bakr al-Baghdadi.

Al-Furqan Media

This was the center where it all began under al-Zarqawi. In 2006, AQI began releasing videos of its campaigns, and the production house for those operations was named al-Furqan. With hundreds of releases, before the group called itself ISIS, al-Furqan was the grand-daddy media organization. Starting with series like *Hell of the Romans and Apostates in the Land of Two Rivers*, al-Furqan mastered the art of jihadist video and terrorism snuff films. The *Hell of the Romans* series was a batch of over a hundred near-minute-long clips showing various AQI attacks from shootings, bombings, grenade attacks on US, or "apostate" troops from around Iraq. These were first released January 20, 2007, and continued until August 30, 2009.

In June 2012, ISII released the first of four videos called *Clanging of the Swords*, which would be recalled repeatedly in other AQI releases as a suggested title for viewing. The hour-long video starts by attacking the Shia as apostates before turning to SVBIED attacks and ending with house raids with silencers.

The second volume, running just under an hour, was filled with footage from a Haditha attack on March 5, 2012, where approximately 40 AQI fighters killed 20 police officers.[2] The video shows how the attackers put the operation together, how they disguised themselves as SWAT team members to get past the checkpoints and attack the police officers. Col. Mohammed Shafar was one of those killed. He had been helping the fight against AQI with "Awakening Movement," a Sunni militia. The video shows the attackers' view of the events of the evening.

In a "Cops"-style first-person video format, the video takes you through three checkpoint raids before they reach Haditha. The officers are first subdued after being swarmed by AQI attackers dressed as SWAT officers and bound. Then later you see them murdered by shots to the head with silencer pistols.

The third *Clanging of Swords* featured footage of the *Destroying the Walls* campaign. Al-Baghdadi called for the campaign in July 2012. One of the stages of the campaign would focus the release of allies from prison. In this video, prisoners from Tafirat prison in Tikrit are featured after they are freed by AQI. Iraqi officials state that files on who was freed were destroyed during the attack.[3] The fourth *Clanging of the Swords* came many months later and opened with a drone video shot.

Al-Furqan shocked the world and thrust ISIS upon the stage with a series of videos launched in the summer of 2014. On July 5, 2014, al-Furqan released perhaps its most important video with Abu Bakr al-Baghdadi's *Khutbah and Jum'ah Prayer in the Grand Mosque of Mosul*, a 21-minute video that updated the face of the leader of the terrorist organization that had the world's attention. Before this video, the image of the mysterious former prisoner was his mug shot.

Weeks later, on August 19, 2014, al-Furqan would shock the world again with the release of *A Message to America*, a five-minute video that introduced the world to ISIS in a new way—via the murder of James Foley. It ended with threatening the death of another, Steven Sotloff. The video featured a hooded British speaker who was later dubbed by the media "Jihadi John." This would only be the beginning, though, as a series of beheadings were carried out on video for the world to see.

On September 2, 2014, al-Furqan would release *Second Message to America*, 2:46 in length, featuring the murder of Steven Sotloff and threatening to kill David Haines. On September 14, 2014, another release appeared titled *A Message to the Allies of America*, a 2:27 video of the murder of David Haines and the threatening of British citizen Alan Henning. Then on October 4, 2015, the group releases *Another Message to America and Its Allies*, a one-minute video of the murder of British citizen Alan Henning and the threat to kill American Peter Kassig. This continued with Japanese captives Kenji Goto and Haruna Yukawa in a *Message to Japan*.

But the group wouldn't stop there. It was responsible for releasing three other videos that shocked the world. Instead of individual beheadings, a video was released in November 2014 showing the mass execution of Syrian soldiers by beheading. Intelligence officials throughout America and Europe were frantically examining the footage for foreign fighters after a few had been seen in the footage including the Frenchman, Maxime Houchard.

They released the video of the Jordanian pilot Muath al-Kasasbeh, burning alive in a cage in March 2015, which sparked a swift response from Jordan. Weeks later, they released another video with a child soldier killing Israeli Muhammad Musallam with a gunshot through the head. Then they capped off the barbaric series of releases with a double mass execution in Libya of Ethiopian Christians in April 2015. Eventually the videos of beheadings shifted from al-Furqan out to the various regional offices where the savagery of executions would eventually go way beyond beheadings as methods varied from region to region. Al-Furqan set the tone for the regional center savagery.

In September 2016, US forces killed the leader of al-Furqan, a man named Wa'el Adel Hasan Salman al-Fayad, the man who had become so synonymous with the group that he was known as "Abu Muhammad Furqan." He was at the center of the rise of the most powerful segment of ISIS propaganda before his death by airstrike in his home in Raqqa.

British journalist John Cantilie is a terrorist hostage of ISIS. On numerous occasions he was forced to make videos designed to attack the United Kingdom, the United States, and Western policies. The videos titled *Lend Me Your Ears* were released through al-Furqan. Two other videos called *Inside Mosul* and *Inside Raqqa* were also filmed with Cantilie. He appeared mid-2016 in a brief video released by the AMAQ news agency in 2016.

Al-Hayat Videos

In the first video release, *There is No Life Without Jihad*, released June 19, 2014, Reyaad Khan (a.k.a. Abu Dujana al-Hindi Britain) and other fighters are featured in the English targeted release. The first speaker was Nasser Ahmed Muthana (Abu Muthanna al-Yemeni-al-Britani), followed by Abdul Raqib Amin (a.k.a. Abu Bara' al-Hindi-al-Britani), Zakaryah Raad (a.k.a. Abu Yahya as-Shami-Australia), Abu Nour al-Iraqi (Australian, damaged left eye), and Neil Prakash.

Al-Hayat was most commonly known because of its non-Arabic titles aimed at the United States, UK, and Europe. It is also responsible for the publication of official *nasheeds* (religious chants) and the shiny near-quarterly magazine *Dabiq*.

Figure 47: ISIS video banner. (Source: TAPSTRI)

Taking the Shot—The Role of the Cameraman

To examine how ISIS videos are filmed and produced, testimony from former fighters and media workers of the group who discussed their activities in or in relation to the media center demands has proven the best source. Additionally, numerous videos and photo packages showed the life of ISIS's "Combat Cameramen." The media teams often showed the glamorous life of cameramen, editors, nasheed singers, or other media personnel that help put the picture together of how a video or photo story comes to be.

There are videos aimed at the media team; its members look like war correspondents with Sony HandyCams. Running alongside Toyota Helix gunner trucks, the videos show the camera crews putting themselves right in the mix of hot combat to get shots that promote the ISIS image of brave fighting men. There are a couple of videos that give a glimpse of head-mounted cams like the GoPro. The GoPro style footage gives the viewer a "Call of Duty" POV shot usually articulated with the barrel of an AK47 in the view.

The *Washington Post* conducted interviews for a piece called "Inside the surreal world of the Islamic State's propaganda machine." The interviews conducted by Greg Miller and Souad Mekhennet discussed how orders are given and how workers are compartmentalized to create the final video spectacle. They told the stories of several returning fighters who worked with the media machine of ISIS.

In the story of a man they identified as "Abu Hajer al-Maghribi" (who was serving time in Morocco after returning from Syria where he worked with the Raqqa media office), he stated he went through a "month-long program for media operatives" that taught him how to film and edit. He was taught how to sound during interviews.

He stated that he would get his daily video assignments issued to him on paper that bore the seal of "the terrorist group's media emir" with location and coordinates. He was involved in filming many of ISIS's more memorable massacres of Syrian troops. He was used to film the British terrorist hostage John Cantilie's *Inside Mosul* release. He claims to have used a Canon camera. He was then ordered to transfer the footage to laptops, then to memory sticks before "delivering those to drop sites."[4] The article doesn't state if he meant a physical or virtual "drop site." The process was rigorously compartmentalized.

Abu Hajer stated that media operatives are paid more than the average fighter. He claims he was paid $700 per month and free of *zakat* (taxes).

Another fighter in the *Washington Post* article under the name "Abu Abdullah" claimed to help arrange dead fighters and other menial tasks. He stated that the media teams control the executions they film. The segments are filmed over and over until the team's director decides to execute. Off camera a person holds a cue card for the monologue of the executioner or execution leader in the case of mass killings.[5]

Abu Hajer was one of many who have stated that executions and other video moments are often very staged and the production of the video takes precedence. Harry Sarfo said this highly scripted method broke the illusion of the invincible army once he was asked to essentially perform for a video filmed in Syria.[6] In both cases, they also felt a repulsion at the violent and disrespectful killing of other Muslims in a manner that didn't match what they learned as Muslims.

The camera teams used by ISIS fell into three categories. First Line Video was any footage from Body Cam-, Helmet-, and Weapon-Mounted shots meant to give Point of View (POV). ISIS developed formal Video Support Teams (VSTs) for second line video, which is second person footage of fighters running, shooting, or driving suicide bomb trucks. Finally, the Third Line teams were the Professional News Teams (PNTs) who create the highest quality of propaganda packages. The materials from these teams would be crafted to go directly to the global news media. These segments are often recorded with more advanced lighting, stands, and scripts and were meant to appear newsworthy.

The Video Gear

The product rendered by ISIS would indicate they understand the need to invest in an arsenal of gear to capture their campaign to destroy humanity in high definition. With a mix of GoPro cameras, handheld Sony and Canon cameras, and small project studios used to mix various segments of the spectacle together, the final picture requires quality gear.

According to the *Washington Post's* interview with a jailed former ISIS fighter who operated as a cameraman, Abu Hajer, video-making gear and computers came through routes out of Turkey.[7] Abu Hajer stated he received gear after his training that included a Samsung Galaxy smartphone and a Canon camera with digital media video recording capability. Videos released by ISIS have shown Sonycams in action in the field.

A new twist on the video recording team efforts was the addition of the Drone Video teams (DVT). By early 2016, the group was using Phantom III aerial drones to record shots including the before, transit, and explosions of suicide bomb truck attacks, as well as to collect intelligence.

Figure 48: Al-Anbar Aerial video footage filmed by ISIS via drone cameras in Wilayat al-Anbar video. (Source: TAPSTRI)

ISIS VIDEO THEMES

Depending on the specific theme, there are repeating formulas for most of the types of releases. There are a handful of themes common in all ISIS videos; some or all of those themes can be combined in a video from time to time.

The Just Will Prevail as It Is Allah's Will

The largely misunderstood view of execution films from ISIS was that they are portrayed as justice in an eye-for-eye manner where the person being killed is paying for their own crime of betraying the caliphate or paying for the crimes of others as their proxy.

The Grand Betrayal

The leaders of the Arab and Muslim world are often the targets of ISIS scorn. They are accused of working against the interests of Muslims and thus are worthy of being targeted for death. The theme of the grand betrayal constantly repeated by ISIS and other extremist groups is also used as a motivating factor when the recruiters manipulate supporters' feelings of grievance to encourage them to attack.

There Is Your Enemy

There are so many ways to become the enemy of ISIS if you wait long enough and try hard enough. But to the followers, there was no doubt that the enemy was the one who does not believe in the strict interpretation of the Quran given to them by the Islamic State. This includes not just the filthy unbelievers but the apostate teachers and leaders of the Muslim world. Thrown directly on the screen for all to see, ISIS doesn't mince words when it labels its enemy. The subject was a driving force in the propaganda in that it makes killing the enemy the preferred way to serve the interest of the caliphate.

The titles of many of the pieces published by ISIS are directed at these targets, as in *Harvest of the Spies* or *Harvest of the Army* where dozens of people are propped up for crowds as traitors or dragged off to a ditch and shot and dumped as traitors to the caliphate and thus to Muslims. First, since the majority of these victims are Muslim, they are condemned on the basis of their confession and told that they couldn't possibly be Muslim (this is called *Takfir*, or declaring a Muslim a non-Muslim so they can be killed). Thus, they deserve death for working for the apostate regime. In each video of this nature, after the victim is made to confess to a crime of spying or perhaps serving as an Iraqi security official, they are executed as an example and warning to the apostates and unbelievers.

The message isn't intended just to respond to would-be critics or threats to the caliphate, but to reward those who want to have an enemy that must be punished. In a large quantity of ISIS official videos, there was a crowd drawn to watch the execution of a person who has been condemned by ISIS for crimes. The crowds are mostly eager to watch this macabre spectacle and even cheer on the activities. In one video in which a man was surrounded and killed by a group of people, his executioners piled on and took turns kicking and beating him until he was lifeless. In other cases, witnesses were asked to come in to pull the trigger on blindfolded captives.

Hijra (The Sooner the Better)

One of the key points of change in radicalization occurs during the *self-hijra* stage. This stage also has a range of graphic and video supplements to encourage this process. By helping viewers to emotionally detach from their friends, family, and surroundings, the cult recruiting of ISIS gives meaning to the transition by reminding the target of this message that the caliphate was thriving, its land is the morally superior place to be and a place where real Muslims find safety to be themselves. Many of the pithy posts that exist on Telegram channels are used to remind ISIS recruits to be "good Muslims" but insist that this means doing what suits the aims of ISIS, including preparing to fight or recruiting friends who may want to fight for the caliphate.

There are stories from the combat outpost (a.k.a. *rabat*) or front lines that are meant to give you a sense of adventure and a conviction that these fighters are indeed on the "front line" of history in the battle against the unbelievers. In most videos, you cannot see the enemy but simply see fighters rushing forward to enemy positions.

The purpose of these videos was to give the viewer a sense of how victorious the fighters are, so, obviously, there are no videos published that show catastrophic defeat. The video also reproaches the passive viewer for merely sitting there and being a witness and thus not really committing to the cause of protecting Muslims from the evil disbelievers. There was always a subtext of "you should be here doing this" directed at the viewer.

In addition to the fighting videos, the celebration of Eid, religious holidays often marked with feasts, was just one of the lures used to evoke a viewer's desire to make the journey to Syria. In these selections, the celebrations are made to underline the superiority of the realm of ISIS over other parts of the Muslim world as well as the plight of the disbeliever who couldn't understand how everyone in the caliphate was so happy.

All Is Great in the Caliphate

The common videos showing *ishtishada* attacks or Suicide Vehicle-Borne Improvised Explosive Device (SVBIED), a.k.a. suicide truck/car bomb attacks, follow an evolving formula that begins with showing an attacker preparing the vehicle for attack, and his friends wishing him well as he drives in under rocket and gun fire to hit his target, cheered on by the screams of his brothers, God is Great! ("Allau Akbar"). The attacker's backstory was most often the lead-in, but there are also examples in which the attacker was merely mentioned just before and after the detonation of their vehicle near an outpost berm. One evolution in how these videos have been filmed was the introduction to drones in a few of the regions. Now there was a bird's-eye view of these attacks in which the same pattern of covering fire from guns and RPGs (Rocket Propelled Grenade) is shown, followed by SVBIED attack. Followed by men with guns rushing in to polish off enemy soldiers.

The Path to Warrior

In some cases, they show stage-by-stage a SVBIED attack with the extended bio and interview with the attacker. Then you see them get into an explosive-filled truck or van that drives off, out of the view of the camera. Cut to the detonation of the vehicle (shown rather dimly in the distance), accompanied by the driver's fellow fighters back at the original location yelling, "Allau Akbar" in the background. The formula doesn't change much from the first time we saw these videos a decade before after the release of AQI videos.

But there are some changes worth noting including the use of drone-mounted cameras, which now have shown details of SVBIED attacks from a position that may enable opposition forces viewing that released footage to help predict and prevent such attacks in the future. But ISIS isn't afraid to use the drones for video now and has done so with videos of drones operating out of what's presently its most strongly held regions of Aleppo, Raqqa, and Mosul.

The End Times Scenario

One of the key distinctions between ISIS and other extremist groups was how its message was truly apocalyptic. The result is a mission focused on the advancing toward end times as the great showdown of good and evil that will come. There are endless references to this grand showdown in videos, photo shows, pamphlets, and the magazine that bears the name *Dabiq*, the presence of the *Dijjal* (false messiah).

THE PRESENTATION

Much has been said about the visual quality of ISIS videos, especially the misappropriated phrase "Hollywood-style" to describe the High Definition footage mixed with HD presentations cooked up by the graphics teams and tied together with a limited narrative that sometimes may resemble a PBS special on Islamic history. There was typically a patient and steady narrative voiceover in many videos. As if produced for a historical documentary segment, many of the titles engage in large narratives that end with attempting to justify ISIS actions before turning to running GoPro filmed footage and the steady main camera shots of an execution. The techniques used to piece these mininarratives together can be applied on laptops and PCs with off-the-shelf video gear easily smuggled into the ISIS territories through routes in Turkey, according to former fighters.

The HD-level images are produced with a variety of cameras including GoPros strapped to the attackers' heads or bodies, run along cameramen using Sony handheld cameras and in some cases cell phone cameras. Other captive fighters who reported that they have worked in the media centers reported that they have used Canon cameras for their assignments. ISIS was keenly aware that the world takes them more seriously because they bring forward terror in high definition.

THE MEME MACHINE

For every event that could relate to ISIS culture there was a meme that will be rendered within minutes. The message of "You're next" after the attack on Paris was sent to Telegram channels in GIMP- or Photoshop-produced panels; the same threats were circulating within hours of the attack in Nice. Then came the images aimed at Germany that indicated it would be facing lone wolf attacks soon. Within a week after Nice came an axe attack in Wuerzburg, Germany, in the name of ISIS by Afghan teenager Riaz Khan Ahmadzai, and within two weeks Syrian Mohammad Daleel killed himself with a backpack bomb filled with nails and metal debris in Ansbach, Germany. Within hours of their respective attacks were celebrity-styled memes celebrating their attacks and taunting the government's inability to protect citizens from these attacks.

Figure 49: ISIS meme cards published on Telegram by Aswirti media.
(Source: TAPSTRI)

Once the theme starts, you can expect to see it a few times before it shifts. Often the group is focused on prodding a leader or a country when things are going badly. If diplomatic missions fail, hurricanes strike, or elections get ugly, the ISIS supporters would be there to fill in the space with ridicule.

When the al-Qaeda affiliate in Syria, Jabhat al-Nusra, decided to break off official relations with the international terror group, ISIS supporters took to the web to poke at Jabhat al-Nusra's leader with a picture meant to insult him.

Figure 50: ISIS fanboys on Telegram poke fun at the Jabhat al-Nusra leader in graphic. (Source: TAPSTRI)

One channel that appeared on Telegram in support of ISIS posted graphics of facts about Muslim history under the header "Did you know?" The series was used to not only praise famous Muslims, but to denigrate critics like Malala Yousifzai and also to feature the anti-Muslim ban called for by a candidate for President of the United States.

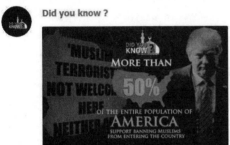

The whole of America itself has been brainwashed to wage a war on Islam, its a nation at war with a single religion. #WaronIslam

Figure 51: Telegram entry on the Did You Know? page. (Source: TAPSTRI)

THE ONLINE PHOTO SETS

Almost daily, ISIS regional offices released photo packets to frame the fight for the regions they oversee with all photos showing victorious fighting, productive services, and the dedication of ISIS members. The photo sets vary in number but are a daily snapshot from the view intended to convince the members all is great in the caliphate.

There are some photo sets that are simply nature shots, pictures of a clear moon, or vibrant greenhouses. These photos are perhaps the most important to convince followers that ISIA is creating a utopian society, one that is stable, productive, resilient, and healthy.

Like the video releases, the photo sets are loaded with grievance. It was a strong theme in many photos that are filled with destroyed buildings and injured civilians, especially children. The images are released with tag lines that blame either coalition forces in many cases, or the Russians and Assad's forces.

THE MAGAZINES

In the lead-up months to the announcement of the return of a caliphate, ISIS was putting together two magazines called the *Islamic State News* and the *Islamic State Report*. They were released starting in late May and early June of 2014 before the announcement of Abu Bakr Al-Baghdadi as the Caliph. Then came the magazine that became synonymous with ISIS, *Dabiq*. The apocalyptic title conveyed the primary goal of the organization, a showdown with the army of the *kufar* on the lands in Syria.

Figure 52: Magazine montage. (Source: TAPSTRI)

To get the word out, the organization would need to reach the other regions with titles and articles that concern them, and the al-Hayat Media Center was the place to do it. Working out of a two-story house in Raqqa, those producing the magazines ensured they measured up to the quality and precision found in the finest article-friendly magazines. Like the AQAP magazine, *Inspire*, these publications gave a professionally packaged and attractive presentation of the beliefs and actions of a regime devoted to killing lots of people.

Packed with features on regional reports, ongoing religious arguments against other rival groups, or profiles and interviews of the favorite ISIS fighters and leaders, the magazines are glossy and well produced yet vary in their release schedules.

The "unbelievers and apostates" eagerly anticipate and read them for the morsels of intelligence they may provide, but months can go by between editions. Some editions may have revealed more personal information on targets like Jihadi John or the Paris attacker, Abdelhamid Abaaoud. After the Paris attacks of November 2015, most of the attackers were featured in a video and a poster in *Dabiq*.

Figure 53: Dabiq magazine. (Source: TAPSTRI)]

Dabiq—English Publication

With its high-definition photos presented in high-quality magazine layout, *Dabiq* is proof that the message from its true publisher, ISIS, was serious. The themes inside each edition projected what ISIS officials want the world to believe about the organization by running features on new alliances, expanded operations, philosophical explanations of its mission, clear condemnation of enemies, and promos for the latest video releases. One edition even had hostage information (*Dabiq* 11) in full-page "ads" at the end of the publication.

The number of pages in each edition can run from as few as 40 (Fifth Edition) to as many as 83 (Seventh Edition). There seems to be little concern about this variation.

Dabiq runs a section every month that features an Enemy Number One of the Islamic State. The column "In The Words of The Enemy" has appeared in every edition. The first piece was "The Return to the Khilafah." In that initial piece, Col. Douglas A. Ollivant, the former Director for Iraq at the National Security Council, was featured. Edition #15 featured Pope Francis and Grand Imam of al-Azhar, Ahmed Muhammad Ahmed el-Tayeb.

Here is the list of the first fifteen Enemies of the State:

In The Words of the Enemy

- Douglas Ollivant—Edition 1
- John McCain—Edition 2
- Barack Obama—Edition 3
- Chuck Hagel—Edition 4—Revisited 6
- Andrew Liepman—Edition 5
- Benjamin Netanyahu—Edition 6
- Patrick Cockburn—Edition 7
- Rick Santorum—Edition 8
  Gary Berntsen—Edition 8
  Richard Black—Edition 8
- McCain and Lindsey Graham—Edition 9
- Rami Abdulrahman—Edition 10
  Ahmed Rashid—Edition 10
  Yaroslav Trofimov—Edition 10
- Michael Scheuer—Edition 11
- Abu Firas as-Suri, Jabhat al-Nusra spokesman—Edition 12
- Tamim bin Hamad al-Thani, Qatari Emir, Erdegon—Edition 12

- Michael Morell—Crusader-Edition 13
- Ban Ki Moon—Edition 14
- Pope Francis-Ahmed el-Tayeb— Edition 15

Figure 54: Dar al-Islam. (Source: TAPSTRI)

Dar al-Islam—French Publication

With nine editions published by 2016, the *Dar al-Islam* magazine was focused at the French-speaking audience. In comparison to *Dabiq*, the *Dar al-Islam* was started as a shorter magazine, but it expanded steadily from 16 pages in the first edition to 114 in the eighth edition.

Figure 55: Konstantiniyye. (Source: TAPSTRI)

Konstantiniyye—Turkish Publication

For the Turkish audience, al-Hayat has the *Konstantiniyye* magazine. Published in Turkish, the magazine is filled with some overlapping themes from *Dabiq* publications but often with the focus on the secular society of the neighbor to the north. Attacks on Turkey's relationship with Russia, Europe, or the United States are always fodder for the magazine.

Figure 56: Istok. (Source: TAPSTRI)

Istok—Russian Publication

With the long-standing jihadist fight against the renowned atheist state to its north, ISIS started publishing a magazine aimed at the Russian-speaking audience. The content of the four releases before September 2016 was largely Russian reprints of *Dabiq* content aimed at Chechnya and other former Soviet countries. ISIS has largely relied upon the Furat media group to handle translations of videos and texts for the Russian audience.

Figure 57: An-Naba. (Source: TAPSTRI)

An-Naba—Arabic Publication

The "Weekly Newsletter" features the latest ISIS attacks and campaigns, with text accompanied by a few images. It is printed, published, and widely distributed in the areas controlled by ISIS.

Figure 58: Kybernetiq. (Source: TAPSTRI)

Kybernetiq—German Publication

This ISIS-affiliated German language magazine was focused on the cyber jihad and was released December 2015; it is focused on encryption, metadata, and apps, including a look at the features of the encryption app Asrar al-Mujahideen, otherwise known as Mujahedeen Secrets. Only one edition had been released by September 2016.

Figure 59: Rumiyah. (Source: TAPSTRI)

Rumiyah—English Publication

Virtually identical in content to *Dabiq*, a new magazine was launched by ISIS in September 2016 with essentially the same content. It seemed to be hastily slapped together, possibly because the news of Abu Muhammad al-Adnani's death had come only days before the on-press date. The articles in the first edition were a mix of criticisms aimed at those on the typical enemies list—Egypt's Muslim Brotherhood, Abu Muhammad Al-Maqdisi, the mentor to Abu Musab al-Zarqawi, et al. It even featured a lone wolf threat directed at a random florist in Manchester, England, Stephen Leyland, with a picture of him smiling at work in his shop to show their reach could touch even those at a low level.[8]

Figure 60: Iraqis gather to grab a copy of the latest an-Naba *weekly newsletter.*
(Source: TAPSTRI)

THE NASHEED CHANTS

Every movement, revolution, or generation needs a soundtrack. In the background of the majority of ISIS videos are the *nasheed*s or the *anasheed jihadiya*—Gergorian chant-like songs about fighting for the caliphate. The themes are simple and symbolic tributes to dead fighters, celebrating successful campaigns or singing the praise of someone like al-Baghdadi or Osama Bin Laden. But despite the strong association of these simple redundant melodies with ISIS, *nasheeds* have been around for many battles across decades. As required by strict Sunni fundamentalists, there are no instruments used in ISIS nasheeds. However, other groups have used musical instruments to accompany the singers. It was clear that ISIS uses Auto-Tune on its vocal tracks, and there was one official *wilayat* video that shows a *nasheed* singer multitracking the song with a dynamic cardioid microphone and small recorder connected to a laptop.

ISIS has used *nasheeds* in its recruiting and inspirational efforts for current fighters. Ajnad Media was founded in August 2013 to focus on *nasheed* and *surah* (chapters from the Quran) readings. Simple and repeating lyrics that are easily internalized, they produce an almost hypnotic effect upon the listener. Mixed with Quranic allusion. In addition to Arabic, they have been released in other languages including English, German, Chinese, Bengali, Bosnian, Pashtu, Turkish, Urdu, and several in French. For example, their greatest hit "Clashing of the Swords" was released in June 2014 during the seizure of Mosul and Raqqa:

Clashing of the swords: a nasheed of the reluctant.
The path of fighting is the path of life.
So amidst an assault, tyranny is destroyed.
And concealment of the voice results in the beauty of the echo.

By it my religion is glorified, and tyranny is laid low.
So, oh my people, awake on the path of the brave.
For either being alive delights leaders, or being dead vexes the enemy.

So arise, brother, get up on the path of salvation,
So we may march together, resist the aggressors,
Raise our glory, and raise the foreheads
That have refused to bow before any besides God.

With righteousness arise,
The banner has called us,
To brighten the path of destiny,
To wage war on the enemy.
Whosoever among us dies, in sacrifice for defense,
Will enjoy eternity in Paradise. Mourning will depart.

While other groups, including, al-Qaeda, create *nasheed*s, the overt integration of *nasheed*s into ISIS videos has had a powerful effect. Behnam Said, who has dedicated his PhD research to studying *nasheed*s, said that the use of *nasheed*s dates back to the late 1970s during the "Islamic resurrection."

Figure 61: Al-Hayat video featuring British citizens appealing for fighters to join
them in Syria. (Source: TAPSTRI)

THE TERROR SHOCK VALUE VIDEOS

Perhaps the thing ISIS was best known for was its publication of execution videos, including the murders of James Foley, Steven Sotloff, David Haines, Alan Henning, Peter Kassig, Kenji Goto, and Haruna Yukawa. There have also been other execution videos that featured Syrian fighters and Egyptian Coptic Christians who were executed en masse.

This modern macabre spectacle has its video roots in the beheading of a Russian soldier in Chechnya. The first American beheaded
on video was Daniel Pearl. Al-Qaeda beheaded Pearl in 2002. He
was forced to read a series of grievances. Demands included release
of all prisoners held at Guantanamo Bay, Cuba, return of Pakistani
prisoners to Pakistan, the end of US activities in Pakistan, and "The
delivery of F-16 planes Pakistan paid for and never received."

The first video of an American being beheaded by al-Qaeda in
Iraq was released in May 7, 2004. Nick Berg's murder was blamed
on the abuses at Abu Ghraib. It was later uploaded to the Muntada
al-Ansar website and given the title *Abu Musab al-Zarqawi shown
slaughtering an American*. The "Acme Commerce Sdn Bhd" web-
hosting company in Malaysia that hosted the website took it
down.[9] The Zarqawi propaganda model under Tawid wal-Jihad
began with Nick Berg and continued with others including Kim
Sun-il, Bulgarian Georgi Lazov, Durmus Kumdereli, Eugene Arm-
strong, Jack Hensley, Kenneth Bigley, and Shosei Koda.

A decade passed between the Zarqawi era of blood and gore
and the rise of ISIS. Zarqawi was killed June 7, 2006, and with his
death a change in the leadership over to Abu Ayyub al-Masri and a
scramble for reaffirming the message. As Zarqawi's group morphed
through its various incarnations from AQI to ISIS, the videos were
still being made, but just not disseminated globally. That would
change with the seizure of a third of Iraq and half of Syria
in 2014.

The first major video, as noted previously, was released on
August 19, 2014 with *A Message to America*. It opens with a statement of grievances. The text stated, "Obama authorizes military
operations against the Islamic State, effectively placing America
upon a slippery slope towards a new war front against Muslims."
After a segment with Obama discussing airstrikes, James Foley was
presented in what has been compared to GITMO orange clothing
alongside an executioner clad in black who was armed with both a
gun and a knife. Foley speaks first as he's forced to read a statement

blaming America and his own brother for his death. The unnamed executioner then addresses some remarks to President Obama about US airstrikes and efforts to remove ISIS from Iraq and Syria.

In what was a first for the United States, the video ends with an edited but real beheading of James Foley followed by a threat against Steven Joel Sotloff. The executioner closes with, "The life of this American citizen Obama depends on your next decision." The video was uploaded to YouTube, Liveleak, and other video-sharing sites. Take-downs followed but the damage was done. The era of beheading videos had begun.

This pattern of release continued on September 2, 2014, when the next video, *A Second Message to America*, came, featuring Steven Sotloff. At a length of only 02:46, it was more direct. Again, ISIS began with Obama comments about continuing the military campaign against ISIS. Then came a forced reading by Steven Sotloff aimed at President Obama to withdraw troops. The video ends with the beheading of Sotloff in the same edited manner as the Foley video. Then the masked executioner from the first video threatens the UK with the murder of David Cawthorne Haines.

On January 3, 2015, the world was locked in horror as ISIS moved from beheading its victims to the execution of Jordanian pilot Muath al-Kasasbeh. Kasasbeh had been captured, and for weeks there were negotiations through backdoor channels to try to secure his release. However, he was murdered by the Islamic State and the film was released showing the terror group burning him alive in a cage. The reaction by Jordan was swift. They not only conducted airstrikes, but executed a captive who was highly sought-after by ISIS in the swap, an Iraqi woman named Sajida al-Rishawi who had been facing the death penalty for her role in a 2005 bombing that killed 60 people.

Over the next couple of years, any doubts about whether ISIS fighters were really beheading people were dispelled as ISIS increasingly made the murders more graphic by doing things like speeding up the camera rate to create up-close slow-motion execution shots.

ACROSS THE WILAYAT

The primary substates or *wilayat* are in Syria and Iraq, where decisions are closely coordinated with the central authority. Each of these media offices specializes in creating ISIS media for their region but also may perform a function for the entire organization. Wilayat Sinai and Wilayat Janoub have been responsible publishing metrics of the caliphate's attacks and resources.

Then there are the external *wilayat* found in Algeria, Tunisia, Libya, Egypt, Saudi Arabia, Yemen, Afghanistan, and parts of the Caucasus regions including Chechnya and Dagestan. The features of the area, the battles with other locals will alter the composition of each region's final product. For example, in Yemen, the videos will highlight battles with the Houthis and AQAP. The Iraqi videos will focus on clashes with Iraqi security and Kurdish forces. Syria will focus on Assad forces, Kurds, and Turkey to the north.

To give a sense of how many titles have been released by ISIS official *wilayat* media offices, by August 1, 2016 here are the release numbers per *wilayat*:

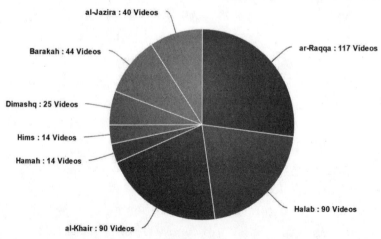

SYRIAN VIDEO RELEASES

al-Jazira : 40 Videos

Barakah : 44 Videos

Dimashq : 25 Videos

Hims : 14 Videos

Hamah : 14 Videos

al-Khair : 90 Videos

ar-Raqqa : 117 Videos

Halab : 90 Videos

Figure 62: Syrian Video Releases. (Source: TAPSTRI)

AS OF AUGUST 1, 2016, TOTAL VIDEO RELEASES PER REGION. (SOURCE: TAPSTRI)

Syria wilayat

Raqqa 117, Halab 90, al-Khair 90, Hamah 14, Hims 58, Dimashq 25, Barakah 44, al-Jazira 40

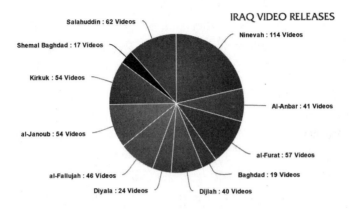

Figure 63: Iraq Video Releases. (Source: TAPSTRI)

Iraq wilayat

Nineveh 114, Al-Anbar 41, al-Furat 57, Baghdad 19, Dijlah 40, Diyala 24, al-Fallujah 46, al-Janoub 54, Kirkuk 54, Shemal Baghdad 17, Salahuddin 62

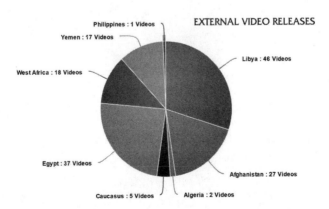

Figure 64: External Video Releases. (Source: TAPSTRI)

Other wilayat
Libya 46 (Barqa 22, Tarabulus 24), Egypt 37, Afghanistan 27, West Africa 18, Yemen 17 (Aden 3, Hadramaut 5, Sana'a 4, Shabwa 5), Caucasus 5, Algeria 2, Philippines 1

AFFILIATED MEDIA AGENCIES

There are dozens of nonofficial media groups that reedit existing ISIS material to recycle the message but are not sanctioned by ISIS. ISIS has specified what are its official centers in both video and printed materials. Some of the groups include "al-Battar," "al-Nusra al-Shameya Media," "Al-Yaqeen Media Center," "Asawirti Media," "Grandchildren of Aisha," "al-Samoud Foundation," and a group called "The Constancy." In many cases, the video quality released by these groups was significantly lower and some almost un viewable because retread video was taken from other videos that had been highly compressed for the web or had audio levels that were too high, too low, or muffled.

A group was formed of many of these unofficial media houses under the banner "Al-Jabhah al-I'ilamiya li-Nusrat al-Dawlah al-Islami-yah" or the "The Media Front for Support to the Islamic State." This group would do what other ISIS media groups including al-Battar, Al-Ghuraba, Markaz al-Aisha, Al-Wafa, al-Minhaj, al-Wagha media, and Rabitat al-Ansar would do.

THE PROPAGANDA MACHINE IN MOTION

We can see that the early incarnation of ISIS known as al-Qaeda in Iraq or AQI was intent on spreading its terror via video and that early on al-Qaeda objected to these images for fear that they would be used against the effort to gain recruits and defeat the American, European, or Israeli interests. Instead, AQI was over the top because of its beheading videos under Abu Musab al-Zarqawi.

In order to remind followers that they have a role to play in getting the message out, ISIS media leaders tell them to propagate widely and makes distinctions mainly between inside and outside channels. For the insiders, there are reminders of their duty to remain pious Muslims, serve the caliphate, and avoid being lazy. There was the occasional instruction to share links to like-minded cult members.

The Media Pitch

Islamic State supporters online have exceeded tens of thousands. However, a great number of them only watch video releases and follow the news.

> To those, I send this message: Supporting brother, you are a part of the Islamic State media on the Internet; don't be a liability by just watching videos and following only, but learn how to upload, share, transcript, translate, program and work towards having an impact on the ongoing war against the disbelieving Crusaders.
>
> Just as a society, Islamic State supporters include very diverse people with different skills and abilities; use what you now to do best to support the Islamic State. If you don't, learn how to download/upload releases, get the know-how from an efficient supporter.
>
> Ask yourself, what have you done to support the Islamic [State]? Are you here to effectively support the Khilafah or to spend your free time? Supporting the Islamic State is by work, not by sitting watching idly. Leave the laziness of excuses and ask

yourself what can you do to support the Mujahideen who defend the honor of the Muslims, facing the nations of Kufr and disbelief, giving their blood in battles in the east and the west?

Stand up, dear brother, and learn new skills, this is an obligation upon you now that all the nations of Kufr have stood together to face the Islamic State—may Allah give it glory—and be a thorn in the throats of the disbelievers. Share the truth about the Islamic State to the Muslims. How many Muslims have been guided and saw the reality of this war thanks to Allah then to a video release, a picture report, and article or just a tweet from an Islamic State supporter?

It's our duty dear brother, put your trust in Allah, take the necessary online precautions and support the Mujahideen with everything you can.

Translated from Arabic by Maghrebi Witness —MW

Like many messages from ISIS, the aim of this message was to be spread widely.

The Propagation Channels

Figure 66: Khilafah News banner. (Source: TAPSTRI)

Khilafah News
Fed by official headlines from around the caliphate, Khilafah Internet News shares the daily lists of attacks, excerpts from speeches by leaders, or other headlines created by the actions of ISIS leaders. Khilafah news was often found on posting sites like JustPasteIt and on Telegram.

Figure 67: Telegram advertisement of Nashir's new Portuguese channel from ISIS. (SOURCE: TAPSTRI)

NASHIR Telegram Channel

This channel posts photo slide shows, official ISIS announcements, and link clusters to the latest official ISIS videos. Unlike several other channels, it does not engage in propagating links for unofficial sources or the various echo chamber videos. It will also publish the links to the latest official ISIS print media like *an-Naba, Dabiq*, or other releases.

When the channel announced it would start broadcasting in Portuguese, there were analysts who took this to mean that ISIS had established a foothold in Brazil. The concerns were largely tied to security concerns around the Summer 2016 games in Rio. The games were completely without incident.

Figure 68: Al-Bayan Telegram advertisement from ISIS. (Source: TAPSTRI)

Al-Bayan Radio

Daily dispatches from events in the ISIS region and with occasional announcements from across the world. Releases are featured as mp3s along with .doc and .pdf releases of the headlines in both Arabic and English. The outlet has also been featured in short-lived website form as both stand-alone domain and as a wordpress.com page.

Figure 69: AMAQ Agency Telegram advertisement from ISIS. (Source: TAPSTRI)

Amaq News Agency

Amaq News Agency is the source that was almost synonymous with ISIS claims of responsibility even though it is not listed by ISIS as an official agency. Though never listed in the official centers under ISIS, it acts more in conjunction with ISIS than any other satellite organization. Though little is known about its staff or hierarchy, it was revealed after his death that ISIS minister of information and head of al-Furqan media, Wa'el Adel Hasan Salman al-Fayad, was a board member of Amaq. Despite this, al-Furqan's video *The Structure of the Khilafah* did not list Amaq despite listing al-Bayan (radio), *an-Naba* (newsletter), Ajnad (nasheeds, sermons), Al-Hayat (non-Arabic publications), and *Maktabat al-Himmah* (print publications).

The group films and photographs events in the same manner as normal news agencies around the world, but with ISIS pointing the finger at the Assad regime, the coalition forces, and the various militias who are fighting ISIS in Syria and Iraq.

Amaq News Agency ran several Telegram channels in English and Arabic. They developed their own news feed app for Android phones.

OFFICIAL DISTRIBUTION

In the early days of jihadist media, the communication and propaganda was disseminated via cassettes, VHS, or Hi8 tapes. Eventually that gave way to digital media like CDs, DVDs, jump drives, and smart cards. AQI Spokesperson for Zarqawi, Abu Maysara al-Iraqi, used YouSendIt to send files after running into perpetual issues at the time with file hosting on free pages like Yahoo.[10]

The materials are introduced to the web via uploads to any number of these dead drop sites, or sites intended to dump data anonymously, and now also via Telegram downloads. Once on the web, the messages on Twitter and Telegram often post links to a dozen or so sites that are file sharing-related and the "official" version uploaded to Archive.org. For a while, Archive.org was rather slow to take the clips down, but by mid-2016 they were becoming very effective in responding with file deletion of audio-video material from ISIS sources. In some cases, videos would be posted and within two hours or less it was a dead link at Archive.org and/or YouTube. By then, Twitter and Telegram messages that contained these links would be useless.

But there are occasional stand-alone pro-ISIS media archive sites that migrate frequently around the web. These outlets keep up with the video releases. Though they are becoming less common, they are still published occasionally on Telegram channels. By 2016, the most common means of finding ISIS videos would be Telegram. All day long there are download links published and direct links for getting the file via channels on the social media platform.

The Modern Day "Digital" Dead-Drop

In literature and life, spies used to have rocks, boxes, and other strange locations to do "dead-drops," an old intelligence term for a place where items such as a film minicassette and money could be left without the agent waiting around to be discovered. But for the modern-day terrorist, Internet pasting pages are the prime location used to send files, save files, or otherwise share data with conspirators without hassle—digital dead-drops. The terrorists before YouTube had to come up with a way to share videos. Abu Maysara al-Iraqi was one of the first to simply go to YouSendIt to share files with AQI supporters.[11]

Some of the sites used by ISIS in the first few years include JustPaste.it, Google Drives, YouTube, Cloud.mail.ru, Dailymotion.com, Archive.org, My.mail.ru, Sendvid.com, Userscloud.com, and Samaup.com.

Using these sites, the followers fill up repeaters of the original file, making it harder to eliminate the files from the web. In some cases, ISIS users have coordinated all the ISIS videos into files with the material organized and categorized by *wilayat* and release numbers. Other sites like TimesOfIS.wordpress.com maintained a running chronology that was reliably updated for months until it was deleted by Wordpress in May 2016. In other cases, sites like ISdarat variations on Wordpress kept track of affiliated releases from al-Battar, al-Samoud, and al-Waad in addition to Amaq and official ISIS media channels.

Distribution on Telegram

In Telegram, you may run across channels that are available to read or "join" without hindrance, but most of the important channels are set to privacy after an initial period of announcement. Posts flow all day with links to other ISIS forums, postings that you have to watch continuously or miss your way in for another day. If you're trying to follow Amaq News Agency, for instance, your access to the channel can last anywhere from a few minutes to a couple of hours before you get "Error-The Invite link is invalid. Technical details here."

The channels of ISIS and AQ material on Telegram have a range of subjects that break down into General news about the caliphate (internal and external), Publications (the latest video, slide show, pamphlet, or magazine), Rebroadcasters (users who only recycle other's postings), Graphics or How To Channels, Operations channels (Online Da'wah Operations, CCA), and of course plenty of cult-level obsession with the passages and interpretations of the Quran. There's even a snarky channel mentioned earlier called "Did you know?" that loves to point out bits from Islamic history to show how uninformed or ignorant the disbelievers can be. "Did you know that Jack Sparrow is really Yusuf Reis?" one says as it seeks to show how Hollywood and American pop culture doesn't, namely, that these figures came from Islamic culture.

Another channel, al-Nusra al-Shameya, spent months posting how-to graphic instructions so you can learn how to cut out horses, fighters, and other figures from the video stream and make your own shiny ISIS video graphic. The tools would be easy-to-use graphic apps, which are often included.

Rely on the News Echo Chamber

ISIS was well aware of how to use the news cycles as their predecessors had before them. Well-timed manipulation of video releases, audio releases, magazines, and other materials keep journalists, analysts, and counterterrorist analysts waiting for the next bit of information. This game continued under ISIS.

When Kim Sun-il was killed in June 2002, Jama'at al-Tawid sent a video tape of his execution to al-Jazeera, which injected the story into the news cycle. Earned media was free media because the shock value of ISIS media content was effective in getting the attention of and a free echo from news outlets, officials, and the chattering class. Point made?

For instance, after the execution of Bulgarian citizen Georgi Lazov, Zarqawi's group, Tawhid wal Jihad, posted a statement, "Await for a video with the execution of the Bulgarian unbeliever" and a single photograph of a fighter holding a severed head.[12]

In June 2016, a release from al-Furqan had counterterror analysts locked to their Telegram and Twitter feeds as they waited to hear an audio clip from Abu Muhamad al-Adnani that called for attacks during Ramadan. The guessing game went on for hours to the point where ISIS followers in Telegram and Twitter channels were laughing at the analysts with eager anticipation. When the audio finally came down and the watching and waiting had yielded a disappointing result—it wasn't a message from al-Baghdadi. Many had believed it would be because it was supposed to come via al-Furqan.

THE BATTLE OF THE #HASHTAGS

The caliphate followers are strong proponents of the use of hashtags and extensively use various tags to promote their latest campaigns. The choice of tag depends largely on the aim of either promoting a message or mocking (trolling) a message. Many times when looking for a new video release you could go to Twitter and type in something like #alfurqan, or if you could read Arabic you could follow the hashtags associated with ISIS channels more directly by following tags that were very topical or referred to regional clashes in Syria, Iraq, or Yemen.

The primary tags associated with ISIS have been #IslamicState and #ISIS. There are times where the tag was aimed at followers like #WeAllGiveBayahToKhilafah from late August 2015.

Sometimes the tag was intended as psychological warfare, like the hashtag that was aimed at the United States during Steven Sotloff's captivity. In one example, there was a picture made with President Obama superimposed over Jihadi John with the phrase, "Why Would I Care about Him," and the hashtag #StevensHeadInObamasHands.[13]

Hijacking Trending Tags

As terror tragedies associated with ISIS hit the news, its followers began to flood posts about reactions throughout the world. Tags like #prayfornice or #orlandoshooting became ripe for trolling by ISIS fanboys to the irritation of those still in shock over the attacks. It didn't take long after the attack in Nice, France, for ISIS Telegram channels to begin encouraging mocking (trolling) hashtags reflecting the tragedy. While trolling, their members could not only excite the hatred against the group, but discern where they had sympathy or potential recruits.

The group also often attacks random targets in order to get attention, instill fear, or both. In January 2016, ISIS fanboys attempted to hijack #JustinBieber with a banner for an execution video.

One group that regularly invades hashtags is the Online Dawah campaign; it is the almost official troll brigade online. With a Telegram channel in hand, they set their daily aims on pages with comment sections in order to harass participants, Muslim and unbeliever alike.

Made Ya Look

ISIS took their method of getting the world's attention up a notch in the late spring of 2016. On a Saturday morning in May of 2016, notification went out that there was a new al-Furqan release coming soon. With a technique as simple as advertising an upcoming release, ISIS via al-Furqan demonstrated that it was able to capture the attention of the analyst and law enforcement world in a long waiting game played out on that Saturday in May. First, al-Furqan released a "coming soon" banner then followed it in multiple languages across multiple platforms and channels including Telegram and Twitter. Analysts were guessing at what the content would be for hours. Was it a claim of responsibility for the missing Egypt Airbus? Was it going to be al-Baghdadi?

Figure 70: That They Live by Proof banner. (Source: TAPSTRI)

The hashtag #alfurqan started trending—being widely picked up on by Internet users—but by late morning found that what had been so keenly anticipated was merely an audio message from al-Adnani called "That They Live by Proof" calling for ISIS followers to launch attacks wherever they happened to be in the name of ISIS. There had been great hope that the release would be a claim of responsibility for the downing of EgyptAir MS804. A month later, the same hashtag would be used to advertise al-Furqan's video *The Structure of the Khilafah*, a presentation aimed at demonstrating that it was a vibrant state.

But the battle wasn't one-sided, as the hashtags #DefeatingDaesh and others were in play. Counterefforts were often given hashtags including #khawarij, a term the terror group particularly did not like.

#AllEyesOnISIS

Launched by Twitter handle @Ansaar999, this hashtag was dubbed the source of an ISIS "Twitter Storm" in late June 2014 as ISIS swept across Iraq and Syria, declaring the founding of a caliphate at the end of the same month. Seemingly from all over the world, followers were posting pictures of their locations and stating they were supporting the caliphate. Yet many of these photos had been previously published months earlier and were unrelated to the upcoming "Twitter Storm." One from @ahmetmatar11 (featuring a still of al-Bilawi) had a picture of pink cupcakes topped with ISIS flags and a flag in the background with "Support from South Africa" in the tweet.

In a way, #hashtags are very representative of what makes groups like #ISIS hard to defeat. You can eliminate the @users, but the hashtag theme (#idea) has taken shape in a manner that was harder to knock down.

THE SHIFTING LANDSCAPE

As the technology shifts, we can expect to see the methods of creation, dissemination, and the medium of delivery change. We can also expect to see a change in the emphasis as conditions on the ground for ISIS change. At the time of this writing news just broke from Syria of the death of Abu Muhammad al-Adnani, who was highly involved in the media campaigns.

Additionally, there are few notable anti-ISIS media campaigns undertaken to challenge the propaganda coming from the voices of ISIS, official or unofficial alike. The lack of substantial pushback to their message emboldens their voice. The only notable anti-ISIS media, ironically, come from al-Qaeda and AQ affiliates like Jabhat Al-Nusra, al-Qaeda in the Arabian Peninsula, and al-Qaeda in the Maghreb. There are Muftis and clerics who have challenged ISIS, but there have been no notable campaigns to get their message out to the masses in a manner that compares to the propaganda onslaught of ISIS.

Chapter 10

ISIS Digital and Strategic Communications Tool Kit

There are two primary purposes for which cyber jihadists use digital tool kits: Communications and Security.

COMMUNICATIONS

Key to ISIS activities is their ability to broadcast across the organization and out to the world. With use of smartphone apps, social media sites, and free file hosting, the organization exploited most of the commonly available online communication tools.

End-to-End Communication

Terrorist organizations have an urgent need for apps that enable them to communicate. In order to recruit, conduct operations, or inform the followers of the latest events or expectations, these groups need the technical means to do so without all the trappings found in account setups, cell phone accounts, or email communications. The prime pick of apps used for end-to-end communications by summer of 2016 were Telegram, WhatsApp, Surespot, and Signal. Communication tools are picked based on the belief that they are secure end-to-end communications. When news hits the mainstream technical magazines of a breach or vulnerability, ISIS and other groups grow suspicious and often migrate to a new platform for communications.

Propagation

The second need was to propagate the message of the caliphate to targeted audiences. This might include their current or potential cult members or the broader international audience. Entries on Telegram channels may contain attached downloads or, just like JustPaste.it posts, offer direct links to the latest videos on Archive. org, Google Drives, and other file sharing sites. This gives supporters alternative ways to share the ISIS materials widely in order to guarantee access. They must accomplish this in the face of a constant effort to take down these materials by both government efforts and grassroots activist intervention.

Apps like Amaq or al-Bayan radio make the latest news headlines from ISIS available. Need to know what the latest da'wah campaign is doing? Or need to know the latest news out of Syria? There's an app for that. Communication between operatives or from ISIS or AQ central to followers requires using a great many of the tools in the cyber jihadist tool kit.

Examples: Telegram was both an end-to-end messenger and an online location on which one could read the latest discussion, news, and announcements from ISIS, AQ, and other organizations. Due to the addition of channels, Telegram has in many ways replaced the jihadist website of years gone by. As the takedown efforts of Twitter started to have their effect, users were migrating to Telegram to get the latest information. For some leaders in the media department, Twitter is still recommended as an effective means to propagate the ISIS message on the Surface Web.

Community

A major component of web usage by international terrorists was the need to form bonds. Ironically, the need to avoid detection by legal authorities runs into the need of the terrorist community to identify and express itself in ways no different from the ones that subcultures around the world employ to express themselves. For instance, the sharing of pro-ISIS humor that may upset Americans or Europeans quickly elicits unifying laughter from followers on Twitter or Telegram. This "humor" has included superimposing leaders' heads over a doomed captive facing beheading or one particularly upsetting graphic in which injured US soldiers were mocked by ISIS followers on a Telegram channel.

There was a clear need for community in the communications of ISIS. The us-versus-them language was rampant, and the target-of-the-day postings are meant to unify a powerful and targeted resentment. It also serves to further unify the ISIS followers who enjoy being in on the "jihadi-cool" found in much of the chatter on Telegram and Twitter, as true believers in the ISIS cause enjoy the same punchlines at the expense of the disbelievers or the apostates. They share in the glee of the fall of their enemies and the worship of their dead fighters. Whether Telegram or Twitter, the app tools help to foster a sense of community.

Commentary

Apps are used to participate in the many political discussions of the world, enlivened by comments with a slant only ISIS followers could provide. This includes discussions on breaking news events— the attempted coup in Turkey, downed airliners, or domestic events in countries that can be spun into validation of the caliphate's goals. It is also where the followers of these groups turn to for the latest message from ISIS or AQ officials or to enjoy the irreverent postings against the disbelieving *kufar*. ISIS keeps up with American and European news and often comments on the headlines along with graphics posted in Telegram channels taken from cell-phone screen shots.

THE NEED FOR SECURITY

The other imperative for using the tools available was to provide security. While almost all the tools have some application to maintaining security, there are specific uses for certain tools, in particular the ones used for encrypting messages or ones used for eluding detection, leaving no footprint, and destroying materials to prevent the opposition from obtaining them.

The level of support for an app was dictated by the perceived security of the tools being used to conduct these activities. When security was perceived to be an issue for a forum online or for an app on a phone, ISIS/AQ media warnings follow and migrations to other tech options occur. It was very common to have tech tools discarded quickly upon the mere speculation that intel agencies had a hand in making them.

ISIS-related tech groups and channels keep up with conventional tech columns and forums, specialists' Twitter accounts, and news flashes that let them know what is currently happening in the technology realm and subsequently advise the ISIS faithful to follow new recommendations. In some cases, posts made on Twitter by recognized tech experts wind up as Telegram posts within minutes, with news on encryption, net security, hacking, or other security matters.

Terrorists also pay attention to what happens to their own followers after an operation. Trend Micro, a cyber security firm, noted a decline in the usage of Facebook's communications app, WhatsApp, after arrests led to investigations of the usage of the web tool by terrorist suspects.[1]

Potential targets of investigation are very aware of the use of metadata to capture them or their colleagues. In one example, noted in the Boston beheading plot of June 2015, David Wright was alleged by prosecutors to have been told by Usama Rahim to destroy the phone and wipe the laptop clean by resetting and clearing the hard drive.[2]

THE ISIS-APPROVED MOBILE PHONES

"(duh. . . .Please don't attempt to make hijra if your parents confiscated your phone)," reads the Hijrah guide produced by ISIS. The "Hijrah to the Islamic State" publication purportedly put out by ISIS states: "Also remember to never use iPhones, Androids are securer."[3] It also says "Buy a SIM card at the airport, but don't buy any SIM card, buy a Turkcell SIM card." After you've done this, of course you have to call the "Office of Borders of Dawlah," the guide continues.

It's clear that ISIS and AQ use a range of tools based on availability. There are preferences based on user recommendations and security considerations. Then there are phones actually confiscated. The largest group of users are on Android phones, and some are on iPhone. The preferences of phone are limited by availability, so it was not possible for ISIS to maintain a steady operation in terms of equipment. In the Paris attacks of November 2015, a Samsung smartphone was used.[4] Weeks later in San Bernardino, Saed Rizwan Farouk was using an iPhone 5c provided by the county agency he worked for when he and his wife attacked coworkers on December 2, 2015. The phone was under a password-protected lock, and after strenuous attempts by the US government to make Apple Inc. provide access, the FBI announced on March 28, 2016, that it had successfully unlocked the phone.

Phones can be used not only for texting on apps, but for sending voice messages, a common way followers seek to avoid detection, since there will be no metadata to read from the audio file. One mother, Karolina Dam, even had a friend of her son's play back messages from him seeking to recruit him into ISIS. Her son, Lukas, died in Syria, and she kept in touch with him via the messaging app Viber until he died in Syria.[5]

Chapter 11

All Is Great in the Caliphate

ISIS has manipulated much of the Western news media into believing it speaks for Islam. Their videos and photos portray them as being the judge, jury, and executioners of the Muslim faith. We will show how this image is false and when propagated by the West to attack ISIS it actually achieves ISIS's goals for them. What does "achieves ISIS's goals for them" mean? When ISIS makes the decision about whether you are a believer or unbeliever, but also whether you are a proper believer, a video is made, crafted to your belief system. With thousands of hours spent delivering this message, it's clear that the real targets of ISIS aggression recruitment are other Muslims, and in their campaign of recruitment, the Western news media was their best enabler.

ISIS videos have characteristics that are quite unlike media previously produced and disseminated by groups in the jihadist world. It is from the concept of the caliphate itself that ISIS draws its rhetorical strength, and it is the caliphate that ISIS portrays as expanding and resilient. Through this message, all campaigns, all festivals, all bay'āt ceremonies, and messages to others are framed. The first message level was sent to other Muslims, as ISIS claims to fulfill a prophecy from a dim, distant past for the benefit of Muslims today. The graphic content of many ISIS videos may mask the central narrative message—ISIS speaks to the pure Muslim who has found the path of righteousness by accepting the ISIS media's version of Islam.

There are two primary audiences for ISIS videos, Us and Them. But in the "Them" category you have many subcategories. The ISIS narrative always paints ISIS as the noble victim who has become the noble victor. To justify its campaigns and attacks, ISIS cites grievances accumulated over centuries. The expression of historical grievance takes up much of the first part of all of their videos. Contrary to the logical assumption that the next and most intense focus would be on the *kufar* or disbeliever, the rage of ISIS is initially reserved for people it labels apostates or spies.

In order to justify its attacks on other Muslims, ISIS finds endless numbers of people who have committed a crime against the state. The most heinous crime would be allowing the anti-ISIS forces to destroy the caliphate. Such arch criminals include Iraqi and Syrian nationals who are fighting to defeat ISIS within their borders. This includes Turks who are obstructing the flow of fighters through Gaziantep and other border towns. It includes Egyptian police and military who have been fighting in the Sinai region for years and suffering many casualties.

Thus the first objective of ISIS's struggle to create a perfect world for Muslims involves killing a great many Muslims. The massacres are rarely covered in American or European news media—or even if they are, the coverage is minimal and soon forgotten. For example, compare the amount of coverage given the attacks in Brussels or Nice to the coverage of just one Baghdad bombing in July 2016 that killed over 300 people. The coverage of American and European attacks was massive, with follow-up stories continuing over days and weeks after the incidents that included the names and stories of those who lived and those who died, the background of the killers, and much more. But how many people in the Western countries know the names and stories of those killed in Baghdad?

REMOVING THE GRAY ZONE IN ISLAM

It is accepted that a Muslim can essentially excommunicate another Muslim, or resort to *Takfir*, the act of declaring a Muslim a nonbeliever or *kufar*. It was just one of the prevailing themes in the videos and other media created by the ISIS Media Machine. Repeatedly the videos, image shows, and pamphlets show a dramatic battle of "good" vs. "evil" in the starkest terms, and the ISIS lens depicts the enemy in very two-dimensional terms, reserving the harshest condemnation for disbelievers and apostates. There are no nuanced judgments, no gray areas—it is all black versus white.

The ISIS publication *Dabiq*, edition 1, page 9, gave us "breaking news": "The World Has Divided into Two Camps," and those two camps are the "camp of Islam and faith" and "the camp of the kufr (disbelief) and hypocrisy-The camp of the Muslims and the mujahidin everywhere, and camp of the Jews, the crusaders, their allies, and with them the rest of the nations and religions of the kufr, all being led by America and Russia, and being mobilized by the Jews."

A page later, the ISIS publication says, "Muslims everywhere, whoever is capable of performing hijrah to the Islamic State, then let him do so, because hijrah to the land of Islam is obligatory." Then they continue with a "special call" to the Islamic scholars and judges, military, and administrative experts to perform hijrah as part of their religious obligation.

As for cases in which hijrah may not be possible, ISIS encourages engaging in murdering either disbelievers or apostates.

"THE GOOD MUSLIMS"—THE JIHADI LIVING AND DEAD

Key to the plan of the cult of death, ISIS divides the Muslim world into good Muslims and bad Muslims on a regular basis. They believe that they are the sole arbiters of who is a good Muslim and who is a bad Muslim. By using this division, ISIS pits brother against brother, son against father. They use divisions to drive their followers to kill anyone who deviates from the ISIS-provided doctrine.

The Soldiers of the Caliphate

If there was one unifying theme in the media campaign, it was that the mujahideen or holy fighter is fighting the ultimate battle of good vs. evil. It follows that the video and photo presentations released are then used as repeated examples of the Good in the form of the holy fighter vs. the Evil apostates, dictators, spies, and, of course, the *kufar*. Much of the running time in all types of ISIS videos is devoted to this unyielding battle of good against evil. Only those living in the ISIS world see themselves as the pious ones blessed by the will of Allah and standing against Shaytan.

The second theme in these releases was that punishing the iniquities of the khilafah, currently thought to infest Syria and Iraq with footholds in Libya, Egypt, Yemen, and Afghanistan, united ISIS fighters in a nation state. The objective of this blanket condemnation was to compel the Muslim faithful everywhere to support the caliphate against all aggression. In July 2016, al-Furqan released a video called *The Structure of the Khilafah*, and though it was filled with hierarchical information about the ISIS structure, its main purpose was to demonstrate to its followers that it was vibrant, statelike, taking care of its citizens, all thanks to the efforts of ISIS. The video was released just after the fall of Fallujah and the subsequent campaign to take Mosul.

In ISIS media, the fighters are "Defenders of the Religion," as the title of a video from Wilayat al-Furat indicates. This is a repeated refrain in ISIS propaganda designed to persuade young men to become pious fighters for al-Baghdadi.

Figure 71: A fighter saddles up to be a human bomb in this heavily plated vehicle. (Source: TAPSTRI)

Dabiq cites the initial example of Afghanistan, then Kurdistan, for the launch of Abu Musab al-Zarqawi's Jama'atut-Tawhidi wal-Jihad, the precursor for al-Qaeda in Iraq, and also singles out "lands with conditions that support jihad"—Yemen, Mali, Somalia, The Sinai, Waziristan, Libya, Chechnya, Nigeria, Algeria, Indonesia, and the Philippines. To emphasize the absolutism of us vs. them, ISIS condemns deadly attacks on Sunni women and children by enemies in the Syrian or Iranian regimes, seen as the puppets of the disbelievers. All of this self-justifying and twisted version of religion opens the door to the individual and mass executions captured in the unspeakable videos produced by ISIS.

An Unhealthy Worship of the Dead

One of the grand hypocrisies committed by ISIS was their endless idol worship of attackers as "martyrs" or how they accord fighters adulation and celebrity. Not only are images of terrorists like Abu Usamah al-Maghribi featured in ISIS media, but those images are also posted by followers on social media sites like Twitter, Telegram, and Facebook. This hero worship attracts followers who ultimately choose to fill the role of an Istishadi, a suicide bomber. According to ISIS media, a man can take pride in the prospect of being killed fighting for the caliphate. This also influences the propaganda aimed at women as they are groomed to become martyrs' wives and give birth to another generation of fighters for the caliphate.

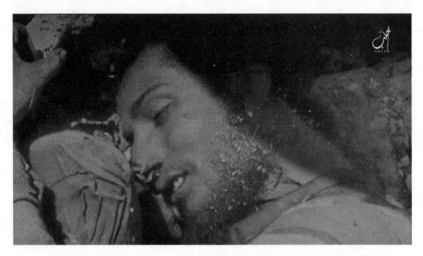

Figure 72: ISIS presents its dead fighter as smiling in Halab photo set.
(Source: TAPSTRI)

At the heart of all ISIS propaganda is the worship of the dead fighter who met God while dying for the religion. In video segments featuring foreign fighters explaining why they went to Syria to fight for ISIS, it becomes clear that the story of the holy warrior inspired them to leave home and die. Of course, some who came to Syria to be holy warriors or suicide bombers find themselves digging latrines or performing other menial tasks. Martyrdom postponed.

The macho projection of the warrior was presented as the role of the "good Muslim," and much of this aim was reflected in the titles of videos like *Resolve of the Brave* (al-Anbar) or *Knights of Victory* (al-Fallujah). Dead fighters sometimes become the latest avatar on social media. One example is followers' veneration of the holy warrior al-Bilawi's image in the summer of 2014 after he was killed by Iraqi forces.

Celebrated and Dead Foreign Fighters Featured in Dabiq

Dabiq Issue 9—Abu Mus'ab al-Almani and brother, originally from Germany, who died in attack under Wilayat Shemal Baghdad 4th Regiment Base attack.

Daqiq Issue 10—"Join the Caravan of Islamic State Knights in the lands of the crusades" with a batch of examples of dead fighters attributed to the Islamic State.

Dabiq Issue 11—Celebrated Najd attacker "Abu Sinan an-Najdi" Abu Ja'far al-Almani, German fighter.

Dabiq Issue 12—Abu Junaydah al-Almani (Moroccan German). Abu Shurayh as-Silani (Sri Lanka).

Dabiq Issue 13—Abu Muharib al-Muhajir (a.k.a. Jihadi John , a British Arab).

Dabiq 14—Abu Sulayman al-Baljiki, Khalid al-Bakrawi (a.k.a. Abu Walid al-Baljiki), Muhammad Bilqa'id (a.k.a. Abu Abdil Aziz al-Jaza'iri), Najm al-Ashrawi (a.k.a. Abu Idris al-Baljiki)—Belgium attackers;

Abu Jandal al-Bangali-Dhaka fighter, traveled to Syria to be shot by 23mm autocannon.

Most of the al-Hayat videos featured a foreign fighter who was portrayed as brave for traversing all the dangers to get to Syria or Iraq to fight for the caliphate. From the first releases on the messages remains the same. For example, *al-Ghurabaa: The Chosen Few of Different Lands—Abu Muslim from Canada* (video from July 12, 2014), *Abu Suhayb al-Faransi* (video from March 7, 2015), and *Stories from the Land of Living—Abu Khaled al-Cambodi from Australia* (video from April 21, 2015) were all designed to exalt the holy warrior image as the face of ISIS instead of the face of cult members who were killed for the ambitions of a terrorist organization.

Figure 73: Canadian Andre Poulin appeared in third al-Hayat video designed to encourage recruits to leave Canada. (Source: TAPSTRI)

Taliban leader Khadim was killed, and shortly after Wilayat Khurusan acknowledges it with tribute and worship. *al-Shaykh Khadim has passed and the revenge is coming* released in March 2015. In March of 2016, a video was released applauding the contributions of dead Emir "Abu Ali Al-Anbari," who was killed in a drone strike.

REPENT OR DIE

In the first edition of *Dabiq*, ISIS claims that hundreds of Iraqi police, law enforcement, and military "repented" (*tawba*) in Diyala, Kirkuk, al-Anbar, and Salahuddin. In a few official ISIS video releases, we also see officials "repent" their previous role in working for the Iraq government and be claimed by the Islamic State. But the message from ISIS remains "Repent Before We Apprehend You," which has a video title all its own released through the Syrian regional ISIS media office, Wilayah Dimashq. Being "repentant" and then joining ISIS can also result in getting you featured in death. A man identified by ISIS as Abu Muhammad al-Ansari, who was a Syrian officer (Nusayri soldier) who turned to ISIS, died in Minnigh. His brief story was highlighted in *Messages from the Land of Legends 2*, released in August 2013 under the al-Furqan Media Foundation, the lead media center for ISIS materials and the original publishing foundation for the organization since its founding under Abu Mus'ab al-Zarqawi.

THE WOMEN OF THE CALIPHATE

Despite the vast amount of propaganda released by the Islamic State or al-Qaeda, very little of it features women. The few bits that have been released come from their print institutions, such as ISIS official publisher Maktabat al-Himmah's pamphlets and the official magazine, *Dabiq*. The articles usually tell the stories of women who found sanctuary in the Islamic State and understanding from her new peers and an awareness of her noble mission. While it is known that women are involved in recruiting and other clandestine operations, there are no images released by the Islamic State showing what the lives of women were like during al-Baghdadi's brutal reign.

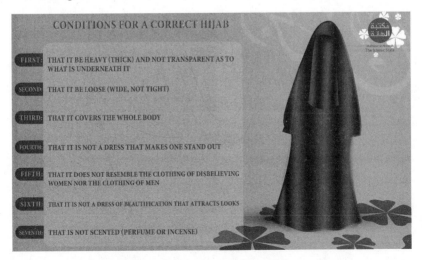

Figure 74: A graphic from Maktabat al-Himmah.

The Voice of Umm Sumayyah al-Muhajirah

In print, the life of women under ISIS was a vastly different world than the one seen in the violent videos featuring the men. In order to tap into the spirit of the women the terrorist group wanted to indoctrinate, there had to be a voice that could speak to the women about their role in the caliphate.

Addressing "my Muslim sister, the wife of the mujahid and mother of lion cubs," Umm Sumayyah al-Muhajirah first appeared in *Dabiq* Issue 8 with the article "Twin Halves of Muhajirin" and then reappeared in *Dabiq* Issue 9 with "Slave-girls or prostitutes." She appears again in Issues 11, 12, 13, and 14. But when the fifteenth issue of *Dabiq* came out in July 2016, a new voice spoke for and to women: Umm Khalid al-Finlandiyyah recounted "How I came to Islam," a testimony of a woman who came from a "Christian" nation. In her story, she describes going to join ISIS after her husband was released from prison.

Narratives like the ones found in the *Dabiq* entries all come down to what ISIS wants from women—marrying ISIS fighters and bearing their children. There have been unofficial clips uploaded to the web of the al-Khanssaa Brigade or unofficial footage showing the treatment of women. One well-known clip included the stoning of a woman for adultery while her father watched. The treatment of women in the caliphate is mostly known through the testimony of women who have escaped.

YOU MUST COME TO THE CALIPHATE—THE HIJRAH MESSAGE

ISIS media constantly reinforces "obligations" for Muslims, and the first one is "hijrah from wherever you are to the Islamic State" and to "Rush to perform it" or "Rush to the shade of the Islamic State with your parents, siblings, spouses, and children. There are homes here for you and your families."

Figure 75: Al-Hayat video uses blame to encourage Muslims to leave their homes and travel to Syria. (Source: TAPSTRI)

If you can't go to the Islamic State, then ISIS has a fallback option: "try in your location to organize bay'āt (pledges of allegiance to the Khalifah Ibrahim). Publish them as much as possible. Gather people in the masajid, Islamic centers, and Islamic organizations, for example, and make public announcements of bay'ah.

But if you can't do that openly, ISIS has yet another fallback option: "If you live in a police state that will arrest you over such bay'āt, then use means of anonymity to convey your bay'ah to the world."

The reason was clearly stated in *Dabiq* Issue 2:

> "Your publicized bay'ah has two benefits. First it is a manifestation of the Muslims' loyalty to each other and to their body. (And those who disbelieved are allies of one another.). . . Second, it is a way to fill the hearts of the kuffār with painful agony."

YOU MUST JOIN THE CALIPHATE—THE BAY'ĀT MESSAGE

A very common type of releases across the ISIS video spectrum is segments of young men holding up their hands with the index finger pointed up and swearing their loyalty as fighters to al-Baghdadi. This was typically the first video sent from any new region or from existing groups seeking to be acknowledged by ISIS and subsequently by everybody else. In addition to videos that come from the groups that pledge loyalty to al-Baghdadi, there are the videos that come from the *wilayat* that express jubilation at the announcements coming from abroad. *Joy of the al-Khilafa Soldiers for the baya'a of their brothers in Nigeria* was a release from al-Khair like several that came out in March 2015 after Boko Haram swore its loyalty to the al-Baghdadi. Then came videos from Dijlah, al-Furat, and others who joined in the theme.

There are times when the videos are sent ahead of a bay'āt, made by groups abroad as an invitation, like the Wilayat al-Furat release *Message to the Muslims in Somalia* released May 21, 2015. It was one of a half-dozen videos released. It was clearly intended to persuade al-Shabaab fighters to make alliances with ISIS instead of AQ. At the time, al-Shabaab fighters and leaders were split on this decision. In the case of Algeria Wilayat, the only video that exists from the *wilayat* was the bay'āt video.

جانب من نشاط مركز العلاقات العامة لشؤون العشائر "صلح بين أهل قرية فولان تبا"

Figure 76: Clans in Nineveh renew their pledge to al-Baghdadi.

In other releases like *Clans of al-Sham and Iraq renew their bay'a to al-Khilafa* from June 7, 2015, you can see tribal leaders renew their oath of loyalty.

"THE BAD MUSLIMS"

ISIS is not simply focused upon exalting the righteous. In their publications, much of the content is aimed at shaming Muslims by accusing them of submitting to the dictators under the unbelievers or for engaging in what ISIS calls forbidden practices. They also frequently call others apostates and declare *Takfir* or excommunication on them. This divide-and-conquer tactic is root to their message and agenda.

The Rafidah (Shia Militias, Shrines, and Markets)

The first group that has to be dealt with are parts of a gray zone in which versions of the Islamic faith obscure their belief that the Sunnis embody the true and pure Muslim faith. First are the Rafidah, or Apostates (Muslims who came to Islam but who left it for another religion). This term was applied to Shia Muslims by various Salafist groups, especially in ISIS media aimed at the Iranians. The title of the thirteenth issue of *Dabiq* was "The Rafidah: From Ibn Saba' to the Dajjal"[1] and focused its efforts on explaining that the Rafidah were "a party of shirk and apostasy." In addition to quickly branding them as murtaddin (apostate), they also make the contrast quite stark. A *Dabiq* Issue 7 article's title was "From Hypocrisy to Apostacy" with a picture of imams standing with "Je Suis Charlie" images after the Charlie Hebdo attack. The subtitle said it all: "The Extinction of the Greyzone."[2]

The *Rafidah* are the source of much angst for ISIS. One has only to watch ISIS media to see their aims. There are video clips of its members attacking the "rafidah" (Apostates or Muslims who left Islam), articles about their historical crimes or apostasy, and justifications for their mass murder by selective interpretations of the

Quran by scholars including Ibn Taymiyyah. The conclusion was that the Rafidah are *mushirk* (loosely translated, "those who engage in Shirk" or polytheism, the belief in more than one God).

It has led to the torture and execution of various bloggers and media activists who were condemned for sharing information deemed offensive to the caliphate. It seems that the caliphate alone has the authority to decide who will be killed and for what offense.

In Syria, ISIS's rhetorical attacks on Assad's army are largely due to the ISIS involvement in a civil war and the fact that Assad is an Alawite, a minority Shia sect.

The differences between the two sides are so great that any reconciliation is out of the question. The ISIS videos made in Syria often show what happens to government officials and members of the Syrian army detained by ISIS forces.

In Iraq, their videos focus on the Shia militias from Iran and Iraq (called "the Safavid armies") who are involved in fighting ISIS to increased hatred. ISIS posts pictures to justify its campaign by showing dead Sunni children killed by Shia militias, as well as Iraqi or Syrian forces.

Morsi and the Egyptian Brotherhood

ISIS referred to the Muslim Brotherhood as a cancer in *Dabiq* Issue 14. Despite sharing ideological roots dating back decades, ISIS maintains the position that the Muslim Brotherhood is now a nationalist organization, seeking to be involved in secular institutions while participating in the politics of a sham democracy.

The Taghut and the Liberators

The insult of *taghut or "idolator"* is often used by ISIS to label other Muslim religious leaders as ignorant, like the pre-Islamic Arabian peoples who worshipped idols. Based on the revelations in the Quran, all authority and legitimacy comes from Allah. According to ISIS, all leaders not part of the ISIS hierarchy have no legitimacy or authority and are to be insulted with the word taghut.

ISIS routinely aims its threats at leaders in North Africa, the Arabian Peninsula, the entire Middle East, and Central Asian regions. It calls for the overthrow of all these leaders and their regimes so that Allah's will will be fulfilled and the faithful liberated to live under ISIS rule.

Figure 77: ISIS video released in January 2016 aimed at leaders of North Africa.
(Source: TAPSTRI)

The other implication in the word was that the *taghut* serve their own self-interests. The word taghut describes a person who has ignored the will of Allah and is corrupt. The images in videos of regional leaders who are directly impacted by ISIS are meant to show the citizens of those countries that their leaders are beholden to outside forces, including the United States, France, Russia, and the United Kingdom.

For example, *Dabiq* 9 was titled "They Plot and Allah Plots" with a picture of Secretary of State Kerry meeting with other leaders, including imams, to broker a deal to destroy the Islamic State. ISIS regards this as not only a betrayal by Muslim countries involved in this conspiracy, but also a betrayal of Muslims and a grave sin in the eyes of Allah.

Masoud Barzani, president of Iraqi Kurdistan Region since 2005, was portrayed as a puppet of the US. A *Dabiq* 10 feature dismisses the Syrian Kurd YPG as merely proxies for American efforts. Other examples come from regional releases like those from Wilayat Khorasan, which labels the Pakistani Army as "apostates" in releases like *Targeting the Apostate Pakistani Army in the Area of Khaybar with Mortars.*

The Moderates and Scholars Are Apostates

ISIS is not hesitant to attack Muslim scholars who have criticized their destruction of traditional Islamic life. Segments in videos show Muftis and Imams who have denounced the Islamic State for its hijacking their religion. Then there are the segments in their magazines: *Dabiq 6*'s "Misleading Scholars" or *Dabiq 7*'s "From Hypocrisy to Apostasy: The Extinction of the Grayzone," featuring two imams with small printed signs saying "Je Suis Charlie" at a demonstration of solidarity after the Charlie Hebdo attacks in Pars.

In order to wage full war on Islam, the Islamic State has targeted the *ulema*, learned scholars, in order to discredit their calls for ISIS to cease its gross perversion of the religion. Targets of their spite and threats include Hamza Yusuf, Yasir Qadhi, Suhaib Webb, Hisham Kabbani, Bilal Philips, and Pierre Vogel.

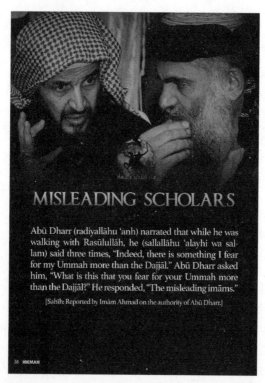

Figure 78: Abu Muhammad al-Maqdisi is a frequent target of attack by ISIS media releases like this panel from Dabiq. (Source: TAPSTRI)

There are no scholars immune from the attacks. The mentor of ISIS "godfather" Abu Musab al-Zarqawi was as much a target as the moderates. The noted Salafist Abu Muhammad Al-Maqdisi has been the subject of many attacks by the Islamic State, which regards him as a confused apostate. In *Dabiq* 11, ISIS again asked the question, "who are the true fuqaha and scholars?" followed by "and who are the evil scholars?" The article had photos of al-Maqdisi and others.

Another target of constant attacks was the Saudi Grand Mufti, Abdul-Aziz ash-Sheikh who has condemned ISIS and called them a cancer and existential threat to Islam. *Dabiq* 13 condemned the Grand Mufti Abdul-Aziz as an apostate.

Those Who Help the Kufar Are Apostates

In a release via Wilayat al-Furat in Iraq, there was a segment where an Iraqi confesses his sins against the Islamic State and expresses a sense of relief that he has finally gotten this burden off his chest. He no longer has to hide his transgressions from the Islamic State. He was then executed for his sins as a reminder that those who took action against the State would be severely punished.

Releases like this often have titles like Wilayah Khorasan's "Healing the Chest for the slaughtering of the spy" or "Harvest of the Spies." Victims are forced to confess spying or working against the caliphate in some way when they were either entirely innocent of the charge or actually worked for the Iraqi, Syrian, Libyan, Egyptian, or other governments that ISIS currently is at war with.

The videos and photo slideshows follow a pattern: accusation, confession, and then punishment to show a simple system of accountability under the rules set by the Islamic State. In some cases the victims look into the camera and plead for others to "listen to me please, don't be foolish," as if it may save their lives.

The Media War with Al-Qaeda

ISIS has been fighting with al-Qaeda through media since the days of Zarqawi. Moreover, the AQ leader ordered him to lower his profile and think long-term. ISIS continues to assail the veteran terrorist organization as out of touch and impotent.

A fighter interviewed in *Dabiq* told them that many fighters were leaving al-Shabaab precisely because the terror group didn't give bay'ah to al-Baghdadi. He also said that many of the fighters are from other countries in East Africa who go to Somalia for hijrah.[3]

THE GOOD GUYS PAY ZAKAH

As further proof that ISIS was a functioning state was a collection of *zakah* (tax) throughout its territories. The videos released are intended to show viewers that good citizens willingly pay their *zakah*, while those who do not will suffer dire consequences. The video claims to show that money collected is distributed fairly and supports a viable society with the judicial means to resolve disputes and take care of those in need.

Figure 79: Screenshot from al-Furqan release "And They Give al-Zakat" from June 2015. (Source: TAPSTRI)

THE DESTRUCTION OF SHIRK

ISIS received wide and mostly unfavorable news coverage for the destruction of antiquities throughout areas under its control. The videos and photographs of the destruction of cemeteries in Iraq and Libya, wrecking the ancient city of Palmyra in Syria, blowing up the city of Nimrud have captured worldwide attention. The presentations begin with an ISIS representative standing before the camera and explaining why it was forbidden to worship the shrines and monuments of the past and that it was their duty to watch for "manifestations of shirk" that could lead Muslims astray.

Videos from Nineveh have shown the destruction of the Lamassu, Tomb of Jonah, and other ancient Assyrian and Babylonian relics. Other videos from Libya show fighters kicking over graves. Clips from Iraq show the detonation of Shia shrines or the toppling of Christian churches in which the cross was removed and a black flag replaced it. Concerns for competition aren't limited to Syria and Iraq when it comes to Shirk. Libya's Tarabulus Media released "Removing Manifestations of al-Shirk" on March 16, 2015.

Figure 80: A bulldozer destroys a Sufi shrine in Libya. (Source: TAPSTRI)

Dabiq 8 described these destructive operations as "Erasing the legacy of a ruined nation," one way to characterize the death cult's attempt to erase the history of Iraq and replace it with a new history under ISIS tyranny. The terrorist organization prides itself on the destruction of early temples that predate the Prophet Muhammad. For example, *Dabiq* 11, covered the destruction of the "Temple of

Baalshamin," which ISIS blew up in August, 2015. It had stood for nearly 2,000 years.

Figure 81: ISIS graphic aimed at discouraging nationalism. (Source: TAPSTRI)

ABANDON NATIONALISM

One of the constant criticisms of other terrorist organizations by ISIS was that they served to bolster nationalism because this is contrary to the will of Allah. This was a way for ISIS to gain hegemony over other terror organizations, including the Taliban.

PROPHECY

The constant evocation of the "End Times" and the Day of Judgment pervades ISIS propaganda in *Dabiq* and elsewhere. For a cult

Figure 82: ISIS outdoor da'wah (preaching) event from November 2014.
(Source: TAPSTRI)

steeped in death and destruction, this is hardly surprising. Before the day of wrath arrives there will be a showdown with unbelievers. This confrontation is forecast in videos, flyers, and elaborate pamphlets—most of the printed material is in Arabic and features sermons on how to prepare for the end of days.

REACHING THE LONE WOLF AUDIENCE

ISIS materials, like those of al-Qaeda's before them, urge extremists throughout the world to carry out lone wolf attacks. Unfortunately, the unstable of the world are receptive. Justin Nojan Sullivan, a.k.a. "The Mujahid," was charged with material support on June 22, 2015. He told an undercover law officer: "I liked IS from the beginning then I started thinking about death and stuff so I became Muslim." Sullivan gave the undercover officer advice on how to build a silencer by passing on instructions he had gotten via the Internet.

Abu Muhammad al-Adnani was the latest terrorist leader to call for Loner attacks in May 2016, just before Ramadan. He called for improvised attacks around the world as a sign that the caliphate was strong while calling for Muslims to prepare for the Holiest month of the Muslim calendar.

THE PERCEPTIONS OF MUSLIMS USED BY ISIS

"Put simply, extremist groups use the stereotypes of their targets."
—*Mia Bloom*[4]

When we first started dealing with jihadist videos, we were often trying to find a martyrdom video to learn what we could about an attacker. Even as ISIS media were preparing to release Flames of War, we thought we had seen the different levels of capability in these violent groups. The more we dug to see who was publishing and how they were getting it out on the web, the more we started seeing videos of the group with smiling kids. Despite the onslaught against their "nation" state, they continue to push the fantasy through videos that theirs is a paradise dangling on the precipice of destruction, they continue the fantasy of paradise though their video messages. There, one will enjoy only the best bread, properly killed sheep, and good water, all reserved for the Good Muslims who have sworn their allegiance to Abu Bakr Al-Baghdadi; these are presented in a level of propaganda equal to that of Saddam Hussein or the Nazis. There are two major tools of the ISIS media campaign. First, the initial release of products for consumption. Second, the reactive nature of both supporters and the targets of their campaigns. Using the Internet to upload files was only the beginning of their strategy to show the caliphate as heaven on earth.

The general public perception of ISIS was understandably shaped by the videos of the executions of Americans and Europeans or the mass executions of Iraqis, Syrians, Yemenis, Libyans, Egyptians, Afghani, and others. But those seeking to be part of something big are attracted to the caliphate despite such horrors. Repetition. Already said.

Figure 83: ISIS photosets show repair and upkeep of power.

"Jannah" Gonna Believe This, but the Services Are Under Control

There are many ISIS slide shows and videos that show a functional state in which roads are repaired, maintained, and well lit, clean water is supplied to residents, and the government looks after their welfare—if you are a believer. In *Dabiq* 4, they claimed that "soldiers of Allah do not liberate a village, town or city, only to abandon its residents and ignore their needs" and included photographs with captions such as "repairing a bridge in al-Khayr" or "restoring electricity in the city of ar-Raqqah." They additionally promise "cancer treatment for the children of Ninawa" and "street cleaning services."

Some videos and related slideshows, however, show things like the hisbah patrol (religious police) keeping an eye out for people breaking laws about everything from the way one is dressed to someone sneaking a cigarette. They demonstrate what can happen if you disobey the Islamic State, burning cartons of forbidden cigarettes or flogging a prisoner for disobedience—or exacting severe punishments ending in death. However, they also portray the support of the people, with onlookers always cheering on punishment of the apostate, spy, or, worse, a disbeliever.

THE MUJATWEETS

A series of eight videos that came out in 2014 aimed at conveying a positive image of ISIS by making it appear that the fighters were happy, children under the caliphate were happy, food made in the caliphate was healthy, and other scenes encouraging fighters to come to the new utopia.

EID, THE BEST TIME OF YEAR

According to the media utopia of ISIS, there was prosperity under the shariah as enforced by ISIS. This prosperity was highlighted by video and photo releases covering the observance of Eid al-Fitr or like the title *Eid Spirit in Wilayat al-Furat* from Sept 26, 2015, celebrating Eid al-Adha or The Feast of Sacrifices, a commemoration of the story of Abraham's willingness to obey God and sacrifice his son, Isaac.

THE EDUCATION SYSTEM

ISIS released videos showing children learning basic Arabic as well as basic weapons training starting from an early age. The education is geared to making future jihadists. The terrorist group has also released various pdfs to further indoctrinate supporters' children into the death cult.

Figure 84: Child learning Arabic. (Source: TAPSTRI)

In addition, there are dozens of training camp videos and videos featuring the "cubs of the khilafah," or the child soldiers who are trained to be the next generation of fighters. In one case, a child named Abdallah was featured first in a school with other children before appearing a year later in a video in which he is killing a Russian FSB officer.

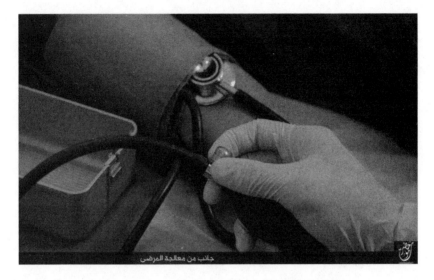

Figure 85: Health Care Pulse. (Source: TAPSTRI)

Figure 86: Fresh Fish Market. (Source: TAPSTRI)

THE FOOD IS HEALTHY AND DELICIOUS

Abundant food provided by the caliphate was the theme of several feature photo sets and videos. There are many pictures of greenhouses bursting with well-tended produce or markets filled with good healthy food. The hisbah patrol stops in to make sure items sold are compliant with halal rules, while the image suggests there's a world of good health under the caliphate.

The image of the Islamic State as provider is a powerful message aimed at both the local and international recruiting targets.

Figure 87: Cigarette Burn Pile. (Source: TAPSTRI)

No More Smoking

ISIS was keen on stomping out smoking. You might be sentenced to death for other vices under ISIS rule, but at least you would have healthy lungs. The pictures typically show a pile of recently confiscated cartons of cigarettes, cases of alcohol, cannabis, or other pro-

Figure 88: Member of the Hisbah patrol reads out the vices of others before a crowd. (Source: TAPSTRI)

hibited substances being burned. There are periodic photo sets released to remind people in the caliphate that indulging these vices are grounds for flogging citizens. Or worse.

No More Vices, Thanks Hisbah!

"Clamping down on sexual deviance" was very important to the caliphate. In *Dabiq* 7, ISIS blamed what it called "sexual deviance" on the "sexual revolution" that occurred "five decades ago" in the West. ISIS had ways of "curing" such deviance, which included throwing gay men off towers, stoning men and women to death for adultery, or flogging those caught possessing pornography.

ISIS routinely releases hisbah patrol videos that show them as law and order enforcers for any number of violations from improper preparation of food, selling cigarettes, or playing musical instruments. Pictures are infrequently published of piles of instruments in burn piles.

The Gold Dinar

To complete much of the ISIS shift off the grid, there was the campaign known as "Return of the Gold Dinar" in which the Islamic State announced it would simply print its own currency based on gold. It came with hashtags #return_of_the_ gold_dinar and a series of videos and photo sets and was featured in several editions of *Dabiq*.

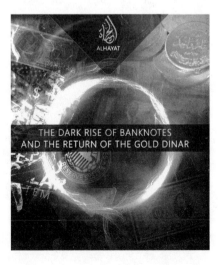

Figure 89: Al-Hayat advertises its videos on the Return of the Gold Dinar.
(Source: TAPSTRI)

Chapter 12

The Anti-ISIS Cyber Army

Who is standing up to ISIS online? A coalition of governments, a coalition of private enterprises, and a range of private individuals who have, like cyber vigilantes, taken on an effort to eradicate ISIS from the Internet. The United States Government's efforts via the Pentagon, State Department, and intelligence and law enforcement agencies are constantly being tested, since terrorist sometimes stay a step ahead.

There the little consensus on how to balance public safety and the assumed right to privacy online. Government has a duty to protect its citizens. Private enterprise tech firms have a commercial goal that was undermined by the presence online and association with bad actors of any kind. Private citizens who are skilled in using the tools of the Internet have mounted take-down efforts against the ISIS media materials and channels.

THE UNITED STATES EFFORT AGAINST ISIS ONLINE

The Pentagon and the State Department have active campaigns to confront online recruiting and terrorist or criminal operational use of the Internet. Congress's efforts have been limited, since it remains in perpetual deadlock. The White House has used its influence and power to call on tech leaders for input about what can be done to combat the online presence of ISIS. During the 2016 elections, the presidential candidates called for a declared cyber war against ISIS.[1]

The House of Representatives

In December 2015, the Combat Terrorist Use of Social Media Act (H.R.3654) was passed by the U.S. House of Representatives. It requires the President to submit a strategy to congress within 180 days of enactment that will serve counterterrorism efforts on social media. The key provisions include:

- "an evaluation of the role social media plays in radicalization in the United States and elsewhere;
- an analysis of how terrorists and terrorist organizations are using social media;
- recommendations to improve the federal government's efforts to disrupt and counter the use of social media by terrorists and terrorist organizations;
- an analysis of how social media is being used for counterradicalization and counterpropaganda purposes, irrespective of whether such efforts are made by the federal government;
- an assessment of the value to law enforcement of terrorists' social media posts; and
- an overview of training available to law enforcement and intelligence personnel to combat terrorists' use of social media and recommendations for improving or expanding existing training opportunities."

The US Senate

In July 2016, the US Senate Homeland Security Committee passed S. 2517-Combat Terrorist Use of Social Media Act of 2016, a companion bill to H.R. 3654.

On July 11, 2016, the US Senate Homeland Security Committee passed S.2418-The Countering Online Recruitment of Violent Extremist Act. This act expands the resources for DHS in order to develop programs to counterterrorism including how to counter the propaganda used for recruitment, creating alternatives for those who are potential recruits. "If we can shut down their communications, they cannot radicalize people to conduct terror attacks like what we saw in San Bernardino," says Representative Michael McCaul.[2]

The battle to find the right balance in the law, law enforcement, civil liberties, and private enterprise continues to be active and quite dynamic. Many governments are enforcing blocks on end-to-end encrypted technology or in other cases banning use of Virtual Private Network (VPN), an internal network that acts like a closed loop of communication. There are many areas where the demands of law enforcement conflict with the needs of tech firms and social media companies like Twitter, Facebook, and others to assure their customers that they will do everything possible to protect them online. All parties involved have to understand that excessively lowering the level of protection provided to individual citizens entails a risk that others with advanced skill sets would be able to breach the communication systems used by ordinary citizens or even government agencies. The fact is that in the last three years there have been major breaches of data in the public and private sectors, and despite the best firewalls and other security measures, we still remain frighteningly vulnerable to hacking. The tech companies have made a case for self-policing and limited government interference in their operations. Leading companies like Twitter and Facebook justify avoiding limited government regulation and interference by engaging in aggressive takedowns of ISIS propaganda.

United States Law Enforcement Activities
Federal Level activities by the FBI and DOJ include a range of outreach efforts to social media organizations for input and coopera-

tion. In February 2015, the US Justice Department met executives from Apple, Twitter, Snapchat, Facebook, and MTV.[3]

Then, in January 2016, US anti-terrorism officials again met with Silicon Valley executives in a closed-door summit to discuss online counter-ISIS measures, with both sides realizing that government efforts alone might not be enough. The government was wary of encroaching on First Amendment rights.[4]

The predominant method used for years by the FBI and other law enforcement agencies for monitoring ISIS jihadist activity has been a combination of acting on tips from concerned citizens and using undercover officers, informants, and authorized surveillance. Many of the 90+ cases before the federal courts involved a combination of informants and undercover confidence building with the suspects. In many cases there were overlapping suspects, all of whom were intending to go to Syria or in some cases carry out US attacks from within.

US Department of State—"Think Again, Turn Away"

The US State Department has been building coalitions to fight ISIS under Secretary of State John Kerry. The department that spends its time dealing with international diplomacy has been tasked to confront terrorism and online recruiting in several ways. The unit inside the State Department asked with confronting the issue was the Center for Strategic Counterterrorism Communications, or the CSCC. The CSCC was established in September 2010.[5]

The State Department has said it was well aware of the intrinsic relationship jihadist expansion has with the use of the Internet and social media. Deputy Secretary of State and former Deputy National Security advisor Tony Blinken said the department could see a decrease in the space in which ISIS can operate online and that efforts via suspensions were taking their toll.[6]

The "Think Again, Turn Away" project was launched in 2014 before the declaration of the creation of the Islamic State. The purpose of the project was to confront extremism with alternative messages. Using the twitter handle @ThinkAgain_DOS, the channel intended to spread counter-extremist ideas. But without knowing who the target recipients were or what channel would be used by them, the government use of a Twitter channel would not result in getting counter- or alternative messages to those likely to be attracted to watching jihadist materials in the first place.

After the world saw what ISIS was capable of doing, the CSCC prepared a four-minute video called *Welcome to the Islamic State* that sought to use the savage imagery of ISIS to counter recruiting with images of tortured Muslims, mosques being blown up, and other terrorist outrages. The video was released September 5, 2014.[7] There was no evidence the video led to any success in stopping the recruiting of foreign fighters.

The efforts of the State Department include using voices of Muslim scholars to refute the religious claims of ISIS. In doing so, ISIS then retaliates on those scholars, smearing them as apostates for working with Western governments, especially the United States.

US Military vs. ISIS Cyber

As noted in the Operation Vaporize section of Chapter 1, the US military and coalition forces have been busting media centers related to ISIS since it was called AQI. With big hauls of CDs, computers, jump drives, and terabytes of data, the kinetic effort to destroy ISIS media cannot be underestimated. When coalition forces put pressure on all the towns around Mosul in 2016, there were reports of ISIS media and IT techs leaving the group.[8] An anti-ISIS activist named Raafat al-Zarari told ARA News that many who fled were American citizens who have left the Iraq-Syria area for Turkey.

In January 2016, French Air Force fighter jets bombed a building purported to be a key ISIS media center in Mosul. In response to the strike, Amaq stated that ten of the Mosul media crew were killed.[9] On August 31, 2016, the US military killed the ISIS spokesman, Abu Muhammad Al-Adnani. The operations continued days later with the death of the Minister of Information, Wa'el Al-Rawi.

The Launch of a New Offensive by Cyber Command

In March 2016, Defense Secretary Ash Carter and Joint Chiefs Chairman Gen. Joseph Dunford announced the intent to use active, offensive cyber operations to "disrupt ISIL's command and control, to cause them to lose confidence in their networks, to overload their network so it can't function."[10] The "Cyber Command" has been focused on state actors like the Chinese, the North Koreans, and the Russians. Based in Fort Meade, Cyber Command has been active since 2009. During the 2016 announcement about launching the new offensive, Carter told CNN, "We are dropping cyber bombs."

Defense Secretary Carter told Congress that these were the new orders to Cyber Command:

- interrupt their command and control of forces
- interrupt ability to plot
- interrupt finances
- interrupt ability to control population
- interrupt ability to recruit

ANTI-ISIS EFFORTS ABROAD

While the laws in the United States continue to adapt to the changes driven by ISIS activities, countries in the rest of the world have their own ways of dealing with terrorism and abuse of social media. These range from imposing heavy sentences for viewing materials associated with ISIS to shutting down or blocking entire communication platforms in an attempt to prevent abuse of services like Twitter, WhatsApp, and Facebook to coordinate terrorist attacks or, as critics of those plans also note, to crack down on legitimate dissent around the world.

Muslim Coalition Against Isis

The efforts against ISIS in the Muslim world vary, but in the first two years after the invasion of Iraq in 2003 there was little in the way of a coalition despite the damage done to countries in proximity to and immediately threatened by ISIS. Jordan and Egypt have stepped up strikes against ISIS after attacks on their citizens. In both cases, strikes occurred just after videos were released showing execution of their citizens.

In IT responses, many countries already practice strict controls over their communications and Internet usage. In particular, though, some countries have acted upon the concerns of cover planning hidden by encryption. Bangladesh resorted to blocking many social media platforms to cut off communications to potential terrorists. UAE imposed a fine of $545,000 for those caught using a VPN to bypass their strict one-IP system.[11]

European Effort against ISIS Cyber

Even as the UK exits the EU, the efforts to deal with technology and militants continues. The UK has a Twitter channel like the US State Department that was aimed at dissuading terrorist recruiting. As of September 2016, the Twitter channel had 18.1k followers and 4,689 posts starting from July 2015, advising users to follow the channel for the latest information and to use the hashtag #DefeatingDaesh. The US State Department has morphed again, and the @ThinkAgain_DOS channel has 67 followers and two tweets. Its replacement channel, @TheGEC or Global Engagement Center, had 26.8K followers as of September 1, 2016. Not very impressive!

The UK has also cracked down on several radicals including Anjem Choudhury and Abu Haleema. Choudhury was convicted in late July 2016 and sentenced to five years after years of incendiary speeches and explicit taunting of UK authorities by openly and widely expressing extremist views. Finally, after he proclaimed his loyalty to Abu Bakr al-Baghdadi and ISIS, and then encouraged others, the British authorities stepped in and charged him under Section 12 of the Terrorism Act of 2000.[12]

Like Choudhury, one of the livelier characters on YouTube and via Telegram was extremist Abu Haleema, who regularly rants in videos and posts via Telegram and Twitter. He speaks in repeated phrases intended to cause the thoughts to sink in to the listener. In early January 2015, Twitter shut down his channel as part of an effort, reportedly directed by a combination of MI5 and CIA efforts.[13]

Investigatory Powers Bill

Regarding legislation, Parliament has been debating a bill that calls for the banning of encrypted messaging for potential terrorists including usage of Facebook, WhatsApp, and iMessage.[14] In addition, the bill calls for increasing data collection of traffic between suspects of targeted investigations. The bill was met with resistance from privacy advocates, but it passed in the House of Commons.[15]

France

In the aftermath of the attacks in Paris in November 2015, France sought to work with the tech giants to deal with terrorist use of advanced encryption tools and the Internet for recruiting. Officials met with Facebook, Twitter, Microsoft, Google, and Apple.[16]

In an effort similar to that of the US State Department, the French authorities launched a hashtag campaign under "StopJihadisme" meant to teach parents to look for indications that their children might be getting radicalized. Yet critics suggested the campaign was a waste that failed to reach the audience of people who would most likely turn to ISIS. The campaign included a video that was similar to the one released in the United States, a recut of ISIS videos meant to destroy the notion of a utopian destination for the pious Muslim.[17]

Europol

The European Police Office, or Europol, began efforts to find those behind publication of ISIS media in July 2015.[18] The agency said the effort would include sending take-down notices with the demand that accounts be removed within two hours of notice. The effort would also include a more concerted attempt to detect noteworthy channels in order to flush out leaders and media centers.

Silicon Valley vs. ISIS

It wasn't something Silicon Valley had experienced before. Since 2003, foreign terrorists were now controlling their operating systems and custom coding them to spread their messages and recruit fighters to attack abroad. The flood of ISIS on the social media stage was initially overwhelming for YouTube, Twitter, and Facebook. The tech giants were dragged into the fight against their will, but they've had no choice but to respond. With the demand to clean up their sites coming from their users and lawmakers worldwide, each of the firms have increased their efforts to stop and prevent exploitation of their systems for terrorist media propagation and recruiting. Beyond these three, communications like Telegram, Wordpress, and Archive.org have stepped up efforts to remove ISIS from their systems. In the case of Telegram, there are intelligence agencies and private analytical firms who express resistance to removing these channels out of a need to keep an eye on the organization instead of driving them further into the dark.

Twitter vs. the ISIS Fanboys

If there was one social media outlet that was perhaps impacted the most during the rise of ISIS on the world stage in the summer of 2014, it was Twitter. While many people do not know about the world of online forums, secret or not, they do know about Facebook and Twitter and have become accustomed to getting news and lifestyle announcements via Twitter. ISIS, AQ, and other jihadist groups are using the same tools for their message but with a quite different set of goals.

Twitter has also announced its own war on ISIS in a company blog post, where it was revealed that since mid-2015 it has suspended 125,000 pro-ISIS or terrorist accounts. Twitter's blog reported they had increased the staff dedicated to the task of keeping up with reports on suspicious profiles and posts submitted by users:

"We have increased the size of the teams that review reports, reducing our response time significantly. We also look into other accounts similar to those reported and leverage proprietary spam-fighting tools to surface other potentially violating accounts for review by our agents. We have already seen results, including an increase in account suspensions and this type of activity shifting off of Twitter."[19]

"We condemn the use of Twitter to promote terrorism and the Twitter Rules make it clear that this type of behavior, or any violent threat, was not permitted on our service," the blog post read. "As the nature of the terrorist threat has changed, so has our ongoing work in this area."[20]

After the Bastille Day attack, Twitter demonstrated it understood how ISIS would exploit the tragedy on their platform and rapidly suspended accounts that appeared to be pro-ISIS applauding the truck attack during the holiday in the southern town of Nice. When users posted under "#BlessedNiceAttack" or the "#BattleOfNice" tags and more, they were suspended in far less time than past suspensions had taken.

The company defended its performance in keeping up with the proliferation of ISIS profiles by noting that experts in the field suggested it was impossible to develop the magical algorhythms that would perfectly detect who was participating in terrorism. They disclosed that they do use methods similar to their spam tracking that identify activities associated with accounts that have been identified with ISIS activities.

Facebook vs. ISIS

Much like Twitter, Facebook has been very active in removing suspect profiles, pages, and groups from its website. Facebook, in the past, has cracked down on ISIS-related accounts, including banning a company profile that was supposedly owned by the San Bernardino Shooter Tashfeen Malik. However, the social media website relies heavily on users bringing profiles to a moderator's attention by either "liking" the page or "flagging" it for violating its community standards.[21]

Google and YouTube vs. ISIS

Interwoven giants Google and YouTube are still used by pro-ISIS supporters but with far less frequency than just after the announcement of the caliphate in the summer of 2014. The use of the video tools, personal profile pages, email, and Google drives have made this tech giant very appealing to the jihadists.

One of the key tech giants infected with the ISIS bug was Google. Through its email systems, personal websites, google drive sharing, and of course the very powerful YouTube, Google became the center of attention in the beginning of the battle with ISIS in the summer of 2014. With postings of beheadings grabbing the news, Google's subsidiary video site YouTube was caught in the cross fire between the terrorists of ISIS and the demands of free speech in its home country of the United States.

The use of YouTube by ISIS was an easy choice considering the open source nature of the platform, but it wasn't the only video sharing site being used by the terrorist organization. The propagation teams use dozens of lesser-known sites including sites that are beyond the reach of U.S. legislative control. Yet Google wasn't simply picked for YouTube; the terrorists exploited Google both for its email and its Google drives for hosting video, audio, and document files.

Tech juggernaut Google announced that it would take the fight to ISIS by introducing an alteration of its search results. Jigsaw, an advanced research outfit, will redirect anyone searching pro-ISIS terms and phrases to antiextremist messages and videos. The campaign behind this was called the "Redirect Method."[22]

Google hopes to inspire anti-ISIS campaigns by using Jigsaw instead of automatically integrating it into its search results. The campaign seemed to be effective during an eight-week trial from January to March of 2016, reaching at least 320,000 people who searched for one of more than 1,000 Islamic State-related keywords.

The method placed ISIS-related search results close to ads that had links to counterradicalization links. Jigsaw and other groups affiliated with the method did not create new anti-ISIS content, but simply redirected searchers to preexisting content on YouTube. The effort led by Jigsaw, now a division of Alphabet, Google's parent company, follows other initiatives to counter extremist messages on the web. The Jigsaw project comprised 30 ad campaigns and 95 unique ads both in English and Arabic.

Archive.org

There are few places more interesting on the web than Archive.org, and ISIS knows it. They reliably use Archive.org as their primary depot for the highest-quality versions of their video releases, and the source location for their audio and pdf releases like *Dabiq*. But unlike their early efforts at exploiting it, ISIS began having difficulty successfully keeping materials posted there for long, as Archive. org caught on and undertook changes to be more responsive in taking down the propaganda materials.

The Internet archive, an enormous digital library, was hacked because it hosts ISIS materials. The Twitter account @AttackNodes took credit for the hacks with the hashtag #opISIS, which was affiliated with Anonymous. However, Anonymous members have not gotten in contact with Attack Nodes.[23]

CORPORATE FIGHT VERSUS LEGISLATIVE OR EXECUTIVE OVERREACH

There has been a balancing act between private corporations and the power of the US government given its desire to stop terrorism and the desire of the tech firms to be able to retain customers who value their privacy. The tech industry has long pushed back at congress regarding outside policing of their systems and instead tends to offer plans and evidence of action to assure the legislative body that the industry is quite capable of taking care of itself and that customers have expressed concerns over privacy to the companies. As noted earlier, the most substantial battle came when the FBI asked Apple to help breach the phone at the center of the San Bernardino attack in December 2015. Apple refused on the grounds that breaking the encryption with a backdoor for law enforcement was not an option it would pursue. Apple claimed that it could not break the encryption without wiping the iPhone, but the FBI finally managed to succeed.

BRAINPOWER VERSUS ISIS— THE THINK TANKS

There are several organizations and private analysis firms and think tanks that are involved in the daily effort to defeat ISIS online. The research programs are blooming as the need for more awareness of what motivates people to join extremist groups like ISIS is on the rise.

While there are organizations that simply observe and report what they see, others are engaged in direct efforts in counterradicalization, counterrecruitment, counterintelligence, and more.

Muflehun

Humera Khan, an executive director for Washington, D.C.-based Muflehun (Arabic for "those who will be successful"), said that it's not enough to just shut down ISIS websites. A more coordinated effort was required. "The ones who are doing these engagements number only in the tens. That is not sufficient. Just looking at ISIS-supporting social-media accounts—those numbers are several orders of magnitude larger," says Khan. "In terms of recruiting, ISIS is one of the loudest voices. Their message is sexy, and there is very little effective response out there. Most of the government response isn't interactive. It's a one-way broadcast, not a dialogue."[24]

Quilliam Foundation

A British counter-extremism think tank founded by Ed Husain, Maajid Nawaz, and Rashad Zaman Ali, has used its own antiradicalization videos to combat terrorist ideology.[25] The foundation was established in 2007.

Brookings Institution

A Washington, D.C.-based public policy organization. A study led by J.M. Berger of the Brookings Project found that pro-ISIS Twitter accounts had an average of about one thousand followers. Pro-ISIS accounts were also found to be more active than anti-ISIS ones. ISIS's successful spread of its ideology can be attributed to a "small group of hyperactive users numbering between five hundred and two thousand accounts, which tweet in concentrated bursts of high volume."[26] The report also found that while a minimum of one thousand pro-ISIS accounts were suspended from Twitter between September and December 2014, there was also possible evidence of thousands more.

The Soufan Group

The highly respected counterterrorism advisory firm, The Soufan Group, has done extensive research into the use of media for recruiting foreign fighters that prove invaluable to researchers worldwide. They also publish a daily newsletter with up-to-the-minute analysis on terrorism around the world.

STUDENT POWER

Outside of tech companies, college students have been recruited in the fight against ISIS. The US departments of State and Homeland Security, Facebook, and Ed Venture Partners have created a competition to challenge college students to promote anti-ISIS ideology via social/digital media.

In 2015, students from Missouri State University won the competition with their campaign called One95. The campaign had a website, testimonial videos, and a tweet-a-thon. The group's efforts turned into 200,000 Facebook and Twitter impressions. Eventually, the One95 Global Youth Summit against Violent Extremism was held in the fall of 2015 at the UN in New York.[27]

THE GRASSROOTS FIGHT

In what may be a precedent in the history of cyber war, citizens were continuing to get involved in the fight. With a range of forces from moms who decided they had to confront the terrorists who radicalized their sons to lone cyber warriors like "Jester the mystery hacker," who posted credits for taking down forums and inflicting other mayhem against the Islamic State to the news headline-grabbing fight between Anonymous and the terrorist group.

Figure 90: Anonymous Logo. (Source: TAPSTRI)

Anonymous vs. ISIS

Evolved from users of 4chan, an imageboard website launched in 2003, Anonymous has become the most recognizable name in hacking and activism or the more common portmanteau term "hacktivism." Anonymous gained attention through its history of focusing campaigns against Scientology in its "Project Chanology" in 2008; Operation Payback in 2010, which consisted of a series of DDoS attacks against companies and law firms fighting online piracy; and their operations focused on groups seen to be racist or bigoted by Anonymous including the KKK (2015), Storm Front (2015), and Westboro Baptist Church. It has intervened in cases like the Steubenville rape case of 2013, or the Ferguson, Missouri, shooting case of Mike Brown, or even launched a DDoS attack over police officer Jeffrey Salmon's shooting of a dog, which was captured on video in June 2013.

Anonymous also has little fear about threatening violent organizations. In October 2011, the group threatened the Mexican drug cartel, Los Zetas, with releasing personal information that could harm the Zetas if they didn't release an Anonymous member. The group attacked the CIA's website in 2012 and the Interpol website in 2012.[28]

#OpISIS Begins
How Anonymous went to war with ISIS:

> ISIS; We will hunt you, Take down your sites,
> Accounts, Emails, and expose you. . .
> From now on, no safe place for you online. . .
> You will be treated like a virus, And we are the cure. . .
>
> —Anonymous

In response to the shootings at the Charlie Hebdo offices on January 7, 2015, in Paris, Anonymous declared war on al-Qaeda and what would become ISIS in its campaign to destroy jihadist websites and social media accounts. #OpCharlieHebdo was crafted to attack jihadist online resources in retaliation for the murder of twelve people.[29] The first site Anonymous claimed to have knocked down, ansar-alhaqq.net, was only down for a few hours before it reappeared. On February 9, 2015, Anonymous claimed to have removed 800 terrorist Twitter accounts and a dozen Facebook accounts.[30]

Paris Attacked Again

In November of 2015, days after the terrorist attacks in Paris that killed 129 people, Anonymous issued a video promising retaliation against the group. "The War has been declared," the voice started in French. "Prepare yourselves. These attacks cannot remain unpunished. This is why the Anonymous from all over the world will hunt you down. Expect many cyber attacks." The video then closed with expressions of condolence for the victims and families of the attacks that rocked the French capital.

Shortly after it initially began its "war" with ISIS in November, Anonymous claimed to help get 5,500 ISIS Twitter accounts taken down, which supposedly jumped to 20,000 by mid-February through its operation "#OpParis."[31] The hacktivist group claims to have foiled an attack in Italy because of its efforts, all a part of its "Operation Isis" campaign.[32]

ISIS Responds to Anonymous

Though ISIS fanboys often pay attention to their opposition, they don't always take the time to respond. However, in a post on November 17, 2015, on a pro-ISIS Telegram channel came a taunt aimed at the virtual nature of the group. "What are they gonna hack?"

The Brussels Attack

ISIS attacked the Brussels Airport in Zaventem and the Maalbeek metro station, killing 32 people and injuring more than 300. Following the attacks on March 22, 2016, Anonymous released a video threatening ISIS again.

"We have laid siege to your propaganda websites, tested them with our cyber attacks, however we will not rest as long as terrorists continue their actions around the world," a masked spokesman said in the video."We will strike back against them. We will keep hacking their websites, shutting down their Twitter accounts and stealing their Bitcoins. We defend the rights of freedom and tolerance."[33]

The Orlando Response

Omar Mateen struck Pulse, a gay night club in Orlando, Florida, on June 12, 2016, killing 49 and injuring 53 others. The event stunned the nation. Following the Orlando shooting, Anonymous hacked pro-ISIS Twitter accounts and flooded them with Gay Pride messages, photos, and banners.[34] The hacker operating under the name "WauchulaGhost" breached several accounts and repurposed the look of their graphics to a rainbow décor and phrases like, "I'm Gay and I'm Proud!"[35]

Effectiveness

Anonymous has its detractors in the counterterrorism game. There are many analysts who have criticized the group for its lack of discernment regarding accounts attributed to ISIS. This results in accounts being falsely flagged for being Islamic in nature and tone but not associated with ISIS. Twitter issued a confirmation that it took down accounts accused of being ISIS that turned out not be ISIS-related.[36]

Ghost Security Group (GSG)

One group that sprung from the Anonymous versus ISIS battle was formed by a hacker named Mikro and directed by another named DigitaShadow. After breaking away from Anonymous in May 2015,[37] Mikro launched two groups to combat ISIS, the Ghost Security Group (GSG) and CtrlSec. Ghost Security Group started with an intentionally different angle from Anonymous that included cooperating with law enforcement and private security firms and being willing to get paid for the work.

GSG describes itself as a "counterterrorism organization" focused on terrorism only, whereas Anonymous was known for shifting focus when an outrage calls. One minute Anonymous may be focused on Charlie Hebdo, and the next it was aimed at Ferguson, Missouri. GSG claims its focus was consistently aimed at ISIS and related groups.

The group doesn't reveal its methods or logistical arrangements as an organization. Gizmodo stated that GSG claimed 16 members in the United States, Europe, the Middle East, and Asia.[38] They also noted that DigitaShadow had come into the crosshairs of law enforcement because of participating in DDoS (Distributed Denial of Service) attacks related to Ferguson, Missouri, protests.[39]

In July 2015, GSG made the claim that it had intercepted information while doing network analysis on Dark Web sites that uncovered a plot to attack a Tunisian market. This would have been a follow-up attack to the June 2016 beach attack in Tunisia. The group cooperated with a private security firm known as Kronos Advisory to then send the information to the FBI. The outcome was not revealed.

There was another group affiliated with Anonymous called "Ghost Security" that has become a rival group due to the criticism of GSG's cooperation with government law enforcement agencies and private security firms like Kronos Advisory. In late November 2015, the GhostSec hacktivists attacked the Isdarat site on the Dark Web used to host videos and gave it a Prozac rebranding.[40]

The Atlantic Profiles GSG Founder Mikro on ISIS

One hacktivist, named Mikro, who was a member of Ghost Security Group, was profiled in an article by the *Atlantic* magazine. Mikro was supposedly an "operations officer" for GhostSec, a group whose mission was to target "Islamic extremist content" from "websites, blogs, videos, and social media accounts," using both "official channels" and "digital weapons."[41] So far, the group claims to have overwhelmed servers in more than 130 ISIS-linked websites in coordinated attacks.[42]

Formation of CtrlSec

Mikro later formed a second group, this time not affiliated with Anonymous. The new group was dubbed CtrlSec. While similar to GhostSec, CtrlSec accepts financial support and has a defined structure and hierarchy, unlike Anonymous. Its goal was to shut down pro-ISIS Twitter accounts. On a near-hourly level, the four Twitter accounts associated with CtrlSec (@CtrlSec, @CtrlSec0, @CtrlSec1, @CtrlSec2) publish links of Twitter accounts targeted for takedowns. Mikro claims to have shut down tens of thousands of accounts with the group.[43]

Figure 91: Jester Logo. (Source: Jester)

The Jester (th3j35t3r)—The Cyber Vigilante

Before there was #OpISIS, there was 'th3j35t3r' and his efforts to destroy jihadist web sites and materials found on the Internet. Described sometimes as a "patriot hacker," Jester has used his skills to confront not only ISIS, but Anonymous, as well. He claims to be a "former military man" and often speaks in military jargon. His fight with targets like Anonymous, Wikileaks, Westboro Baptist Church, and jihadists all intersect at an interest in looking out for the welfare of members of the military. Hitting the Twitter scene in late 2009, Jester has been documenting his fight against online extremists for years and across several platforms including iAWACS (online surveillance), Xerxes (DDoS program), and other homebrewed web tools.[44]

Jester reportedly got into hacktivism in reaction to Wikileaks releases. He claims he was concerned that files exposed by the organization would endanger our troops. Because Anonymous was very much aligned with Wikileaks, the fight expanded to them, too. He's shown strong animus against Anonymous, their rival group Lulzsec, and Wikileaks.

He then moved on to Islamic terrorists.[45] His first claim to fame was taking out a Taliban site, alemarah.info. On January 1, 2010, he Tweeted, "www.alemarah.info is now under sporadic cyber attack. This 'Voice of Jihad' served only to act as a tool for terrorist. OWNED. By me, Jester," after he hit the site with a DDoS attack by his customer customized DDoS tool codenamed XerXes.

JESTER ⚙ ACTUAL³³⁰¹
@th3j35t3r   ⚙ Following

www.alemarah.info is now under sporadic cyber-attack. This 'Voice of Jihad' served only to act as tool for terrorist. OWNED. By me, Jester.

RETWEETS	LIKES
10	17

3:26 PM - 1 Jan 2010

↰   ⇄ 10   ♥ 17   •••

Figure 92: Jester Tweet 1-alemarah.info. (Source: Twitter)

He proceeded for years to take down site after site, each time punctuated with his trademark tag Tango Down. A check of his Twitter time over the years shows a long list of take-downs starting with the January 2010 toppling of the Taliban site. He says he stopped keeping up with how many sites he's taken down after he topped 179.[46]

Figure 93: Jester Tweet 2-cupcake specials. (Source: Twitter)

"Approximately five years ago I realized that there was a growing threat from jihadis online using the Internet to recruit, radicalize, and even train homegrowners," The Jester told NBC Chicago. "I decided to research their favorite haunts, collect intelligence on the users and admins and in many cases remove them by force. I tended to hit some sites a lot and leave others. This had the effect of herding/funneling them into a smaller space. And smaller spaces are easier to watch and monitor."[47]

One of his next operations was to use a Libyan newspaper to spread disinformation. His psychological operations campaign began just before the toppling of Muammar Gaddafi in 2011. He appeared to have fabricated articles in the online feed of the *Tripoli Post* in March 2011 in order to affect troop movements in the region. His method was determined to be the use of a code injection in the link he provided via a bit.ly url, which included an additional link to offsite content that was aimed to suggest that Gaddafi's army was abandoning him.

He has successfully eluded being outed despite a range of opponents, including Anonymous and many nation states, who clearly would love to do so. His websites and social media accounts have been suspended several times over suspected hacks including having his domain name, jesterscourt.cc, seized by the US federal government.[48]

"[T]he bad guys want to slice my head off on YouTube with a rusty blade, and the good guys want to lock me up in an orange jumpsuit . . . along with the bad guys."[49]

Jester's criticisms of Anonymous have been well publicized in the hacker-oriented news blogs. He has stated the amorphous group lacks a check on their efforts to confront ISIS, that they aren't serious, and that they are largely ineffective.

"All they'll do is dump a random list of names from a previous hack and claim it's ISIS members, and they'll report 'ISIS' accounts to Twitter. Pretty standard BS from them," he told Paul Szoldra from *Tech Insider* in Nov 2015.[50]

Compared to the Anonymous hackers who focus on ISIS, The Jester sees himself as more of a patriot, looking to protect US citizens from those he deems a threat.[51] In an article on his official website, in July 2015, he criticized the US government's efforts:

I didn't go out of my way to broadcast my approach except in a select few places. It was quite simple. I made it my mission to "constantly disrupt and/or disable their self-managed offshore servers, to sow distrust among the users and total frustration among the site administrators . . . strive to make it too much of a pain in their puckered asses to bother using their own resources . . . thereby forcing them off those boxes and 'herding' or 'funneling' them into a smaller space. Because smaller spaces are easier to watch and monitor." The whole effort was well-documented and relatively successful, in at least 179 cases (via CNN) and independently confirmed here (by NBC).[52]

In the end, Jester's view is simple: "You can ask an ISP nicely to perform a takedown, but mostly they don't, that's where I seem to fit in."[53]

Interesting bit: When Jester decided to attack the controversial Westboro Baptist Church's website over their protests at soldiers' funerals, he did so with a 3G phone.

Avoiding Spy on Spy

The rush to take down ISIS materials has raised an issue on account-ability related to who should decide what is taken down and how will that be decided and how do take downs affect others. On the real battlefields, coordination between allied forces is paramount to mission success and vital to the safety of friendly forces. In the cyber world, the same rules apply and may even have life-and-death con-sequences. The stakes are high when undercover operations lurk behind the channels of Twitter and Facebook or on websites, forums, or hidden channels. The court records alone indicate exten-sive contact between federal agents or informants and terrorists or soon-to-be terrorists. Therefore, the takedowns of jihadist materials run the risk of blinding or harming those operations.

In 2008, a website used by the CIA and the Saudi Government to conduct intelligence on extremists in Iraq and the Middle-East region was taken down.[54] The site became the focal point of an intense debate in Washington, as policy makers tried to defend the validity of the concerns. On one hand, the CIA was looking to lure terrorists to the website so they could corral and gather intelligence on their activities. On the other, the US military and others argued that the content posted would lead to further threats against US troops, especially in Iraq. In the end, the US military won out, and the site was targeted, just as US Central Command wanted. The group tasked with the assignment was called the Countering Adversary Use of the Internet program under the Fort Meade-based Joint Functional Component Command-Network Warfare.

Another example concerns the use of the web to archive jihad-ist materials. Researchers gather ISIS material so it can be reported to appropriate authorities and analyzed for intelligence value, but non-Arab speakers may not realize the purpose of the site and flag it for removal. A blogger at InfoSecIsland.com published a review of Jester's take-down effort and noted that he had taken down a research site hosted by the blogger. The blogger stated that a little bit of examination might have led a reasonable person to realize that the site owner was a critic of ISIS, not a supporter.[55]

The FBI is known to have used the Internet to lure suspects to click on terrorism cases like Michigan resident Khalil Abu Rayyan.[56] Therefore, it is reasonable to conclude that if the average citizen issues a take-down on a Twitter, Facebook, or other type of profile without knowing what activity is occurring behind that channel, then they may disrupt an ongoing investigation into a terrorism case.

One solution to this problem would be to continue to ensure public participation while having the tech companies who are stuck in the middle turn over the complaints to law enforcement and leave the judgment of terrorist determination to law enforcement. This could provide accountability for operations and places the greater burden of consequences on law enforcement to handle criminal behavior instead of the companies in the middle. A fast track system to the federal government from the social media, hosting, ISP, and other responsible parties who fall between the users of the Internet and terrorists would help facilitate the notification. Those records could be checked against undercover operations and work to prevent disruption of investigations.

Chapter 13

Tracking ISIS in Cyberspace

LOCATING THEIR PHYSICAL MEDIA CENTERS

ISIS media offices are scattered around the terrain they physically control, but this doesn't mean any one of them has to operate in any physically restricted manner. The footage that was released by ISIS media offices still has their local report messages, which indicates that it still takes local teams to film, gather, and disseminate footage. The footage out of Syria was still focused on Assad and the *kufar*, whereas the footage out of Iraq was focused on Shia militias, Kurdish leaders, and, of course, the *kufar*. The same was true of releases from abroad; the tone remains local even if unified. This indicates there are still nodal centers that can be targeted for lethal force or infiltration.

US-driven coalition forces conducted raids on media centers across Iraq several times over the period of occupation. In the past years of fighting ISIS, the coalition forces have targeted media leaders like the Minister of Information (Propaganda) and the Spokesman. From Abu Maysara al-Iraqi to Abu Muhammad al-Adnani, the coalition forces have targeted the spokesman. From Muharib Abdul Latif al-Jubouri to Wa'el Adel Hasan Salman al-Fayed, the

Minister of Information has been targeted right alongside the spokesman. With an evolving battlefield, cyber targets like Junaid Hussaid and Mohammed Emwazi, most commonly known as "Jihadi John," became key targets not unlike the targets on the fields of Syria, Iraq, or Libya.

Figure 94: Locals watch a video presented on one of the many media spots set up by ISIS. (Source: TAPSTRI)

Observing Media Hot Spots

Though it doesn't technically fall into the context of "cyber" or "online" activity, it is worth nothing that ISIS uses "media spots" to aim propaganda at its own people. At these kiosks, stands, or conveniently established centers, ISIS displays its latest videos, audio clips, and editions of *an-Naba* or other publications. There are numerous photo stories and video clips that feature ISIS media spots. ISIS relishes telling the world that its children and youth are taking in this propaganda. They watch with fascination the acts of horror committed by the terrorist regime. These kiosk stands act as nodes for observing, tracking, and identifying media, cyber, and communication centers. This may have been the technique that led the French Air Force to track and destroy a major ISIS production facility in Mosul.

DISCOVERING NETWORKS

Key to finding what ISIS was doing was discovering where they were, and, more important, which areas could be productive in the effort to stop their physical attacks. Finding their areas of communication was an ever-evolving task, but you can increase your chances by tuning into what ISIS was telling its followers about preferred technology, including channels, methods, and tools. If you map out the various ways they currently discuss their use of communication tools, you'll find they are using a fairly easy-to-use set of apps and forum tools that aren't as cryptic as much as the news echo chamber makes them out to be. The average ISIS follower is not ultimately that technologically advanced. But this doesn't mean they can't be trained to do harm.

What methods can be used to determine ISIS activity online?

Human Intelligence (HumINT)

The most reliable method for finding where important ISIS websites and forums exists comes from the members themselves. This happens in Telegram every day. Members of one channel will publish links to other Telegram channels that belong to Amaq, Nashir, or perhaps Online Da'wah Campaign. ISIS Twitter users engage in extensive linking to ISIS material on a regular basis. Without asking a single member where the party was, you can easily hear the sound of *nasheeds* on the net so it can be found.

Another method is to observe the comments found on social media posts where followers drop hashtags and other momentary indicators of their campaigns or concerns. Using this information, you can expand your search to find forums and other social media outlets where supporters are congregating, posting, or sharing.

Media Comparison Tools

The digital thumbprint of media files can help investigators and analysts find additional postings. Even without sophisticated data mining tools, by taking a single ISIS video banner and uploading it to Google's image tools, you'll discover other locations where the photo may exist. This can be used with Twitter avatars or other types of photos to expand the search for locations used in the Surface Web that are being used by ISIS or other groups.

End User Data Seizures

A sure way to be able to examine how ISIS uses the Internet is to examine in detail all of the gadgets and social media tools used by ISIS followers. The communication apps, the choice of gear, the sophistication of the operative all help identify the Internet regions of operations.

Data Mining and Traffic Analysis

Traffic Analysis around keywords or media—The big picture on traffic over files or text can give investigators strong insight on the activities, perceived abilities, and numbers of supporters.

In 2016, Twitter banned US government intel agencies from using Dataminr to mine accounts in search for terrorists.[1] Dataminr services are available to a wide range of corporate customers ranging from news services to financial services firms that can track real-time metadata. One skirmish in the conflict that caught the attention of the news media was when Twitter was taken to task for allowing RT, which was Russian state-run news, to use Dataminr for its services and denying the same tools to the CIA.[2]

Other notable programs available to conduct data collection and analysis include Geofedia, another tool that collects data that can be used to track real-time events based on Instagram, Twitter, Facebook, PATHAR Dunami[3] social media analytics SocioSpyder,[4] and TransVoyant "Live Predictive Intelligence."[5]

DEFENDING AGAINST THE CYBER CALIPHATE ARMY OR OTHER CYBER THREATS

It is without a doubt important to stress the key to security in your IT systems—keep your server's security systems, operating systems, apps, plugins, or any components used on gadgets, computers and websites up-to-date. The very reason updates exist is to patch vulnerabilities in programs or systems. Failing to update these components or systems for any reason leaves the system vulnerable to breaches or attacks. Servers should be stress-tested and put through various penetration tests by professional "white hat" teams to expose vulnerabilities before you are vulnerable to threats from hackers in CCA, other groups, or even common malware.

Content Management Systems

If you use Content Management System (CMS) sites like Wordpress, Joomla, or Drupal, make sure the site's components are up-to-date. Patches for both the CMS core parts and available plugins can be automated in some cases. These systems are prime targets for the hackers of ISIS, according to many of the releases featuring account login information. Content Management Systems are easier targets because of the ubiquitous nature of their core operating parts. Hackers can save time by mastering the vulnerabilities of a narrow but very common system. Websites that display login locations in public view are especially vulnerable.

Plugin Updates

Parts in systems like Wordpress or Joomla always place the admin systems in the same locations. If a hacker can begin to identify those locations by simply typing the same login they would be given if using the same system, then the vulnerability of access begins at the front door. Some systems allow for an alteration of where that login exists. In other cases, plugins are available for several systems that allow customization of the admin logins. Also make sure that usernames are not published on websites; use real names instead. Protecting usernames is half the battle. Hackers can often tell the usernames by reading posts and checking metadata. Make sure websites and other areas where user IDs can be seen are checked and obscured or removed.

Reinforce Technical Training

Make sure the IT staff's technical knowledge of the systems and their potential vulnerabilities is up-to-date. For individuals, remember that computers are very powerful tools that can do more than Solitaire and Paintbrush. Computers running outdated systems are a gold mine for hackers; the system is like a big hunk of Swiss cheese, and hackers will see all the holes. Make sure unattended, seldom-used computers are up-to-date when accessing the Internet.

Be Alert for Social Engineering

Because many hackers are aware that good social engineering on a target may lead to better results, it is good to make sure that companies, employees, educational facilities, staff, students, government officials, military, and financial institutions are well educated about methods for social engineering and how hackers use that information to gain entry to systems.

Password Management

Regularly change passwords and make sure they are complicated. There are many online locations that can help generate high-quality passwords of any string length to meet the highest standards. Many people tend to rely upon memory for passwords out of convenience. This is well understood by hackers who often follow the "Keep It Simple" approach to a breach; "password123" is not a suitable password if the intention is to keep a system secure. Whereas, "W[{1U] L&A?D;#9%K+E" will keep them busy and setting off cyber alarms while they're trying to break in by password guessing.

Avoid Being Phished

Spearphishing is a method used to trick a specific target of a cyber attack into assisting in the attack by clicking on an email that was either laden with malware attachments or has links to malware attachments. The key to the spearphishing campaign is social engineering. Understanding the target allows the attacker to customize details that further lower the guard of the intended target. Getting an email address from a colleague in a small firm or friend-to-friend may not be that difficult, but getting emails on the large-scale institution often only requires looking at the company website.

To avoid being targeted in this manner, make sure never to download attachments that you aren't expecting and verify ahead of time that someone is sending you files you should expect, including and especially formats. Example: "I will be sending you a pdf when we're off the phone" along with the email is a good basic method to avoid confusion over attachments from a friendly source. Additionally, organizations, government agencies, and private enterprise should advise staff about the latest cyber threats that may affect their use of computers. They should also help install quality protocols that prevent anyone unknown to the system from entering it by blending with masses of employees.

Good IT security is only as good as that one employee who didn't know it wasn't "Pete in the computer department here, sorry, we're updating the systems here and I need you to update your password for me. I've sent you an email so we can do this quickly, I'm sure you're busy." The subject looks at the email, and it appears to be legitimate until they click the link and find out eventually the hard way they were the target of a spearphishing campaign. Therefore, it is important that verifications are in place to make sure that breaches do not occur.

ON THE OFFENSE—KILLING THE NARRATIVES

Harry Sarfo, a German fighter who traveled to Syria and wound up in an ISIS video from Wilayah Hims, says he lost faith in the ISIS cause while the group carried out executions in Palmyra.[6] According to an interview with Rukmini Callimachi, once Sarfo realized that the videos were not spontaneous actualities but were in fact arranged with multiple takes and lots of preparation, he realized he'd been had. He says that he was asked to kill one of the captives and that man stated he was a Sunni imam. As a result, he ran for his life back to Germany to face the court.

Capture Raw Footage from ISIS

When caught with raw video footage, many ISIS fighters look like Keystone Cops. In one video obtained by Peshmerga, you can see the ISIS fighters argue over how to fire an rpg, flying gun rounds, and then get taken out by Peshmerga fire. When displayed on unedited video, ISIS doesn't look as heroic as it does in its polished and highly scripted videos and slide shows.

"Thumb Drives Secured!"

Seizure of data in Sensitive Site Exploitation operations, also known as "Shoving everything we capture into a bag," have yielded massive troves of information about ISIS. In 2007, an ISI safe house raid in Sinjar yielded data on fighter networks. The previously described May 16, 2016, Delta Force operation on Abu Sayyaf captured computers, devices, and data from the raid in eastern Syria. The resulting information haul led to more ISIS leaders being located and targeted for airstrikes.[7] Jump drives seized in raids near Manbij have helped unlock more of the keys to the caliphate.[8]

Operation Gallant Phoenix

When a goldmine of information was secured after the fall of ISIS in the northern Syria town of Manbij, the data found its way to the intelligence coordination center in Jordan run by the Pentagon.[9] The reports of the haul indicate that over 10,000 documents and 4.5 terabytes of information on the individuals and operations of the terror group was successfully retrieved after the SDF (Syrian Democratic Forces) and the Kurdish YBS (Sinjar Resistance Units) and YJE (Yazidi Women's Units) militias drove them from the town.

Catalog All Gear Used by ISIS

Every time there was an event tracked at TAPSTRI, we kept records of technical equipment seen in media or identified to us by law enforcement that was used by attackers and accomplices to keep track of the end result of what was used vs. what was available or suggested. Laptops, hard drives, jump drives, flash-media cards, cameras, email accounts, martyrdom video files, and software used to communicate are all vital assets to assess how ISIS was and is communicating with and advising their attackers and support teams. It helps also to compare these end-user tools to advice given to followers in security channels and try to determine whether or not the end user in an attack followed suggested OpSec or deviated. If they deviated, was it intentional, and if so, why?

Counter-Hacking: Use of Malware and Other Asymmetric Operations

The FBI and DEA have used various programs for cover surveillance on targets. It is a method not without its critics. Yet these tactics are available and have been used against ISIS targets by the terror group. ISIS uses these techniques against their enemies, as they did with Abu Majad, a vocal critic of ISIS from Syria. They tried to spear-phish him with an email seeking to steal his login credentials.

Used in reverse, the technique has possibilities for surveillance on the gear used by ISIS to track their whereabouts, capture their keystrokes, observer their contact lists, and even wipe the gear's memory on the way out. The available tool kit against ISIS should have a wide selection of tools for surveillance and data collection targeted at known ISIS members. Applicable laws related to warrants and probable cause could still apply in the US.

Additional intrusions could involve website infiltration and data extraction to gain information on site users. Seizures of forum databases can yield a trove of information on users, admin ranks, and other metadata found in the site logs.

Honey Traps

Entrapping a target into recruiting after luring them with the promise of a relationship with a young woman. Young men from around the world are falling for this method of luring them to Syria.

Areeb Majeed, a young Muslim man from Kalyan, India, fell for a honey trap on Facebook under the name of Tahira Bhatt, a.k.a. "umm-al-homsi," or "umm bakiya-al-hamsi."[10] Majeed was set up via a social networking site. To back up the fiction, a real person with another account under the name "Jaanbaaz Omar" was used to convince Majeed that Bhatt was real and "Jaanbaaz Omar" was her brother.[11] Women in India were told that they would be needed for honey traps. When it came to Majeed, he believed he'd have a wife when he got to Syria to fight and instead found himself unable to participate in battles, delivering water to fighters and cleaning up behind them. His dream of love shattered, he returned to India to face charges.[12]

Use of Infiltration and Informants

Twenty-one-year-old Khalil Abu-Rayyan wanted to get married, and to do so he was willing to brag to a woman online that he fantasized about attacking churches. Unfortunately for Rayyan, the confession was to Jannah Bride, who turned out to be an FBI informant. Use of informants is one of the leading methods for catching suspected terrorists and discovering the networks behind their usernames, although cases involving informants and undercover law enforcement are sometimes met with the accusation that the operation was an entrapment (as in leading someone to say they will do something they really aren't prepared to do). Coaxing a suspect to admit he or she is prepared to commit a violent action uses personal rapport building, still perhaps the best method to find out what a potential terrorist will do.

TROLLING

Anonymous and others have taken to creating parody accounts and seeking to disrupt real accounts in a manner that may have made

Abbie Hoffman proud but begs the question—how effective was it when applied to the big picture? While some members of the #OpI-SIS advocates may enjoy getting the laughs on the time of the ISIS fanboys, some researchers like J.M. Berger suggest this only fuels the other party's antagonism or at the least was not very helpful. According to Berger, "there is a lot of evidence that trolling and antagonistic communications are counterproductive."

Chapter 14

The Ghost Caliphate

In 2007, the Idaho National Laboratory ran an experiment to demonstrate how a cyber attack could destroy the physical devices connected to the national electrical grid by inserting malicious code into a power management computer. In what is known as the Aurora Generator Test, White Hat hackers developed the code that sent a 2.25 megawatt diesel generator out of control; it was destroyed when it exploded within three minutes. The video, which can be found on the Internet, is dramatic, but had this generator been attached to an actual power grid, the effect would have been traumatic.

The cyberwarfare developments of the early twenty-first century were not lost on the Russian intelligence agencies, the FSB and GRU. They captured a set of malware known as BlackEnergy1, created by a private Russian hacker, that was designed to stop web traffic through Distributed Denial of Service (DDoS) attacks. The FSB upgraded this malware into a version called BlackEnergy2. In 2008, they launched it and carried out a DDoS attack that took down the entire Internet system of the nation of Georgia during a military operation by Russian forces. Another variant of the malware, BlackEnergy3, also called Sandstorm, successfully disrupted physical energy infrastructure through the introduction of malicious code. It knocked out three Ukrainian power plants simultaneously, removing power to 80,000 customers.

In 2012, Saudi Arabia's oil company Aramco was hacked by suspected Iranian intelligence agencies in what is considered to be the single largest hack in history. Some 35,000 computers connected to Aramco's Intranet went off-line in one fell swoop. A shadowy group named "Cutting Sword of Justice" claimed responsibility and installed on each computer the image of a burning American flag.[1]

The attack was technically a Fire Sale, the virtual destruction of all aspects of Aramco's internal communications Internet email and removing their ability to process 10 percent of the world's oil sales. The method of malware infection was through a spearfishing virus email sent to an Aramco employee who clicked the link that unleashed the malware.

Between 2012 and 2013, seven hackers connected with the Iranian Revolutionary Guard Corps (IRGC) conducted increasingly disruptive DDoS attacks on the New York-based heart of the US financial industry before they were stopped, but not before the FBI discovered that they attempted to hack and hijack the controls of the Rye Brook dam sluice gate in Westchester County. Local authorities believe that the hacking may have been a test run for attacking the far larger Bowman dam on Crooked River, Oregon. Had either dam been commanded to release its water, there would have been an environmental disaster on an enormous scale.

THE CYBER CORSAIRS

The power of real hacking capability shows the potential of a group, even one with rudimentary capability, to learn lessons and grow. Despite the fact that none of the ISIS hackers or their malware have risen to the level of being an Advanced Persistent Threat (APT), that day will come. ISIS and its E-Mujahideen may be amateur, but with just a bit of technical skill and the ambition to become hacker famous, they could become as notorious as the 9/11 hijackers.

At this point, however, ISIS and other jihadist group are capable of causing a nuisance in comparison to the capability of real advanced threat groups like the FSB and IRGC. They aren't yet capable of hacking industrial infrastructure or doing more than the distribution of propaganda and the dissemination of their dark media.

Yet new hacker technology emerges every day. In August 2016, an NSA subcontractor, Equation Group, was hacked by suspected Russian intelligence hackers who stole terrifying hacker tool kits with names like Epicbanana, Egregiousblunder, and Buzzdirection. These tools could bore through security Firewalls, seize controls of computers, and watch and capture the keystrokes of security officers. They were stolen from the most elite hackers in the world by a group calling itself "Shadow Brokers." It was selling these tools for $500 million in bitcoins. Should any tool kits like these fall into the hands of one or a collective of ISIS supporters, then the attacks on the West would be devastating.

By devolving back into an underground and web-based terror organization, ISIS will be communicating more directly with ambitious young people who have deep cyber knowledge and may acquire exceptional hacking skills.

If there is anything that has been learned about ISIS, it is that it is committed to waging asymmetric warfare, using electronic and propaganda judo to confound their opponents. The future E-Jihadists will do the same. They will form very small groups and adopt the tactics of the Arab pirates of old—a legion of Cyber Corsairs. Like the original corsairs, their platforms, computers, and mobile phones will be used for everyday tasks till they sight a target of opportunity. They will then band together swiftly and harness the fastest, simplest technology to hack with whatever tools they can muster until the older, slower objective is raided, looted, and left a hulk. It worked for centuries off the coast of

Arabia, and it can work again in the cyber coast between the Deep Web and the Surface Web. The Internet is a sea of Islands and makes every wired-in device a treasure ship to be raided. We won't know if they have this capability until the start to strike.

A nascent group of Cyber Corsairs may already be working with a collective. These ISIS hackers, the fanboys and young wannabees, are derided as "script kiddies" because they cannot write really malicious code but use programs from other hackers. They may seem harmless today, but if they get their hands on tools such as those stolen from NSA, they will lack only direction and leadership. The global cyber security world must prepare for higher-quality weaponized tool kits in the hands of the seemingly least capable hacker who has big dreams. Imagineering is the single greatest vulnerability we have in anti-terrorism and cyber security. If Russia or China decided to empower some of their young corsairs with real tools, or if they themselves somehow acquire the capability, they could move from being minor players into a renowned and feared global hacker force that could shut down power plants, disrupt airplane flight controls and destroy oilfield industries.

The strength of ISIS is it has have created a structure of communications, coordination that operates out of the view of the news media and most IT researchers operating on the Surface Web. ISIS cyber capability has always been sounder in the development of its Deep Web IT infrastructure, because it created a secure network of contact points that has allowed it to communicate and disseminate propaganda and establish long-term covert communications pathways between their operatives world-wide. This infrastructure may be the salvation of what remains of the protostate itself.

Make no mistake: ISIS is presently on a path to its ultimate physical destruction. It will lose its capital Raqqa and its suicidal combat forces deployed in several nations besides Syria and Iraq. They will all be destroyed. The caliphate's physical treasury will be looted, and its global financial capital will be stolen by its members or seized by coalition forces. ISIS will be left bereft of its earthly fortune—except for one cash cow that has heretofore remained undetected. Advertising fraud.

THE ISIS ADWARE FRAUD NETWORK

In 2014, an American cyber defense firm discovered, while conducting banking fraud tracking, that for the last three years ISIS has been collecting as much as $100 million through the establishment of a constellation of advertising fraud networks and websites. This network was established by ISIS's supporters in the Gulf States operating within legal web distribution companies in Dubai, Saudi Arabia, and other Arab states. These, along with other ISIS Deep Web operations, were established by former Jordanian, Palestinian, and Russian criminal cyber operatives who set up the same advertising fraud networks across Asia and the Middle East.

Adfraud works by conducting typo-squatting, also called Water Holes—false websites with a only a spelling mistake to distinguish them from the sites they are impersonating. It looks and acts like the original. For example, Quran.com is legitimate but slips up on the spelling—Qiran.com—and it leads you to an identical site that is actually owned by the typo-squatter hacker. This false site can collect credit card information, be a portal for malware, or is just filled with links and pop-up boxes that pay the typo-squatter every time you click on a link or close a pop-up box. Typo-squatting relies on a person to make a mistake when putting in a legitimate URL that takes them to a fraudulent website that is populated with legitimate web advertising links. Once an innocent victim goes to this website via any of the links that they click (or that is clicked for them), the visited site will legally pay a small amount of money to the typo-squatter—from as low as a penny to as high as $25 per click, depending on the site visited. All of the money goes into the bank accounts of ISIS.

The ISIS AdFraud servers also harbor a constellation of self-regenerating advertisement bots that spray out new links onto other legitimate websites. As they are clicked, or closed, they generate revenue. Closing the bots requires one to visit the links, so even experienced cyber attackers or researchers with good intentions manage to directly contribute to the ISIS coffers.

The websites and links of ISIS are arrayed in such a way that legitimate searchers of news and information will misdirect researchers to ISIS Adfraud sites—where they will find links to the legitimate news sites. Again, once any of those links are clicked or closed, ISIS gets paid. However, also embedded within the sites may be links to ISIS terrorism video media, propaganda, and secret pathways to web forms and secure communication portals. In fact, many researchers, intelligence officials, members of the news media, and just the curious who go to many of the web storage sites that have ISIS media embedded are in fact paying the organization for every click they make within these sites. The more people track these Surface Web sites, the more ISIS gets paid. The visitor is materially contributing to the financial future of a terrorist group.

When the caliphate falls the question will be what form the disparate followers of this group will take. Anyone who survives can probably leave the battlefronts of Libya, Syria, Iraq, Yemen, and Afghanistan in an attempt to return home. For a while, they may be out of touch with their Jihadi brothers at home. Those who successfully return to their homeland, particularly Europe and the United States, will have to face a level of scrutiny from national and international intelligence agencies never seen before. But this doesn't matter if they can still inspire, coordinate, and finance operations though the Deep Web. ISIS will live on, and the role of the cyber Jihadis will become the face of the average member.

That said, the ISIS Deep Web communications structure will have to survive, at least initially, on cash rolling in from Internet advertising fraud networks.

The Future of ISIS after ISIS

The future of ISIS is that it will reform in the shape of a Ghost Caliphate.

On its face, the destruction of ISIS will be a historic achievement, but the by-product will be a less centralized terror group that will rely much more on inspiring terror attacks rather than planning them and deploying cells. For the next decade or more, ISIS-inspired terrorists such as the husband and wife suicide team in San Bernardino, the truck driving murderer in Nice, and the mass murder at the gay night club in Orlando, Florida, will become the norm. These types of attackers, who dream up a plan and then execute it without saying a word or leaving a deep digital footprint, are extremely difficult to detect. Once an inspired attacker finds the right target and acquires a weapon, be it a bomb or a tractor trailer, they can kill with impunity and claim ISIS loyalty after the fact. This is future model of ISIS's global disruption campaign. Conversely, ISIS-directed attacks from a central Cyber Caliphate will decrease or disappear as the bases of operations are physically destroyed; the Ghost Caliphate will take its place and remain devoted to terrorism—by proxy.

The Ghost Caliphate will be broader, more covert, surreptitious, and much harder to detect. ISIS will essentially devolve back into the original model al-Qaeda used between 1988 and present day—it will become a covert terror organization that is 100 percent underground—leaving evidence of its activities only after the fact.

To establish the Ghost Caliphate, some of the surviving leadership of ISIS must find a safe haven to have any chance of reconstituting the terror network. Their best chance is to find a small remote area in Yemen, the central Sahara, or a hidden corner of Somalia. There, they can attempt to reestablish communications pathways using satellite Internet or regional mobile phone technology and basic operational security in an effort to connect with other surviving members. Only then can they reestablish a central command that will give the current cyber warriors the support and direction they need. Without some form of leadership, the Ghost Caliphate will be equivalent to trolls on comments sections of digital editions of newspapers.

The Ghost Caliphate will not direct individuals on precisely what to do but will become a completely inspirational organization that will call upon its attackers to join, secretly swear allegiance, and attack wherever, whenever, however. The future battle strategy of the failed Islamic state will essentially abandon all attempts to seize land like they did in Iraq, Syria, Libya, and Egypt.

With this strategy, there will also be an increase in attacks claimed by or attributed to ISIS even when there is no evidence that ISIS was ever in communication with or inspired those who carried out the attack. That would be expected as they break up and dissolve from a solid into a gaseous state of ideology.

The ghost hackers will use advanced tools rather than Kalashnikovs, propaganda in place of bombs, and, like the 9/11 hijackers, they will someday be poised to conduct an asymmetric war at the place, time, and with the methodology of their choosing.

Appendix A

ISIS Magazine Issues

ISIS Magazine Releases

Al-Hayat-Islamic State News
Edition #1—May 31, 2014
Edition #2—June 5, 2014
Edition #3—June 10, 2014

Al-Hayat-Islamic State Report
Edition #1—June 3, 2014: Propagating the Correct Manhaj
Edition #2—June 7, 2014: Giving Zakah
Edition #3—June 14, 2014
Edition #4—June 21, 2014

Al-Hayat-Dabiq
Edition #1—July 5, 2014: The Return of the Khilafah
Edition #2—July 27, 2014: The Flood
Edition #3—September 10, 2014: A Call to Hijrah
Edition #4—October 11, 2014: The Failed Crusade
Edition #5—November 21, 2014: Remaining and Expanding

Edition #6—December 29, 2014: Al-Qaeda of Waziristan: A Testimony from Within
Edition #7—February 12, 2015: From Hypocrisy to Apostasy: The Extinction of the Grayzone
Edition #8—March 30, 2015: Shariah Alone Will Rule Africa
Edition #9—May 21, 2015: They Plot and Allah Plots
Edition #10—July 13, 2015: The Law of Allah or the Laws of Men
Edition #11—September 9, 2016: From the Battles of Al-Ahzab to the War of Coalitions
Edition #12—November 18, 2016: Just Terror
Edition #13—January 19, 2016: The Rafidah
Edition #14—April 13, 2016: The Murtadd Brotherhood
Edition #15—July 31, 2016: Break The Cross

Istok— *ISIS's Russian-language magazine*
Edition #1—May 25, 2015
Edition #2—August 1, 2015
Edition #3—November 30, 2015
Edition #4—May 1, 2016

Dar al-Islam—ISIS's French-language magazine
Edition #1—December 22, 2014
Edition #2—February 11, 2015
Edition #3—March 31, 2015
Edition #4—June 1, 2015
Edition #5—July 21, 2015
Edition #6—September 27, 2015
Edition #7—November 30, 2015
Edition #8—February 6, 2016
Edition #9—April 26, 2016

Konstantiniyye—ISIS's Turkish-language magazine
Edition #1—May 26, 2015
Edition #2—August 1, 2015

Edition #3—November 30, 2016
Edition #4—May 1, 2016

An-Naba

An-Naba was a weekly newspaper released in PDF form online and printed for those living under the authority of the Islamic State. Printed entirely in Arabic, the target audience was very local. The publications are released often midweek and publication segments are often edited up to the last minute including examples where the publication mentioned news from only a day before release.

Rumiyah

Edition #1—August 31, 2016

A new magazine from ISIS was released with the headline, "The Death of Abu Muhamad Al-Adnani."

Appendix B

Al-Hayat Video Database

AL-HAYAT VIDEOS

Video #1. June 9, 2014 *There is no life without al-jihad*: British fighters describe why they left to go fight in Syria in this first video from al-Hayat.

Video #2. June 29, 2014 *End of Sykes-Picot*: Chilean foreign fighter Bastian Alexis Vasquez appeared in "End of Sykes-Picot."

Video #3. July 12, 2014 *al-Ghurabaa: The Chosen Few of Different Lands—Abu Muslim from Canada*: Canadian "Abu Muslim," a.k.a. Andrea Poulin, discusses his hijra and the glorious deaths of ISI fighters in Syria.

Video #4. July 16, 2014 *Those Who Were Truthful with Allah*.

Video #5. July 22, 2014 *Join the Ranks*: Abu Muhammad al-Indonesi pushes Muslims to act on hijra.

Video #6. August 2, 2014 *Eid Greetings*: Eid al-Fitr celebration with foreign fighters who have traveled to the Islamic State.

Video #7. September 16, 2014 *Flames of War* trailer.

Video #8. October 16, 2014 *We Are Also Waiting*: Abu Abdullah from Britain, Abdul Wadoud from France, Abu Dauoud from Germany.

Video #9. November 2, 2014: *A Message from Brother Abu Muhammad ar-Rousi.*

Video #10. November 19, 2014: *What Are You Waiting For*: French-language video that features Abu Osama al-Faranci and Abu Maryam al-Faranci, who demanded, "why haven't you made hijra, aren't you embarrassed yet? If you can't make hijra, kill *kufar* where you find them." *What Are You Waiting For*" also includes Abu Salman al-Faranci.

Video #11. November 21, 2014 *Race Towards The Good*: Kazakh-language film with Russian subtitles. Abdalluh, a child soldier, was asked what he wanted to do when he grows up: "I will be the one who slaughters you, O kuffar."

Video #12. November 28, 2014 *A Visit to al-Mosul*: An ISIS view on how Mosul was captured in 2014 and how the people enjoy Islamic justice under ISIS.

Video #13. January 4, 2015 *From Inside Mosul*: John Cantilie, a hostage, is forced to tour the city in the role of a supposedly ISIS-friendly "journalist."

Video #14. January 6, 2015 *A Message from Brother Abdullah al-Moldouvi.*

Video #15. January 13, 2015 *Uncovering an Enemy Within*: A terrorist hostage, Mamayev Jambulat Yesenjanovich, from Jambul, Kazakhstan, is accused of being a spy. He confesses on video to being a Russian intelligence (FSB) agent and sticking a USB stick into the laptop of an ISIS operative in Turkey. A second hostage, Ashimov Sergey Nikolayavich, was also accused of being an FSB agent. Video ends with a young Kazakh boy, previously identified in video #9 as Abdalluh, shooting both captives through the head.

Video #16. February 9, 2015 *From Inside Halab (Aleppo)*: John Cantilie, a hostage, is again forced to tour Aleppo in the role of a supposedly ISIS-friendly "journalist."

Video #17. February 15, 2015 *A Message Signed With Blood to the Nation of the Cross*: A long-format hostage video where twenty-one Egyptian Coptic Christians are executed by beheading on the Libya seafront (coast of *Wilayat Tarabulus*).

Video #18. March 7, 2015 *Story from the Land of Life*: Abu Suhayb al-Faransi.

Video #19. March 23, 2015 *A Message to the People of Kurdistan*: Short videos featuring deceased fighters (including Kattib, Abu Ishaq, Osama Bin Ladin, Abu Hammam) and ending with execution.

Video #20. April 21, 2015 *Stories from the Land of the Living*: Features Australian Neil Prakash, a.k.a. Abu Khaled al-Cambodi.

Video #21. June 4, 2015 *Honor is in Jihad*: Features a propaganda message to the people of the Balkans.

Video #22. August 29, 2015 *The Rise of al-Khilafa and Return of the Gold Dinar*.

Video #23. October 11, 2015 *The Dark Rise of Banknotes and the Turn of the Gold Dinar.*

Video #24. November 21, 2015 *Turkey and the Fire of Nationalism.*

Video #25. November 24, 2015 *No Respite*: Released in English, French, German, Russian, and Turkish.

Video #26. January 24, 2016 *Et Tuez-Les où que vous les rencontriez (French: Kill Them Where You Find Them)*: Features training segments with the terrorists responsible for the Paris attacks in November 2015.

Video #27. March 6, 2016 *Al Qauqaz: Aliment and Cure* (Russian with Arabic Subtitles).

Video #28. May 30, 2016 *The Religion of Kufr is One.*

Endnotes

Chapter 1:

1. Reuter, Christoph, "Secret Files Reveal the Structure of Islamic State," Der Spiegel Online, April 18, 2015. http://www.spiegel.de /international/world/islamic-state-files-show-structure-of-islamist -terror-group-a-1029274.html

2. Johnson, Patrick B, "Countering ISIL's Financing," November 13, 2014. http://www.rand.org/content/dam/rand/pubs/testimonies /CT400/CT419/RAND_CT419.pdf

3. Irujo, José María, "Network of 250 Spanish butchers and phone shops funding jihadists in Syria," El Pais, February 6, 2015, http://elpais .com/elpais/2015/02/02/inenglish/1422892172_955064.html

4. Moore, Jack, "Hawala: The Ancient Banking Practice Used to Finance Terror Groups," *Newsweek*, February 24, 2015, http:// www.newsweek.com/underground-european-hawala-network -financing-middle-eastern-terror-groups-307984?rx=us

5. U.S. Department of Defense, "Statement from Pentagon Press Secretary Peter Cook on Airstrike against ISISL Senior Leader," Defense. Gov, September 16, 2016, http://www.defense.gov/News/News -Releases/News-Release-View/Article/946983/statement-from -pentagon-press-secretary-peter-cook-on-airstrike-against-isil-se

Chapter 2:

1. McKinsey Global Institute, "Big data: The next frontier for innovation, competition, and productivity," http://www.mckinsey.com/~/

media/McKinsey/Business%20Functions/Business%20Technol
ogy/Our%20Insights/Big%20data%20The%20next%20fron
tier%20for%20innovation/MGI_big_data_full_report.ashx

2.   Arthur, Charles, "What's a zettabyte? By 2015, the internet will
      know, says Cisco," *Guardian*, June 2011, https://www.theguardian
      .com/technology/blog/2011/jun/29/zettabyte-data-internet-cisco
3.   O'Connor, Clare. "How To Use Bitcoin To Shop At Amazon, Home
      Depot, CVS, and More," *Forbes*, http://www.forbes.com/sites
      /clareoconnor/2014/02/17/how-to-use-bitcoin-to-shop-at-amazon
      -home-depot-cvs-and-more/#1f9ae9e86cd4, February 17, 2014
4.   US v Ali Shukri Amin, "Criminal Complaint," June 19, 2015
5.   Greenberg, Andy, "Feds seize Silk Road 2 in major Dark Web drug
      bust," *Wired*, https://www.wired.com/2014/11/feds-seize-silk
      -road-2/, November 06, 2014
6.   Europol, "Global Action Against Dark Markets on Tor Network,"
      https://www.europol.europa.eu/content/global-action-against
      -dark-markets-tor-network, November 7, 2014
7.   Vance, Cyrus, "Manhattan District Attorney's Offices Applies
      Innovative Technology To Scan The 'Dark Web' In The Fight
      Against Human Trafficking," Press Release, http://manhattanda.
      org/press-release/manhattan-district-attorney%E2%80%99s
      -office-applies-innovative-technology-scan-%E2%80%9Cdark
      -web%E2%80%9D-fig, February 09, 2016

Chapter 3:

1.   Nance, Malcolm, *Defeating ISIS: Who they are. How they fight. What
      they believe.* Skyhorse Press, NY, NY, 2016
2.   Alshech, Eli, Apelbaum, Jacob, "Behind the scenes of Virtual Jihad
      IV," MEMRI report, March 03, 2010
3.   Klatell, James, "Web's 'Jihadist James Bond' Gets 10 Years," July 5,
      2007, http://www.cbsnews.com/news/webs-jihadist-james-bond
      -gets-10-years/
4.   Clogherty, Jack, "Virtual Terrorism: Al Qaeda Video Calls for
      'Electronic Jihad," ABC News, May 22, 2012, http://abcnews.go.
      com/Politics/cyber-terrorism-al-qaeda-video-calls-electronic-jihad
      /story?id=16407875
5.   Cloherty, Jack, "Virtual Terrorism: Al Qaeda Video Calls for elec-
      tronic jihad," ABCNews, May 22, 2014, http://abcnews.go.com
      /Politics/cyber-terrorism-al-qaeda-video-calls-electronic-jihad
      /story?id=16407875
6.   Magnusen, Stew. "Al-Qaeda may have plans to manipulate a hack-
      ing group," National Defense Magazine, July 2012, http://www

.nationaldefensemagazine.org/archive/2012/July/Pages/Al-Qaida
MayHavePlanstoManipulateAnonymousHackingGroup.aspx

Chapter 4:
1. Bakunin, Mikhail. "Letters to a Frenchman on the Present Crisis," https://www.marxists.org/reference/archive/bakunin/works/1870/letter-frenchman.htm, September 1870
2. Eunjung Cha, Ariana. "From a virtual shadow, messages of terror," *Washington Post*, October 2, 2004, http://www.washingtonpost.com/wp-dyn/articles/A1570-2004Oct1.html
3. Eunjung Cha, Ariana. "From a virtual shadow, messages of terror," *Washington Post*, October 2, 2004, http://www.washingtonpost.com/wp-dyn/articles/A1570-2004Oct1.html
4. Karadsheh, Jomana, Mahdi, Basim. "U.S. says terrorist in Jill Carroll kidnapping killed," CNN, May 4, 2007, http://edition.cnn.com/2007/WORLD/meast/05/03/iraq.main/index.html
5. Abu Haniyeh, Hassan. "Daesh's Organisational Struction," Al Jazeera, December 4, 2014, http://studies.aljazeera.net/en/dossiers/decipheringdaeshoriginsimpactandfuture/2014/12/2014 12395930929444.html
6. Benson, Pam. "U.S.: Senior al Qaeda in Iraq leader held," CNN.com, July 18, 2007, http://www.cnn.com/2007/WORLD/meast/07/18/iraq.capture/index.html?iref=topnews
7. Gleason, Carmen. "Security Forces, Citizens Decrease Violence in Iraq," American Forces Press Service, http://archive.defense.gov/news/newsarticle.aspx?id=47965", October 28, 2007
8. Kruzel, John. "Antiterrorism Successes Continue in Iraq Despite Foreign-Born Resistance," American Forces Press Service, http://archive.defense.gov/news/newsarticle.aspx?id=46697, July 11, 2007
9. U.S. Department of Defense, "Statement from Pentagon Press Secretary Peter Cook on Airstrike against ISISL Senior Leader," Defense.Gov, September 16, 2016, http://www.defense.gov/News/News-Releases/News-Release-View/Article/946983/statement-from-pentagon-press-secretary-peter-cook-on-airstrike-against-isil-se
10. Ryan, Missy. "Pentagon says Raqqa strike kills Islamic State information minister," *Washington Post*, September 16, 2016, https://www.washingtonpost.com/news/checkpoint/wp/2016/09/16/u-s-strike-kills-another-senior-islamic-state-militant-official-says/
11. Whitehead, Craig. "Did it in '06," Twitter, September 16, 2016, https://twitter.com/CraigAWhiteside/status/77686889059275 1616

12. Abdulhaq, Ethar, "ISIS leaks: more about al-Absi, former mastermind, archive and biography," April 18, 2016, https://en .zamanalwsl.net/news/15295.html

13. Enders, David, "Syria rebels say they killed leader of extremist group that kidnapped 2 journalists," September 7, 2012, http:// www.mcclatchydc.com/news/nation-world/world/article 24736636.html

14. Mortada, Radwan, "Jihadis in Syria: The Cracks Start to Show," October 3, 2012, http://english.al-akhbar.com/node/12796

15. Windrem, Robert, "ISIS says No. 2 leader Abu Muhammad al-Adnani is dead in Syria," NBCNews, http://www.nbcnews.com /storyline/isis-terror/isis-says-no-2-leader-mohammad-al -adnani-dead-n640171 , August 31, 2016

16. Reuters, "Who runs the militant group Islamic State?" http://www .reuters.com/article/us-mideast-crisis-is-penpix-idUSKCN 0HT04J20141004, October 4, 2014

17. Callimachi, Rukmini, "How a Secretive Branch of ISIS built a Global Network of Killers," *New York Times*, http://www.nytimes .com/2016/08/04/world/middleeast/isis-german-recruit-interview .html?_r=0, August 3, 2016

18. Callimachi, Rukmini, "How a Secretive Branch of ISIS built a Global Network of Killers," *New York Times*, August 3, 2016, http://www.nytimes.com/2016/08/04/world/middleeast/isis -german-recruit-interview.html

Chapter 5:
1. Howell O'Neill, Patrick, "Creator of top jihadist online forum sentenced to 8 years in prison," Daily Dot, http://www.dailydot.com /layer8/shumukh-al-islam-forum-arrest-sentenced/, April 7, 2016

2. France24, "France: maçon le jour, cyberjihadiste la nuit . . . prison confirmée pour un Tunisien," May 04 2016

3. Zelin, Aaron, "New Statement from al-Fajr Media's Technical Committee," Jihadology, http://jihadology.net/2013/12/10/new -statement-from-al-fajr-medias-technical-committee-surprise -program-security-of-the-mujahid-for-safe-encrypted-communicatio n/, December 10, 2013

4. Miller, Greg, Mekhennet, Souad, "Inside the surreal world of the Islamic State's propaganda machine," *Washington Post*, https:// www.washingtonpost.com/world/national-security/inside-the -islamic-states-propaganda-machine/2015/11/20 /051e997a-8ce6-11e5-acff-673ae92ddd2b_story.html, November 20, 2015

5. Threatwatch, "Admin of ISIS propaganda website has been hacked," July 17, 2016, http://www.nextgov.com/cybersecurity/threat watch/2016/07/user-accounts-compromised-spearphishing-data -dump/2692/

6. Hijrah to the Islamic State, pg 6

7. Hijrah to the Islamic State, pg 47

8. Department of Justice, "Pennsylvania resident charged with pro- viding material support for ISIL," https://www.justice.gov/opa/pr /pennsylvania-resident-charged-providing-material-support-isil, December 17, 2015

9. Krause, Kevin, "Mesquite man who pledged allegiance to ISIS sentenced to 4 years in prison," May 25, 2016, http://crimeblog .dallasnews.com/2016/05/mesquite-man-who-lied-about -allegiance-to-isis-leader-given-4-years-in-prison.html/

10. Department of Justice, "Massachusetts man indicted on terrorism charges," June 30, 2016, https://www.justice.gov/usao-ma/pr /massachusetts-man-indicted-terrorism-charges,

11. ADL, "Online activity provides insight into MA man arrested for ISIS plot," ADL.org, July 13, 2015, http://blog.adl.org/extremism /alexander-ciccolo-ali-al-amriki-boston-ma-terror-isis

12. Cleary, Tom, "Alexander Ciccolo: 5 fast facts you need to know," July 13, 2015, http://heavy.com/news/2015/07/alexander-ciccolo-ali -al-amriki-massachusetts-terrorism-suspect-son-boston-police -captain-isis-isil-arrested-charged-felon-photos-facebook/

13. ADL, "Online activity provides insight into MA man arrested for ISIS plot," ADL.org, July 13, 2015, http://blog.adl.org/extremism /alexander-ciccolo-ali-al-amriki-boston-ma-terror-isis

14. Associated Press, "Boston police captain's son indicted in ISIS- inspired plot," July 1, 2016, http://nypost.com/2016/07/01/boston -police-captains-son-indicted-in-isis-inspired-plot/

15. Dickey, Christopher, "ISIS Terror killing in Paris streamed on Face- book live," Daily Beast, June 14, 2016, http://www.thedailybeast .com/articles/2016/06/14/isis-terror-killing-in-paris-streamed-on -facebook-live.html

16. Pues, Viktoria, "The Islamic State on Tumblr-Recruiting Western Women," International Institute for Counter-Terrorism, February 2016, https://www.ict.org.il/UserFiles/ICT-ISIS-on-Social-Media -Pues.pdf,

17. Crooks, Lauren, "Runaway British jihadi bride writes shocking suitcase checklist for schoolgirls wanting to join ISIS," *MirrorUK*, http://www.mirror.co.uk/news/uk-news/runaway-british-jihadi -bride-writes-6179441, August 1, 2015

18. Yan, Holly, Elbagir, Nima "Authorities scramble to find teens before they join ISIS," http://edition.cnn.com/2015/02/23/europe/uk-syria-missing-girls/index.html, February 23, 2015

19. Department of Justice, McNeil complaint, https://www.justice.gov/opa/file/792881/download

20. Mezzofiore, Gianluca, "ISIS boy executes 'Israeli spy': Toulouse killer Mohamed Merah's step-brother appeared in Islamic State video," March 11, 2015, http://www.ibtimes.co.uk/isis-boy-executes-israeli-spy-toulouse-killer-mohamed-merahs-step-brother-appeared-1491497

21. Prince, S.J. Heavy, "New ISIS video shows Russian FSB agent beheaded," http://heavy.com/news/2015/12/new-isis-islamic-state-news-videos-pictures-fsb-federal-security-service-agent-spy-chechen-chechnya-russia-russian-moscow-vladimir-putin-raqqa-syria-full-uncensored-youtube-english-translation/, December 2, 2015

22. Tsetkova, Maria, "The double life of a Russian 'spy' beheaded by Islamic State," Reuters, http://www.reuters.com/article/russia-syria-spy-idUSKBN0UC19U20151229 , December 29, 2015

Chapter 6:

1. Teague Beckwith, Ryan, "Read the CIA Director's Thoughts on the Paris Attacks," Time Magazine online, http://time.com/4114870/paris-attacks-cia-john-brennan/ November 16, 2015

2. Dixon Kavanaugh, Shane, Shiloach, Gilad-Vocativ, "ISIS spreads violence and terror with 'Foolproof' App," November 17, 2015

3. Tsotsis, Alexia, "Telegram Saw 8M Downloads after WhatsApp Got Acquired," TechCrunch.com, https://techcrunch.com/2014/02/24/telegram-saw-8m-downloads-after-whatsapp-got-acquired/, February 24, 2014

4. Burns, Matt, "Encrypted Messaging App Telegram Hits 100M Monthly Active Users, 350K New users each day," TechCrunch, https://techcrunch.com/2016/02/23/encrypted-messaging-app-telegram-hits-100m-monthly-active-users-350k-new-users-each-day/, February 23, 2016

5. Rotella, Sebastian, "ISIS via WhatsApp: 'Blow Yourself Up, o Lion!'" https://www.propublica.org/article/isis-via-whatsapp-blow-yourself-up-o-lion, July 11, 2016

6. Sharafedin, Bozorghmehr, "Iran's Revolutionary Guards target popular messaging app in widening crackdown," Reuters, November 15, 2015

7. Rotella, Sebastian, "ISIS via WhatsApp: 'Blow Yourself Up, o Lion!'" https://www.propublica.org/article/isis-via-whatsapp-blow-yourself-up-o-lion, July 11, 2016

8. Telegram, "Winter Contest Ends," https://telegram.org/blog/winter-contest-ends, March 2, 2014

9. Telegram, "Crypto Contest Ends," https://telegram.org/blog/cryptocontest-ends, February 11, 2015

10. Shiloach, Gilad, "ISIS Supporters Warn of Honey Traps on Telegram," Vocativ, http://www.vocativ.com/322316/isis-supporters-warn-of-honey-traps-on-telegram/, May 25, 2016

11. Flisbäck, Ola, "Stalking anyone on Telegram," https://oflisback.github.io/telegram-stalking/, December 16, 2015

12. Avraham, Zuk, "Telegram App Store Secret-Chat Messages in Plain-Text Database," Zimperium, http://blog.zimperium.com/telegram-hack/ February 23, 2015

13. WhatsApp, "Looking ahead for WhatsApp," https://blog.whatsapp.com/10000627/Looking-ahead-for-WhatsApp , August 26, 2016

14. WhatsApp Blog, "One Billion," https://blog.whatsapp.com/616/One-billion, February 1, 2016

15. Barry, Colleen, "Islamic State told Moroccan Living in Italy to Attack Rome," http://www.usnews.com/news/world/articles/2016-04-28/prosecutors-says-is-ordered-italian-resident-to-attack-rome, April 28, 2016

16. Blair, Scott, "Kickboxing champion Abderrahim Moutaharrik arrested 'as part of ISIS terror cell using WhatsApp to plan Vatican attack'," *US UK News*, http://www.newsusauk.com/news/305236-kickboxing-champion-abderrahim-moutaharrik-arrested-as-part-of-isis-terror-cell-using-whatsapp-to-plan-vatican-attack.html, April 29, 2016

17. Rotella, Sebastian, "ISIS via WhatsApp: 'Blow Yourself Up, O Lion!'" ProPublica https://www.propublica.org/article/isis-via-whatsapp-blow-yourself-up-o-lion , July 11, 2016

18. Blount, Jeb, "Brazil court blocks Facebook funds over Whatsapp dispute: report," Reuters, http://www.reuters.com/article/us-brazil-facebook-whatsapp-idUSKCN0ZH3EX, June 30, 2016

19. Varghese, Johnlee, "Bangladesh mulls blocking WhatsApp and Viber to prevent terror activities," International Business Times, http://www.ibtimes.co.in/bangladesh-mulls-blocking-whatsapp-viber-prevent-terror-activities-654305#muD8eI6SjGKic65l.97, November 11, 2015

20. Zweerink, Maikel, "WhatsSpy Public," https://gitlab.maikel.pro/maikeldus/WhatsSpy-Public/wikis/home,

21. Greenberg, Andy, *Wired*, https://www.wired.com/2014/07/free-encrypted-calling-finally-comes-to-the-iphone/, July 29, 2014

22. Tripathi, Rahul, "Dangerous Signal: This encrypted app is helping ISIS members in India to communicate," *Times of India*, http:// timesofindia.indiatimes.com/tech/tech-news/Dangerous-Signal -This-encrypted-app-is-helping-ISIS-members-in-India-to-com municate/articleshow/51773877.cms, April 11, 2016

23. Cordoba, Armando, "A secret app called Wickr has become ISIS one recruitment device," NewsComAu, http://www.news.com.au/ national/a-secret-app-called-wickr-has-become-isiss-number-one -recruitment-device/news-story/07857ae05909639df75 df65dff960137 , April 14, 2015,

24. Bentley Paul, "Revealed: How British jihadi brides are being groomed for ISIS by using a phone messaging app after brainwashing them on Twitter," *DailyMail*, http://www.dailymail.co.uk/news/article -2966116/How-British-jihadi-brides-groomed-ISIS-using -phone-messaging-app-brainwashing-Twitter.html, February 23, 2015

25. Stewart, Cameron, "War on terror: Cracking growing dark code," *The Australian*, http://www.theaustralian.com.au/news/inquirer /cracking-terrors-going-dark-encrypted-code/news-story/8bd8267 0c825a0a576ca3789a0b44e3a, November 28, 2015

26. Maley, Paul, "Jihadist Mohamed Elomar renews online assault," *The Australian*, http://www.theaustralian.com.au/national-affairs /foreign-affairs/jihadist-mohamed-elomar-renews-online-assault /news-story/1a509fe74e6be2110bf272d23cbfcbd6, August 5, 2014

27. Price, Rob, "Germany's most popular paid app is a secure messen-ger loved by millions-now it's taking on the US," Business Insider, June 18, 2015

28. Threema FAQ, "How long do messages stay in queue for delivery," https://threema.ch/en/faq/message_storage

29. Bagchi, Indrani, "Terrorists used app to hide digital footprint," *Times of India*, http://timesofindia.indiatimes.com/world/Terror ists-used-app-to-hide-digital-footprint/articleshow/53070343.cms m July 6, 2016

30. Afaaq Electronic Foundation, "Threema GmbH," https://justpaste .it/threema1 , June 3, 2015

31. Sternstein, Aliya, "This ISIS Endorsed Encryption Contractor says it will now screen who is buying its services," NextGov, http:// www.nextgov.com/cybersecurity/2015/11/secure-messaging -contractor-endorsed-isis-will-now-screen-credit-cards/123839/, November 19, 2015

32. Engel, Richard, "The ISIS Prisoner: A Month in captivity in the Islamic State," NBC News, http://www.nbcnews.com/storyline

/isis-uncovered/isis-prisoner-month-captivity-islamic-state
-n293656, January 25, 2015

33. Varghese, Johnlee, "Bangladesh mulls blocking WhatsApp and Viber to prevent terror activities," *International Business Times*, http://www.ibtimes.co.in/bangladesh-mulls-blocking-whatsapp -viber-prevent-terror-activities-654305#muD8eI6SjGKic65l.97, November 11, 2015

34. Ioffe, Julia, "Mothers of ISIS," Huffington Post, http://highline. huffingtonpost.com/articles/en/mothers-of-isis/, August 12, 2015,

35. Goodin, Dan, "Think Your Skype Messages get end-to-end encryption? Think Again," ArsTechnica, http://arstechnica.com/secu rity/2013/05/think-your-skype-messages-get-end-to-end -encryption-think-again/, May 20, 2013,

36. Rotella, Sebastian, "ISIS via WhatsApp: 'Blow Yourself Up, O Lion!'" ProPublica, https://www.propublica.org/article/isis-via -whatsapp-blow-yourself-up-o-lion , July 11, 2016,

37. Serafini, Marta, "Fatima speaks, Behead in the name of Allah," Corriere Della Sera, http://www.corriere.it/esteri/15_luglio_06/parla -fatima-jihadista-italiana-decapitiamo-nome-allah-612672f2-2421 -11e5-a98d-32629d3b799b.shtml?refresh_ce-cp, July 7, 2015,

38. Roberts, Hannah, "Revealed, how Italy's Lady Jihad convinced entire white Catholic family to convert and join ISIS in Syira," *DailyMail UK*, http://www.dailymail.co.uk/news/article-3264534 /Revealed-Italy-s-Lady-Jihad-convinced-entire-white-Catholic -family-convert-join-ISIS-Syria-Fanatical-daughter-guaranteed -mother-terrorists-washing-machine-leave-pet-kitten-behind .html, October 5, 2015

39. Conley Criminal Compaint, https://cchs.gwu.edu/sites/cchs.gwu .edu/files/downloads/Conley%20Criminal%20Complaint.pdf

40. Taher, Abul, "Filmed on Skype, the chilling exchange between reporter posting as a child and Islamic fighter from London," *DailyMailUK*, http://www.dailymail.co.uk/news/article-3094448/Filmed-Skype -chilling-exchange-reporter-posing-child-Islamic-State-fighter -London-told-pick-going-picking-wife.html, May 23, 2015

41. Erelle, Anna, "In The Skin of a Jihadist," http://www.rd.com/true- stories/survival/romancing-terrorist/

42. TrueCrypt, "TrueCrypt," May 2014, Sourceforge.net, http://true crypt.sourceforge.net/

43. Ratcliff, Evan, "The Strange Origins of Truecrypt, ISIS's favored encryption too," March 30, 2016, http://www.newyorker.com /news/news-desk/the-strange-origins-of-truecrypt-isiss-favored -encryption-tool

44. TOR, "What is the Tor Browser?," https://www.torproject.org/pro jects/torbrowser.html.en

45. Finley, Klint, "Out in the Open: Inside the operating system Edward Snowden used to evade the NSA," *WIRED*, http://www .wired.com/2014/04/tails/, April 14, 2014

46. Finley, Klint, "Out in the Open: Inside the operating system Edward Snowden used to evade the NSA," WIRED, http://www .wired.com/2014/04/tails/, April 14, 2014

47. Al-Qaeda in Arabian Peninsula, Inspire #1, "How to use Asrar al-Mujahideen: Sending & Receiving Messages," June 2010

48. Storm, Morten, "How I helped kill Al Qaeda's terrorist mastermind 'the Sheikh': The nerve shredding story of an MI5 spy posing as a fanatic," *DailyMail*, http://www.dailymail.co.uk/news/arti-cle-2665385/How-I-helped-kill-Al-Qaedas-terrorist-mastermind-The-target-The-worlds-wanted-man-The-dangers-Immense-This-nerve-shredding-story-MI5-spy-posing-fellow-fanatic.html, June 22, 2014,

49. Zahavi Gilad, "Online Jihadist Express Interest in Cyber Warfare and Cyber Security," SenseCy, https://blog.sensecy.com/tag/tash feer-al-jawwal/, February 24, 2014

50. Recorded Future, "How Al Qeda uses encryption post-Snowden (Part 2)," https://www.recordedfuture.com/al-qaeda-encryption -technology-part-2/, August 1, 2014

51. Zahavi Gilad, "Online Jihadist Express Interest in Cyber Warfare and Cyber Security," SenseCy, https://blog.sensecy.com/tag/tash feer-al-jawwal/, February 24, 2014

52. Trend Micro, "Dark Motives Online: An Analysis of Overlapping Technologies Used by Cybercriminals and Terrorist Organizations," May 03, 2016, http://www.trendmicro.com/vinfo/us/security/news /cybercrime-and-digital-threats/overlapping-technologies -cybercriminals-and-terrorist-organizations,

53. Zahavi, Gilad, "Online Jihadists Express Interest in Cyber Warfare and Cyber Security," Sensecy, https://blog.sensecy.com/tag/tash feer-al-jawwal/, February 24, 2014

54. Technical Center of Internet, Techno News, "Snowden scares even Al-Qaeda," https://www.tcinet.ru/en/press-centre/technology -news/1113/, May 05, 2014

55. Zelin, Aaron, "New Statement from the Global Islamic Media Front: Warning about the use of the program 'Asrar al-Ghuraba,'" *Jihadology*, http://jihadology.net/2013/12/04/new-statement-from -the-global-islamic-media-front-warning-about-the-use-of-the -program-asrar-al-ghuraba/, December 4, 2013

56.　Meyer, Josh, "ISIS has Help Desk for Terrorists Staffed Around the Clock," NBCNews, http://www.nbcnews.com/storyline/paris-ter ror-attacks/isis-has-help-desk-terrorists-staffed-around-clock -n464391 , November 16, 2015

57.　Bennet, Cory, "New ISIS 'help desk' to aid hiding from authorities," *The Hill*, http://thehill.com/policy/cybersecurity/268940 -new-isis-help-desk-unifies-encryption-support, February 10, 2016

58.　Cyberkov, Twitter, "Anonymous is blackmailing us with DDoS." https://twitter.com/CyberkovCEO/status/668156868838236161, November 21, 2015

59.　RecordedFuture, "How Al-Qaeda Uses Encryption Post-Snowden (Part 2)," https://www.recordedfuture.com/al-qaeda-encryption -technology-part-2/, August 1, 2014

60.　Recorded Future, "How Al Qeda uses encryption post-Snowden (Part 2)," https://www.recordedfuture.com/al-qaeda-encryption -technology-part-2/, August 1, 2014

61.　Bennett, Cory, "Apple couldn't comply with warrant because of encryption," *The Hill*, http://thehill.com/policy/cybersecurity/252896 -apple-rebuffed-warrant-because-of-encryption, September 8, 2015

Chapter 7:

1.　Knutsen, Elise, "Insight: From Remote Mauritania, hacker fights for Islam worldwide," Reuters, http://www.reuters.com/article/us -mauritania-hacker-insight-idUSBRE95R0D920130628, June 28, 2016,

2.　Twitter profile, Teamr00t, https://twitter.com/teamr00t

3.　Paganini, Pierluigi, "Hacktivists from Ghost Squad Hacker group made revealed the identities of hackers affiliated with the ISIS cyber army called United Cyber Caliphate," *SecurityAffairs*, http://securityaf fairs.co/wordpress/49170/terrorism/gsh-dox-ucc.html, July 8, 2016

4.　Pastebin, "OPpetrol-Total Oil Company System Owned by Anon-Ghost," http://pastebin.com/qP00xctu, June 19, 2013

5.　Dean, Jon, "Pro-ISIS hackers 'Caliphate Cyber Army' release video revealing partnership of evil with cyber terrorists AnonGhost," *MirrorUK*, http://www.mirror.co.uk/news/world-news/pro-isis -hackers-caliphate-cyber-7163124, January 12, 2016

6.　Staff, MeetHackers.com, "Ghost Squad exposes ISIS Hackers-Anon-Ghost vs Ghost Squad," http://www.meethackers.com/2016/07 /ghost-squad-exposes-isis-hackers.html, July 17, 2016

7.　"An interview with Hackers group Anonghost," *Surf the Cyber*, http://sec4track.blogspot.com/2014/03/an-interview-with-hackers -group.html, March 2014

8. Telegram Channel, Cyber Caliphate Army, https://web.telegram .org/#/im?p=c1052567040_17139008826567720683

9. Watkinson, William, "ISIS Threatens founder Mark Zuckerberg and Twitter CEO Jack Dorsey in chilling video," *International Business Times*, www.ibtimes.co.uk/isis-threatens-facebook-founder-mark-zuckerberg -twitter-ceo-jack-dorsey-chilling-video-1545849", February 25, 2016

10. Gallagher, Sean, "As US drops 'cyber bomb,' ISIS retools its own cyber army," *ArsTechinca*, http://arstechnica.com/information -technology/2016/04/as-us-drops-cyber-bombs-isis-retools-its -own-cyber-army/, April 28, 2016.

11. Pymnts, "ISIS google hacking attempt flops," http://www.pymnts.com /news/retail/2016/isis-google-hacking-attempt-flops/, March 4, 2016

12. Aboudi, Sami, "Kuwait detains member of Islamic cyber army: newspapers," Reuters, http://www.reuters.com/article/us-kuwait -security-cyberarmy-idUSKCN1111CT , August 26, 2016

13. Pawlyk, Oriana, "ISIS-linked hackers claim to release personal information of U.S. drone pilots," *AirForceTimes*, https://www.air forcetimes.com/articles/isis-linked-hackers-claim-to-release-per sonal-information-of-us-drone-pilots, May 2, 2016

14. Lanier, Candice, "Pro-ISIS group posts list of names & addresses of Americans-Apparently targeted for attack," *ChristianPost*, http:// blogs.christianpost.com/the-good-fight/pro-isis-group-posts-list -of-names-addresses-of-americans-apparently-targeted-for-attacks -25398/, April 13, 2015

15. Peranick, Matt, "Extremist media group issues cyber threats," EplaceInc, http://blog.eplaceinc.com/cyber/2015/06/09/extremist -media-group-issues-cyber-threats/, June 9, 2015,

16. Gallagher, Sean, " As US drops 'cyber bombs' ISIS retools its own cyber army," *ArsTechnica*, http://arstechnica.com/information-tech nology/2016/04/as-us-drops-cyber-bombs-isis-retools-its-own -cyber-army/, April 28, 2016

17. Hunt, Troy, "An analysis of the ISIS 'hit list' of hacked personal data," August 12, 2015, https://www.troyhunt.com/an-analysis-of -isis-hit-list-of-hacked/

18. Bennet, Cory, "Hackers breach the Warsaw Stock Exchange," The Hill, October, 14, 2014, http://thehill.com/policy/cybersecurity/221806 -hackers-breach-the-warsaw-stock-exchange

19. CyInfo, "Al Qaeda's Electronic Jihad," February 2, 2015, https:// blog.sensecy.com/2015/02/02/al-qaedas-electronic-jihad/

20. Liu, Eric, "Al Qaeda Electronic: A Sleeping Dog?" AEI Critical Threats, December 2015, www.criticalthreats.org/al-qaeda/liu-al -qaeda-electronic-december-2-2015

21. Ibid.
22. Ibid.
23. Ibid.
24. Ibid.
25. Ibid.
26. Deccan Chronicle Staff, "Indian Railways website allegedly hacked by Al Qaeda," *Deccan Chronicle*, March 2, 2016, http://www.dec canchronicle.com/technology/in-other-news/020316/indian-rail ways-website-allegedly-hacked-by-al-qaeda.html
27. Hackers Writer, "WSCC website hacked by Al Qaeda Hacker Team & TKL," Hackers News Bulletin, March 2013, http://www.hack ersnewsbulletin.com/2013/03/wscc-website-hacked-by-al-qaeda -hacker-team-tkl.html
28. Praveen, "Al-Qaeda Hackers defaced website of town of Wanatah," Geekyard, March 3, 2013, http://www.geekyard.com/safe/al-qaeda -hackers-defaced-website-of-town-of-wanatah/
29. Zahavi, Gilad, "Online Jihadists express interest in cyber warfare and cyber security," SenseCy, February 24, 2014, https://blog .sensecy.com/tag/al-qaeda-electronic-army/
30. MEMRI, "Tunisian Cyber Army' and 'Al-Qaeda Electronic Army' Reportedly Hack pentagon and State Department Websites," March 11, 2013. http://cjlab.memri.org/uncategorized/tunisian -cyber-army-and-al-qaeda-electronic-army-reportedly-hack-penta gon-state-department-websites/

Chapter 8:

1. Kovacs, Eduard, "Hackers around the world: It's no TriCk, He's among the Best in the UK," Softpedia, http://news.softpedia.com /news/Hackers-Around-the-World-It-s-No-TriCk-He-s-Among -the-Best-in-the-UK-253652.shtml, February 18, 2012
2. Ries, Brian, "The Mujahideen hackers who 'Clean Facebook,'" *DailyBeast*, http://www.thedailybeast.com/articles/2011/01/27 /the-mujahedeen-hackers-who-clean-facebook-and-the-face book-privacy-breakthrough.html, January 27, 2011
3. Kovacs, Eduard, "Hackers around the world: It's no TriCk, He's among the Best in the UK," Softpedia, http://news.softpedia.com /news/Hackers-Around-the-World-It-s-No-TriCk-He-s-Among -the-Best-in-the-UK-253652.shtml, February 18, 2012
4. Kovacs, Eduard, "Hackers around the world: It's no TriCk, He's among the Best in the UK," Softpedia, http://news.softpedia.com /news/Hackers-Around-the-World-It-s-No-TriCk-He-s-Among -the-Best-in-the-UK-253652.shtml, February 18, 2012

5. Telegraph Staff, "Team Poison hacker who posted Tony Blair's details is jailed," *TelegraphUK*, http://www.telegraph.co.uk/tech nology/internet-security/9432459/Team-Poison-hacker-who -posted-Tony-Blairs-details-is-jailed.html, July 27, 2012

6. Pearce, Matt, "Outside Muhammad cartoon contest in Texas, 2 gunmen are killed and guard is shot," May 3, 2015, http://www .latimes.com/nation/la-na-texas-shooting-20150503-story.html

7. BBCNews, "IS computer hacker Siful Haque Sujan killed in air strike," http://www.bbc.com/news/uk-wales-35206038, December 31, 2015

8. LinkedIn Profile, "Siful Sujan," https://www.linkedin.com/in /sifulsujan

9. Farmer, Ben, "Cardiff businessman turned ISIL cyber expert killed in airstrike," *TelegraphUK*, http://www.telegraph.co.uk/news/world news/middleeast/12075144/Cardiff-businessman-turned-Isil -cyber-expert-killed-in-air-strike.html, December 30, 2015

10. Burman, Jake, "British-trained Islamic State computer hacker WIPED OUT in drone strike," *Sunday Express*, http://www.express .co.uk/news/world/630468/Islamic-State-ISIS-Siful-Haque-Sujan -US-America-Pentagon-Drone-Strike-Britain-Cardiff, December 30, 2015

11. Moon, Terri, "Coalition kill 10 senior ISIL leaders in December," *DoD News*, http://www.defense.gov/News/Article/Article/639489 /coalition-killed-10-senior-isil-leaders-in-december, December 29, 2015

12. Mendelson, Tom, "ISIS hacking chief ran massive money-launder ing operation in Britain," *International Business Times*, http://www .ibtimes.co.uk/isis-hacking-chief-ran-massive-money-laundering -operation-britain-1535768, January 3, 2016

13. Samuel, Henry, "Intelligence agencies access private Telegram mes sages of most notorious ISIL recruiter, prompting arrest of 10 teen agers in one month," Telegraph UK, September 16, 2016, http:// www.telegraph.co.uk/news/2016/09/16/french-intelligence- cracks-telegram-account-of-most-notorious-is/

14. BBC Europe, "Did Jihadist Rashid Kassim lure French youths to plot attacks?" September 15, 2016, http://www.bbc.com/news /world-europe-37340697

15. Triet, Kevin, "Un Roannais fait l'apologie du djihad sur Facebook," Le Progress, January 21, 2016, http://www.leprogres.fr/loire/2016/01/21 /un-roannais-fait-l-apologie-du-djihad-sur-facebook-nljs

16. Seelow, Soren, "Rashid Kassim, the guru of young apprentice ter rorists," *LeMonde*, September 16, 2016, http://www.lemonde.fr

/societe/article/2016/09/16/rachid-kassim-le-gourou-des-enfants
-terroristes_4998559_3224.html

17. BBC Europe, "Did Jihadist Rashid Kassim lure French youths to plot attacks?" September 15, 2016, http://www.bbc.com/news /world-europe-37340697

18. France24, "Paris police identify French IS group suspect 'with key links to terror plots,'" September, 13, 2016, http://www.france24 .com/en/20160912-france-rachid-kassim-terrorism-plots-islamic -state-group-paris-police

19. BBC Europe, "Did Jihadist Rashid Kassim lure French youths to plot attacks?" September 15, 2016, http://www.bbc.com/news /world-europe-37340697

20. Seelow, Soren, "Rashid Kassim, the guru of young apprentice terrorists," *LeMonde*, September 16, 2016, http://www.lemonde.fr /societe/article/2016/09/16/rachid-kassim-le-gourou-des-enfants -terroristes_4998559_3224.html

21. Zennie, Michael, "The American computer wiz running brutally effective ISIS social media campaign," *DailyMailUK*, http://www .dailymail.co.uk/news/article-2743737/The-American -computer-wiz-running-ISIS-brutally-effective-social-media-cam paign-College-educated-son-Boston-doctor-FBI-Most-Wanted -list.html , September 4, 2014

22. Al Arabiya News Staff, "ISIS movie maker, documentary producer 'killed' in Iraq airstrike," http://english.alarabiya.net/en/News /middle-east/2015/05/31/ISIS-movie-maker-and-documentary -producer-die-in-Iraqi-airstrike.html, May 31, 2015

23. Poole, Patrick, "American ISIS propagandist Ahmad Abousamra Reported killed in Iraq airstrike," PJ Media, https://pjmedia.com /blog/american-isis-propagandist-ahmad-abousamra-reported -killed-in-iraq-airstrike, May 31, 2016

24. Hall, John, "Two US jihadis who made ISIS propaganda videos-including one on the FBI's most wanted terrorist list-are killed in Iraqi air strike," DailyMail, http://www.dailymail.co.uk/news /article-3105640/Two-jihadis-ISIS-propaganda-videos-including -one-FBI-s-wanted-terrorist-list-killed-Iraqi-air-strike.html, July 1, 2015

25. US v Mehanna, First Circuit, "Motion," http://media.ca1.uscourts .gov/pdf.opinions/12-1461P-01A.pdf, November 13, 2013.

26. Bohannon, John, "Women Critical for Online Terrorist Networks," *ScienceMag*, http://www.sciencemag.org/news/2016/06/women -critical-online-terrorist-networks, June 10, 2016

27. Winter, Charlie, "Women of the Islamic State: A Manifesto on women by the al-Khanssaa Brigade," Quilliam, http://www.quil liamfoundation.org/wp/wp-content/uploads/publications/free /women-of-the-islamic-state3.pdf, February 2015
28. Ibid.
29. Ibid.
30. Webb, Sam, "British ISIS widow Sally Jones threatens UK cities with bomb strikes over summer in a series of tweets," Mirror.co, http://www.mirror.co.uk/news/uk-news/british-isis-widow-sally -jones-8049896, May 25, 2016
31. U.S. Department of State, Office of the Spokesperson (2015, September 29). Designations of Foreign Terrorist Fighters [Press release]. U.S. Department of State. Retrieved September 8, 2016, from http://www.state.gov/r/pa/prs/ps/2015/09/247433.htm
32. Joshi, P. (2016, August 28). Father says British child killer in Isis propaganda video is his son. International Business Times. Retrieved September 10, 2016, from http://www.ibtimes.co.uk/father-says -british-child-killer-isis-propaganda-video-his-son-1578469
33. Schmidt, M. & Pérez-Peña, R. (2015, December 4). "F.B.I. Treating San Bernardino Attack as Terrorism Case. *New York Times.* Retrieved September 7, 2016, from http://www.nytimes .com/2015/12/05/us/tashfeen-malik-islamic-state.html
34. Tucker, E. (2015, December 6). How ISIS is recruiting a growing following of young women. The Associated Press. Retrieved September 7, 2016, from http://www.pbs.org/newshour/rundown /how-isis-is-recruiting-a-growing-following-of-young-women/
35. Saltman, E., & Smith, M. (2015). "Till Martyrdom Do Us Part": Gender and the ISIS Phenomenon (Rep.). Retrieved September 7, 2016, from http://www.strategicdialogue.org/wp-content/uploads/2016/02/Till _Martyrdom_Do_Us_Part_Gender_and_the_ISIS_Phenomenon.pdf
36. Saltman, E., & Smith, M. (2015). "Till Martyrdom Do Us Part": Gender and the ISIS Phenomenon (Rep.). Retrieved September 7, 2016, from http://www.strategicdialogue.org/wp-content /uploads/2016/02/Till_Martyrdom_Do_Us_Part_Gender_and _the_ISIS_Phenomenon.pdf
37. Storey, K. (2016, April 22). The American Women of ISIS. Marie Claire. Retrieved September 7, 2016, from http://www.marieclaire .com/politics/a20011/western-women-who-join-isis/
38. Storey, K. (2016, April 22). The American Women of ISIS. Marie Claire. Retrieved September 7, 2016, from http://www.marieclaire .com/politics/a20011/western-women-who-join-isis/

39. Bennhold, K. (2015, August 17). Jihad and Girl Power: How ISIS Lured 3 London Girls. Retrieved September 7, 2016, from http://www.nytimes.com/2015/08/18/world/europe/jihad-and-girl-power-how-isis-lured-3-london-teenagers.html?_r=0

40. Wockner, C. (2016, May 9). Australian jihadi bride broker Shadi Jabar's Telegram Posts. News Corp Australia Network. Retrieved September 10, 2016, from http://www.news.com.au/lifestyle/real-life/true-stories/australian-jihadi-bride-broker-shadi-jabars-telegram-posts/news-story/6989badd02486ce5e8df268945fb9ce8

41. Ibid.

42. Wockner, C. (2016, May 9). Australian jihadi bride broker Shadi Jabar's Telegram Posts. News Corp Australia Network. Retrieved September 10, 2016, from http://www.news.com.au/lifestyle/real-life/true-stories/australian-jihadi-bride-broker-shadi-jabars-telegram-posts/news-story/6989badd02486ce5e8df268945fb9ce8

43. Ibid.

44. Wockner, C. (2016, May 9). Shadi Jabar: Australian who lured jihadi brides for ISIS. News Corp Australia Network. Retrieved September 10, 2016, from http://www.dailytelegraph.com.au/news/special-features/in-depth/shadi-jabar-the-australian-name-behind-islamic-states-bride-broker/news-story/71cf641c489a6d70b3c7a8d2ead47a24

45. Cook, P. (2016, May 5). Department of Defense Press Briefing by Pentagon Press Secretary Peter Cook in the Pentagon Briefing Room [Press Conference]. U.S. Department of Defense. Retrieved September 10, 2016, from http://www.defense.gov/News/Transcripts/Transcript-View/Article/752789/department-of-defense-press-briefing-by-pentagon-press-secretary-peter-cook-in

46. Ibid.

47. Ibid.

48. Calbert, S. & Grossman, A. (2015, April 3). Philadelphia Woman Keonna Thomas Charged With Attempting to Join ISIS. Retrieved September 8, 2016, from http://www.wsj.com/articles/philadelphia-woman-keonna-thomas-charged-with-attempting-to-join-isis-1428078216

49. United States of America v. Keonna Thomas (United States District Court for the Eastern District of Pennsylvania April 3, 2015).

50. Ibid.

51. Hall, E. (2015, April 17). "Gone Girl: An Interview With An American In ISIS," BuzzFeed. Retrieved September 8, 2016, from https://www.buzzfeed.com/ellievhall/gone-girl-an-interview-with-an-american-in-isis

52. Ibid.

53. U.S. Department of State, Office of the Spokesperson. (2015, September 29). Designations of Foreign Terrorist Fighters [Press release]. U.S. Department of State. Retrieved September 8, 2016, from http://www.state.gov/r/pa/prs/ps/2015/09/247433.htm

54. Emilie König, Cette Bretonne fichée par les Etats-Unis (2015, September 30). *Paris Match*. Retrieved September 7, 2016, from http://www.parismatch.com/Actu/International/Emilie-Koenig-cette-Bretonne-fichee-par-les-Etats-Unis-837707

55. Piel, S. & Vincent, E. (2015, October 1). Emilie, Maxime, Peter, Boubaker ... ces djihadistes français blacklistés aux Etats-Unis. Le Monde. Retrieved September 7, 2016, from http://www.lemonde.fr/international/article/2015/10/01/terrorisme-itineraire-et-profil-des-quatre-francais-inscrits-sur-la-liste-noire-des-etats-unis_4779081_3210.html

56. Hall, Ellie. (2014, September 11). "Inside The Chilling Online World of The Women Of ISIS," BuzzFeed. Retrieved September 7, 2016, from https://www.buzzfeed.com/ellievhall/inside-the-online-world-of-the-women-of-isis

57. Freytas-Tamura, K. (2015, February 24). "Teenage Girl Leaves for ISIS, and Others Follow," *New York Times*. Retrieved September 7, 2016, from September 7, 2016, from into life in SyriaIS http://www.nytimes.com/2015/02/25/world/from-studious-teenager-to-isis-recruiter.html

58. Hall, Ellie. (2014, September 11). "Inside The Chilling Online World of The Women Of ISIS," BuzzFeed. Retrieved September 7, 2016, from https://www.buzzfeed.com/ellievhall/inside-the-online-world-of-the-women-of-isis

59. Dettmer, J. (2014, September 3). The Bride of ISIS Revealed. The Daily Beast. Retrieved September 7, 2016, from http://www.thedailybeast.com/articles/2014/09/03/the-bride-of-isis-revealed.html

60. Winter, Charlie, "Women of the Islamic State: A Manifesto on women by the al-Khanssaa Brigade," Quilliam, http://www.quilliamfoundation.org/wp/wp-content/uploads/publications/free/women-of-the-islamic-state3.pdf, February 2015

61. Umm Layth. Internet Archive. Retrieved September 7, 2016, from https://web.archive.org/web/20150224163437/http://fa-tubalilghuraba.tumblr.com/

62. Umm Layth. Internet Archive. Retrieved September 7, 2016, from https://web.archive.org/web/20150224163437/http://fa-tubalilghuraba.tumblr.com/

63. Shoichet, C., Bilginsoy, Z. & Yan, H. (2015, March 23). 'Brain-washed' foreign medical students went to Syria, Turkish lawmaker says. CNN. Retrieved September 8, 2016, from http://www.cnn.com/2015/03/23/middleeast/syria-isis-medical-students/

64. Sandford, D., Swann, S. & Hashim, M. (2015, July 17). UK medical student "recruited for IS" at university in Sudan. BBC. Retrieved September 8, 2016, from http://www.bbc.com/news/uk-33502534

65. Clifford, S. (2015, April 2). "Two Women in Queens Are Charged With a Bomb Plot," *New York Times*, Retrieved September 8, 2016, from http://www.nytimes.com/2015/04/03/nyregion/two-queens-women-charged-in-bomb-plot

66. Ibid.

67. United States of America v. Noelle Velentzas and Asia Siddiqui (United States District Court for the Eastern District of New York April 1, 2015).

68. Ibid.

69. Ibid.

Chapter 9:

1. Cha, Ariana Eunjung, "From a virtual Shadow, Messages of Terror," *Washington Post*, http://www.washingtonpost.com/wp-dyn/articles/A1570-2004Oct1.html, October 4, 2004

2. Healy, Jack, "Gunmen in Uniforms Kill 20 Police Officers in Iraq," *New York Times*, http://www.nytimes.com/2012/03/06/world/middleeast/police-killed-in-iraq.html, March 5, 2012

3. BBC News, "Iraq Militants attack Tikrit prison, freeing 90 inmates," http://www.bbc.com/news/world-middle-east-19750039, Sept 28, 2012

4. Miller, Greg, Mekhennet, Souad, "Inside the surreal world of the Islamic State's propaganda machine," *Washington Post*, https://www.washingtonpost.com/world/national-security/inside-the-islamic-states-propaganda-machine/2015/11/20/051e997a-8ce6-11e5-acff-673ae92ddd2b_story.html, November 20, 2015

5. Miller, Greg, Mekhennet, Souad, "Inside the surreal world of the Islamic State's propaganda machine," *Washington Post*, https://www.washingtonpost.com/world/national-security/inside-the-islamic-states-propaganda-machine/2015/11/20/051e997a-8ce6-11e5-acff-673ae92ddd2b_story.html, November 20, 2015

6. Callimachi, Rukmini, "How a secretive Branch of ISIS built a global network of killers," *New York Times*, http://www.nytimes.com/2016/08/04/world/middleeast/isis-german-recruit-interview.html?_r=0, August 3, 2016

7.   Miller, Greg, Mekhennet, Souad, "Inside the surreal world of the Islamic State's propaganda machine," *Washington Post*, https://www.washingtonpost.com/world/national-security/inside-the-islamic-states-propaganda-machine/2015/11/20/051e997a-8ce6-11e5-acff-673ae92ddd2b_story.html, November 20, 2015

8.   Fruen, Lauren, "Blooming Scary, Florist's shock at appearing in ISIS magazine," September 7, 2016, https://www.thesun.co.uk/news/1741246/manchester-florist-shocked-to-be-pictured-in-isis-propaganda-magazine/

9.   Kuwait news Agency, "Malaysian web-hosting company terminates server of Muntada al-Ansar," http://www.kuna.net.kw/ArticlePrintPage.aspx?id=1476906&language=en, May 14, 2004

10.   Eunjung Cha, Ariana, "From a virtual shadow, messages of terror," *Washington Post*, October 2, 2004, http://www.washingtonpost.com/wp-dyn/articles/A1570-2004Oct1.html

11.   Ibid.

12.   Novinite, "Bulgarian Beheading Video On the Net," http://www.novinite.com/articles/37501/Bulgarian+Beheading+Video+on+the+Net , July 28, 2004

13.   Trowbridge, Alexander, "ISIS swiping hashtags as part of propaganda efforts," CBSNews http://www.cbsnews.com/news/isis-hijacks-unrelated-hashtags-in-attempt-to-spread-message/, August 26, 2014

Chapter 10:

1.   Trend Micro Report, "https://www.trendmicro.com/vinfo/us/security/news/cybercrime-and-digital-threats/overlapping-technologies-cybercriminals-and-terrorist-organizations?ClickID=anrstkrwlan5vz5stvrrsns5syksok0yrrl," May 3, 2016

2.   Wright Criminal Complaint, "US v David Wright," https://cchs.gwu.edu/sites/cchs.gwu.edu/files/downloads/Wright%20Criminal%20Complaint.pdf, June 2, 2015

3.   Islamic State, "Hijrah to the Islamic State," pg 47

4.   Smith, Chris, "Forget iPhone encryption, the FBI can't legally touch the software ISIS uses," BGR http://bgr.com/2016/03/31/isis-attack-paris-brussels-iphone-encryption/, March 31, 2016

5.   Ioffe, Julia, "Mothers of ISIS," *Huffington Post*, http://highline.huffingtonpost.com/articles/en/mothers-of-isis/, August 12, 2015

Chapter 11:

1.   Dabiq #13, "The Rafidah: From Ibn Saba' to the Dajjal"

2.   Dabiq #7, cover

3.   Dabiq 12, "Interview with Abu Muharib as-sumali"

4. Bloom, Mia, "The Changing Nature of Women in Extremism and Political Violence," Location, http://f3magazine.unicri.it /?p=1093,

Chapter 12:

1. Blinken, Antony J., "New Frameworks for Countering Terrorism and Violent Extremism," U.S. Department of State. U.S. Department of State, 16 Feb. 2016. Web. 10 Sept. 2016.

2. Williams, Katie Bo, "Legislation to combat ISIS propaganda faces pushback from Dems," *TheHill*, http://thehill.com/policy/cyber security/277662-gop-bill-to-combat-isis-propaganda-faces-push back, April 26, 2016

3. Yadron, D., & Wong, J. C., "Silicon Valley appears open to helping US spy agencies after terrorism summit," *TheGuardianUK*, 2016, January 08, https://www.theguardian.com/technology/2016 /jan/08/technology-executives-white-house-isis-terrorism-meeting -silicon-valley-facebook-apple-twitter-microsoft

4. Acosta, J. (2016, February 25). "First on CNN: Government enlists tech giants to fight ISIS messaging." Retrieved September 08, 2016, from http://www.cnn.com/2016/02/24/politics/justice-depart ment-apple-fbi-isis-san-bernardino/

5. U.S. Department of State, "Ambassador Alberto Fernandez Appointed Coordinator of the Center for Strategic Counterterrorism Communications," State.Gov, March 26, 2012, http://www .state.gov/r/pa/prs/ps/2012/03/186790.htm

6. Blinken, Antony J., "New Frameworks for Countering Terrorism and Violent Extremism." U.S. Department of State. U.S. Department of State, 16 Feb. 2016. Web. 10 Sept. 2016.

7. Labott, Elise, "State Department releases graphic anti-ISIS video," CNN.com, September 8, 2014, http://www.cnn.com/2014/09/05 /world/state-department-anti-isis-video/

8. Yousef, Sarbaz, "Dozens of IT experts, media workers desert ISIS in Mosul," *AraNews*, http://aranews.net/2016/04/dozens-experts -media-workers-desert-isis-mosul/, April 30, 2016

9. Yousef, Sarbaz, "France hit ISIS media center in Mosul," *AraNews*, http://aranews.net/2016/01/france-hit-isis-communication -center-in-mosul/, January 16, 2016

10. Baron, Kevin, "US now launching cyberattacks against ISIS, defense secretary says," Defense One, http://www.nextgov.com /defense/2016/03/us-now-launching-cyberattacks-against-isis -defense-secretary-says/126318/, March 1, 2016

11. Iyer, Kavita, "Using VPN in UAE could get you in prison & a fine upto $545,000," TechWorm, http://www.techworm.net/2016/07 /using-vpn-uae-get-prison-fine-upto-545000.html, July 28, 2016

12. BBC, "Radical preacher Anjem Choudhary jailed for five years," September 6, 2016, http://www.bbc.com/news/uk-37284199

13. Wright, Simon, Dorman, Nick, Cortbus, Colin, "Twitter shuts down ISIS supporters and jihadists as MI5 launch anti-terror social media crackdown," *Mirror*, http://www.mirror.co.uk/news/uk-news /twitter-shuts-down-isis-supporters-5038305, January 24, 2015

14. Ballenger, Grace, "US, UK Develop Strategies against ISIS Media Use," *The News Hub*. The News Hub, 4 Aug. 2015. Web. 10 Sept . 2016.

15. Investigatory Powers Bill 2015–16 to 2016–17." Parliament.uk. Parliament of the United Kingdom, n.d. Web. 10 Sept. 2016.

16. Shah, Saqib, "France Holds Counter-terrorism Talks with Twitter, Facebook," Digitaltrends.com. *Digital Trends*, 04 Dec. 2015. Web. 10 Sept. 2016.

17. DiGiovanni, Janine, "Simple Ideas to Counter Terrorism in France," *Newsweek*. N.p., 17 Mar. 2016. Web. 10 Sept. 2016.

18. Dodd, Vikram, "Europol web unit to hunt extremists behind ISIS social media propaganda," Guardian UK, June 21, 2015, https:// www.theguardian.com/world/2015/jun/21/europol-internet-unit -track-down-extremists-isis-social-media-propaganda

19. Twitter, "Combating Violent Extremism," Twitter.com, February 6, 2016, https://blog.twitter.com/2016/combating-violent-extrem ism

20. Twitter, "Combating Violent Extremism," Twitter.com, February 6, 2016, https://blog.twitter.com/2016/combating-violent-extremism

21. R. (2015, December 07). Social media sites quietly join fight against ISIS. Retrieved September 08, 2016, from http://nypost .com/2015/12/07/social-media-sites-quietly-join-fight-against- isis/

22. Detsch, J, "How Google aims to disrupt the Islamic State propa- ganda machine," *Christian Science Monitor*. September 07, 2016, from http://www.csmonitor.com/World/Passcode/2016/0907 /How-Google-aims-to-disrupt-the-Islamic-State-propaganda-ma chine

23. Jeong, S. (2016, June 15). Anti-ISIS Hacktivists Are Attacking the Internet Archive. Retrieved September 08, 2016, from http:// motherboard.vice.com/read/anti-isis-hacktivists-are-attacking-the -internet-archive

24. J. (2015, July 7). Cyber Jihad 2.0 – Where We're going Wrong. Retrieved September 8, 2016, from https://jesterscourt.cc/2015 /07/07/cyber-jihad-2-0-where-were-going-wrong/

25. O'Gara, E. (2015, September 05). THINK-TANK RELEASES ANTI-RADICALISATION VIDEO TO COUNTER ISIS PROPAGANDA. Retrieved September 08, 2016, from http:// europe.newsweek.com/think-tank-releases-anti-radicalisation -video-counter-isis-propaganda-331225

26. Berger, J., & Morgan, J. (2015, March). The ISIS Twitter Census. Retrieved September 8, 2016, from https://www.brookings.edu /wp-content/uploads/2016/06/isis_twitter_census_berger_morgan .pdf

27. Wagner, K. (2015, December 15). U.S. Enlists College Students to Fight ISIS Online. Retrieved September 08, 2016, from http:// www.recode.net/2015/12/15/11621450/behind-the-u-s-govern ments-anti-isis-plan-on-facebook-and-youtube

28. Quinn, Ben, "Interpol website suffers 'Anonymous cyber-attack,'" *GuardianUK*, http://www.diplomaticourier.com/2015/03/19/tor -and-the-bitcoin-an-exploration-into-law-enforcement-surveil lance-capability-online/, February 28, 2012

29. Anonymous, YouTube Video, "Anonymous #OpCharlieHebdo," https://www.youtube.com/watch?v=oqbwqmb8P00, January 10, 2015

30. Anonymous, Pastebin.com, "#OpISIS-Expose & Destroy by Anonymous Red Cult" http://pastebin.com/G663HnDa, February 9, 2015

31. Bryanschatz. (2015, November 24). "When they're not attacking each other, hackers say they're targeting ISIS." Retrieved September 08, 2016, from http://www.motherjones.com/politics/2015/11 /anonymous-hacking-isis-ghost-security

32. Griffin, A. (2015, December 28). "Anonymous war on Isis: Online activists claim to have foiled terror attack on Italy as part of "Operation Isis," Retrieved September 08, 2016, from http://www.inde pendent.co.uk/life-style/gadgets-and-tech/news/anonymous-war -on-isis-online-activists-claim-to-have-foiled-terror-attack-on -italy-as-part-of-a6788001.html

33. Mills, K. (2016, March 23). "Brussels attacks: Anonymous declares war on ISIS in chilling video vowing "we will find you" - *Mirror Online*. Retrieved September 08, 2016, from http://www.mirror .co.uk/news/world-news/brussels-attacks-anonymous-declares -isis--7615029

34. "Anonymous hacks pro-ISIS Twitter accounts, fills them with gay pride." (2016, June 15). Retrieved September 08, 2016, from http://www.cbsnews.com/news/anonymous-hacks-pro-isis-twitter -accounts-fills-them-with-gay-pride/

35. Pascaline, Mary, "After Orlando Shooting, Anonymous Hacker Turns ISIS Twitter Accounts Pro-LGBT," June 17, 2016, http:// www.ibtimes.com/after-orlando-shooting-anonymous-hacker -turns-isis-twitter-accounts-pro-lgbt-2383317

36. Cameron, Dell, "Twitter says Anonymous list of alleged ISIS accounts is highly inaccurate," *The Daily Dot*, http://www.dailydot .com/layer8/twitter-isnt-reading-anonymous-list-isis-accounts/, November 20, 2015

37. Russon, Mary-Ann, "Ghost Security Group: How Anonymous hackers grew up to help save the world from ISIS," *IBTimesUK*, January, 23, 2016, http://www.ibtimes.co.uk/ghost-security-group -how-anonymous-hackers-grew-help-save-world-isis-1539618

38. Knibbs, Kate, "is this vigilante group fighting ISIS or just feeding the media a fat load of crap?" Gizmodo, February 3, 2016, http:// gizmodo.com/is-this-vigilante-group-fighting-isis-or-just-feeding-t -1755489934

39. Knibbs, Kate, "is this vigilante group fighting ISIS or just feeding the media a fat load of crap?" Gizmodo, February 3, 2016, http:// gizmodo.com/is-this-vigilante-group-fighting-isis-or-just-feeding-t -1755489934

40. Cuthbertson, Anthony, "Hackers replace dark web ISIS propaganda site with advert for Prozac," http://www.ibtimes.co.uk/hackers -replace-dark-web-isis-propaganda-site-advert-prozac-1530385, November 25, 2015

41. Cottee, S. (2015, October 8). "The Cyber Activists Who Want to Shut Down ISIS." Retrieved September 08, 2016, from http:// www.theatlantic.com/international/archive/2015/10/anonymous -activists-isis-twitter/409312/

42. Ibid.

43. Ibid.

44. Pagliery, Jose, "Meet the vigilante who hacks jihadists," *CNN Money*, http://money.cnn.com/2015/01/16/technology/security /jester-hacker-vigilante/index.html, January 16, 2015

45. Szoldra, P. (2015, November 17). This hacker has fought terrorists online since 2010, and he's not impressed by Anonymous. Retrieved September 8, 2016, from http://www.techinsider.io/anon-war-isis -jester-hacking-2015-11

46. Pagilery, J. (2015, January 16). "Meet the vigilante who hacks jihadists." Retrieved September 08, 2016, from http://money.cnn.com/2015/01/16/technology/security/jester-hacker-vigilante/

47. Szoldra, P. (2015, November 17). "This hacker has fought terrorists online since 2010, and he's not impressed by Anonymous." Retrieved September 8, 2016, from http://www.techinsider.io/anon-war-isis-jester-hacking-2015-11

48. O'Neill, Patrick, "Who's laughing now? U.S. government seizes The Jester's website," TheDailyDot, August 2, 2013, http://www.dailydot.com/news/jester-jesterscourt-website-seized-ice-hacker/

49. Freed, Anthony, "More Talks with Anti-Jihadi Hacker The Jester," Febraury 4, 2010, http://www.infosecisland.com/blogview/2805-More-Talks-with-Anti-Jihadi-Hacker-The-Jester.html

50. Szoldra, P. (2015, November 17). "This hacker has fought terrorists online since 2010, and he's not impressed by Anonymous." Retrieved September 8, 2016, from http://www.techinsider.io/anon-war-isis-jester-hacking-2015-11

51. Pagilery, J. (2015, January 16). "Meet the vigilante who hacks jihadists." Retrieved September 08, 2016, from http://money.cnn.com/2015/01/16/technology/security/jester-hacker-vigilante/

52. Jester. (2015, July 7). "Cyber Jihad 2.0 – Where We're going Wrong." Retrieved September 8, 2016, from https://jesterscourt.cc/2015/07/07/cyber-jihad-2-0-where-were-going-wrong/

53. Freed, Anthony, "More Talks with Anti-Jihadi Hacker The Jester," Febraury 4, 2010, http://www.infosecisland.com/blogview/2805-More-Talks-with-Anti-Jihadi-Hacker-The-Jester.html

54. Nakashima, Ellen, "Dismantling of Saudi-CIA Web site illustrates need for clearer cyberwar policies," March 19, 2010, http://www.washingtonpost.com/wp-dyn/content/article/2010/03/18/AR2010031805464_pf.html

55. InfoSec Island Admin, "The SANS report: The Jester, A Lesson in Assymetric Warfare," March 05, 2012, http://www.infosecisland.com/blogview/20599-The-SANS-Report-The-Jester-A-Lesson-in-Asymmetric-Warfare.html

56. Aaronson, Trevor, "Listen to an FBI 'Honeypot' On the Job." April 21, 2016, https://theintercept.com/2016/04/21/listen-to-an-fbi-honeypot-on-the-job/

Chapter 13:
1. Stewart, Christopher, Maremont, Mark, "Twitter bars intelligence agencies from using analytics service," *Wall Street Journal*, http://

www.wsj.com/articles/twitter-bars-intelligence-agencies-from -using-analytics-service-1462751682, May 8, 2016

2. Crovitz, L. Gordon, "Twitter Picks Russia over the U.S.," *Wall Street Journal*, http://www.wsj.com/articles/twitter-picks-russia-over-the -u-s-1463346268, May 15, 2016

3. Ibid.

4. Winston, Ali, Reveal, "Facebook reactions are a gift to advertisers and law enforcement alike," https://www.revealnews.org/blog/face book-reactions-are-a-gift-to-advertisers-and-law-enforcement -alike/, March 1, 2016, July 23, 2016

5. Fang, Lee, "The CIA is investing in firms that mine your tweets and Instagram photos," Intercept, https://theintercept.com/2016/04/14 /in-undisclosed-cia-investments-social-media-mining-looms-large/, April 14, 2016

6. Callimachi, Rukmini, "How a Secretive Branch of ISIS built a global work of Killers," *New York Times*, http://www.nytimes .com/2016/08/04/world/middleeast/isis-german-recruit-interview .html,

7. Schmitt, Eric, "A Raid on ISIS Yields a Trove of Intelligence," *New York Times*, http://www.nytimes.com/2015/06/09/world/middleeast /us-raid-in-syria-uncovers-details-on-isis-leadership-and-finances .html, June 8, 2005

8. Schmitt, Eric, "U.S. Secures Vast New Trove of Intelligence on ISIS," *New York Times*, http://www.nytimes.com/2016/07/28/ world/middleeast/us-intelligence-isis.html, July 27, 2016

9. Schmitt, Eric, "U.S. Secures Vast New Trove of Intelligence on ISIS," *New York Times*, July 27, 2016, http://www.nytimes. com/2016/07/28/world/middleeast/us-intelligence-isis.html?_r=0

10. Nanjappa, Vicky, "How ISIS lays honey traps to recruit people," OneIndia, http://www.oneindia.com/feature/how-isis-lays-honey -traps-to-recruit-people-1769698.html, June 8, 2015

11. Indorewala, Sharmeen Hakim, "ISIS honey trap offered to 'marry' Majeed on FB," *MumbaiMirror*, May 30, 2015

12. TimeOfIndia, "I cleaned toilets while in ISIS, Kalyan youth Areeb Majeed tells NIA," http://timesofindia.indiatimes.com/india /I-cleaned-toilets-while-in-ISIS-Kalyan-youth-Areeb-Majeed -tells-NIA/articleshow/45328623.cms, November 30, 2014

Chapter 14:

1. Kaplan, Fred, *Dark Territory: The Secret History of Cyber War*. Simon & Schuster, NY, NY, 2016, pp. 213–14

Index